Doc Down Under

An American Emergency Doc's Family Adventures in Australia & New Zealand

Francis Nolan, M.D.

Published by Ferndle Publishing in 2022.

Ferndle Publishing
Cooperstown, NY 13326

Cover art by Central NY Mobile Marketing and Francis Nolan, M.D.
Interior formatting by Central NY Mobile Marketing

Doc Down Under is dedicated, with all my love and admiration, to my wife, life partner and best friend Stephanie, who made the great leap of faith into the unknown with five young kids in tow. Also, to our five wonderful children; Luke, Claire, Aidan, Cate and Owen. They rose to the many challenges presented with courage and consistently positive attitudes. To me, they help redefine the phrase "grace under pressure" for a new generation of young travelers. We persevered and prospered primarily because of their commitment and child-like faith that I actually knew what I was doing. Go figure... We could never have accomplished any of it without their steadfast love and support.

AUTHOR'S NOTES

Blog entries are *italicized,* with later observations and mental discursions following in standard font.

I've been as diligent as possible in fact-checking. In this modern age, most has been done online, using Google, Wikipedia, Google Earth, Brisbane Times etc., as well as trusting my aging memories of things witnessed, books read, conversations had, and random facts plucked from the ether. While never letting a precise detail upend a "good tale - well told", I take full responsibility for any factual inaccuracies or cultural misinterpretations herein and appreciate reader feedback to correct the same going forward.

Finally, a brief selected bibliography of books I've enjoyed and used to gain a deeper understanding of the region and its history, has been included at the back of the book to assist anyone interested in further literary exploration of Australia and New Zealand, and to perhaps provide some guidance to anyone contemplating a trip or similar re-location to the very ends of the earth.

Now, on with the show...

Australia

Indian Ocean

Darwin
Gulf of Carpantaria

Katherine

Coral Sea

Derby
Cairns

Broome

NORTHERN TERRITORY

Mount Isa

Mackay

WESTERN AUSTRALIA

Alice Springs

QUEENSLAND

Carnarvon

Charleville

Meekatharra

Brisbane

SOUTH AUSTRALIA

Leigh Creek

Bourke

Kalgoorlie

Ceduna

Broken Hill

Port Macquarie

Perth
Fremantle

Port Pirie
Adelaide

NEW SOUTH WALES

Esperance

Canberra

Sydney

Great Australian Bight

VICTORIA

Melbourne

Bairnsdale

Tasman Sea

0   500 Kilometers
0   500 Miles

TASMANIA

Hobart

Indian Ocean

Tasmania

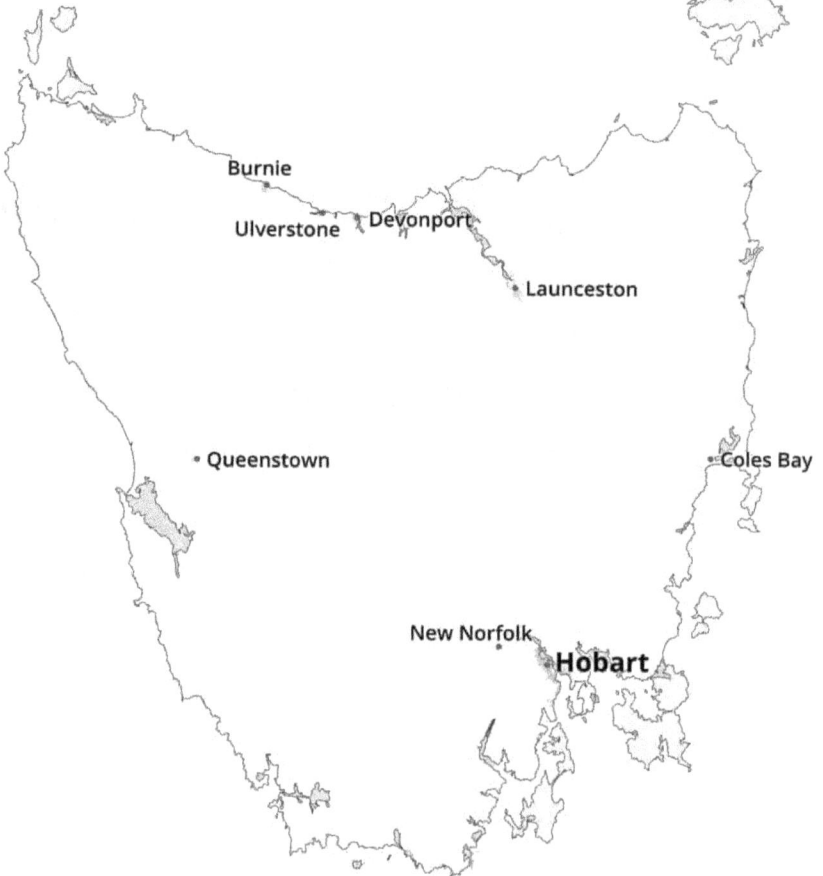

New Zealand

CAPE REINGA

NINETY MILE BEACH

Kaitaia

Kerikeri

NORTHLAND

Dargaville

Whangarei

Great Barrier Island

Coromandel
COROMANDEL PENINSULA

Auckland

Thames

Tauranga

Hicks Bay

WAIKATO

Hamilton

Otorohanga

Whakatane

EAST
CAPE

Rotorua

Taupo

Gisborne

Waikaremoana

New Pymouth

CENTRAL
PLATEAU

TARANAKI

Napier

HAWKES BAY

Wanganui

WANGANUI/
MANAWATU

Palmerston
North

Kapiti Is.

NELSON/
MARLBOROUGH

Paraparaumu

Wellington

WAIRARAPA

Motueka

Nelson

COOK STRAIT

Blenheim

Picton

Westport

Punakaiki

Greymouth

Kaikoura

Hokitika

Hanmer Springs

Arthurs Pass

CANTERBURY

WEST COAST

Christchurch

Mt Cook

BANKS PENINSULA

Haast

Timaru

Milford Sound

Wanaka

FIORDLAND

Queenstown

Oamaru

OTAGO

Te Anau

Manapouri

SOUTHLAND

Dunedin

Invercargill

FOVEAUX STRAIT

Half Moon Bay

STEWART ISLAND

TABLE OF CONTENTS

PROLOGUE

Twilight. Mary River, Northern Territory, Australia

May 2013

Curiously, my first, blinding thought – "She's gonna kill me..."

Sitting in the enveloping silence, after the outboard's metallic grind and shudder - silence - except for the droning whine of myriad mosquitoes, rising to their evening's feed, and the stifling heat, still present, even into late fall here in the far Northern Territory (NT). The skiff is hard aground on an unseen rocky ledge. I'm praying that we haven't snapped the shear pin in sacrifice to saving the propeller. The river water is the sickly gray-brown of old coffee cut with skim milk. Visibility - inches. And there are two Crocodiles, hovering silently, only yards from our stern: snouts, eye ridges, spines and tails unmoving; easily mistaken for water-logged branches. And several more watching close by; motionless on the sloped, sandy wash of both banks. Everything held in sudden anticipation, like a startled breath.

We'd been working our way for several miles up some unnamed tributary of the Mary River; excited after catching a large, silver-sheened, late season Barramundi from under a massive, fallen eucalyptus snag, its crown buried top down in the murk. The classic, much-desired sportfish in these parts, and our first ever; the local consensus was that the cooling weather had shut down much hope of hooking up. But the fish struck suddenly and hard. Aidan, just ten, set the hook and the fish dived. We were shocked into action after hours of empty casting. His steady pumping of the upright rod tip soon brought an indistinct, bright swelling-up from the depths, like focusing a dirty lens, as the mud-roiled water parted. The gasping quarry, almost platinum and three feet long, rose broadside to the surface, entangled in a bundle of blackened, broken branches. Expecting the fish to panic and roll, snapping the line, I instinctively reacted - leaned over the side and, cradling the whole chaotic mess with both arms, threw it all into the boat; barely feeling the stray hook sinking into my hand through the blinding adrenaline rush. Success - against the odds! It was Aidan's peak fishing moment and made the entire trip already a winner.

We'd traveled to the far North purposely in May, to avoid the drenching heart of the "Wet", but still in time to enjoy the terminal lushness of these waterways before the extended, and increasingly desiccated, annual "Dry" set in to linger for months. Flushed with the unexpected catch, we moved deeper into the bush. The river here was not especially scenic, but wilder and vaguely foreboding under the lengthening light of the cloudless fall afternoon. The coffee-gray river ran low between sloping, flood-scoured sandbanks; remnants of the seasonal flood and flow as these vast interior river flats drained north, towards the Timor Sea, some thirty miles distant. Raw evidence of past floods remained in the messy piles of stranded detritus, wrapped around the upstream bases of shaggy gum trees, and resting now some twenty feet above the water's current height. An entirely alien landscape.

Working still further upstream, the banks closed together; the sandy, cleared zones to the water's edge narrowing, and showing signs of recent disturbance; the overhanging treetops now touching to form a sinister, beckoning tunnel. Here will lie the largest, most elusive prey. And very soon we began passing Crocodiles, living remnants of an ancient epoch, dozing undisturbed in their beds of alluvial sand. But rousing now, sensing some new disturbance.

As the day waned, the retiring sun lost its hot, metallic edge, drifting lower into the trackless Australian bush, gray-green in the placid, filtered light. The entire river-course drifted into shaded, diffuse twilight long before full dark. Up ahead, the flat, rich water, flowing seaward imperceptibly to this point, was broken by a small waterfall that flowed gently over a low sedimentary ledge, tumbling over a twenty-foot interval, and dropping several feet at most. A trickle really, the only thing moving, but a barrier still; it marked a good point to turn around and head back downriver toward camp. A gentle swing on the outboard tiller... and then the shocking shudder and metallic grind. Hard aground on an unseen extension of the ledge! Broken, and stranded in the lengthening twilight, Crocs rousing to our plight; silently aware, and closing in...

With no radio, and miles upstream. A sudden realization, then surging panic.

"Nobody get out of the boat." I ordered sternly, trying to keep my voice calm...

My two trusting sons, Luke and Aidan, on the first night of our ten-day venture into the wild heart of Kakadu National Park, looked alarmed and close to panic.

"Look, worst case: we sit here until dark, and they'll launch a search party if we're not back by then. We might be out here most of the night, though." I offered reassuringly - to myself most of all.

Luke, the elder, and always the more skittish one, started in:

"Why didn't we turn back sooner? We have no food, only a little water."

All the thrill of our recent triumph, vaporized. Think, don't overreact...

"Don't try to start the engine; hopefully the pin hasn't sheared."

Sweat blossoming, and not due to the humidity. She's gonna kill me...

"Luke, get up here on the bow with me. Aidan, take the engine."

The bow sags towards the water's surface under our combined weights, as the Crocs subtly shift position without rippling the surface. Then, the stern lifts slightly, as we edge out as far as we dare without falling in, to be surely and savagely mauled.

"Aidan, turn it over." Our younger son leaps into the driver's seat, turns the key... The familiar high-pitched, torquey whine, a slight shudder, and the engine purrs to life.

"Pop it into reverse."

I fully expect it to sit at idle, with the prop-less shaft spinning in the warm murk. But the clutch engages, the skiff lurches slightly and begins to reverse off the unseen ledge. Movement! Oh, sweet relief!

"Thank God", I offer a silent thanks. And just how did I get us into this situation so quickly-so deep, and on the first outing of the trip?

The stern sinks as I move aft and take the tiller, almost not believing that we are underway again, then gently backing off, until I think we're well clear of the ledge; but I can see nothing below. Now gracefully swinging the skiff downstream and guiding it between the narrow banks. And suddenly, we are heading away from this nameless place, downriver towards camp and safety. Everybody exhales...

The Crocodiles observing all, remain motionless, but likely disappointed, as we start to whoop and high-five... And away we go, by the skin of our teeth, certain death and dismemberment cheated!

"Don't tell your mother..."

The engine revs smoothly up to full rpms and we leave the mozzies and reptiles behind in our dirty, foaming wake. Back downriver, with only the tale to tell; and a good one at that. All limbs intact. And on day one, no less!

But what else does this strange country hold in store for us, I wonder silently?

We arrive at the rough-sawn timber dock right on full dark, tie off and read the suddenly pertinent warnings with a sense of real relief.

"CAUTION" declares one sign with a graphic, simple profile in flat-black relief, of a Croc with mouth agape:

"Do Not Clean Fish or Camp Near Water's Edge"

4

Luckily, our tent is already pitched in a grassy spot fifty feet or more from the bank. This is the Mary River after all, known to have one of the highest Crocodile densities per mile of any river in the NT, and that increasing dramatically since the prohibition of Croc culls over the last several decades. The rivers of the NT are fair dinkum swarming with the creatures, and human attacks are becoming more frequently reported.

Thus, we survived the first episode of our ten-day Kakadu National Park/ Northern Territory Outback adventure, full chapter (21) to follow. The boys, who seemed like young men at the time, were only fourteen and ten. I look back at the photos today and just shudder...What was I thinking? Our guardian angels must've been wearing flak jackets, for sure.

To amplify the point, several months later, as we've settled safely back at home in Brisbane, the Brisbane Times reported that at the exact same spot, in the very same campground on the Mary River, a bunch of local teens were hanging out. I suspect they were doing what teens everywhere do, and especially so in the Northern Territory. Most likely partying, drinking a lot, and daring each other to do some stupid shit or other. Apparently, two friends challenged each other to swim across the Mary River, leaping in from this very same dock. Old coffee, gray-brown, serene; flowing imperceptibly seaward, and here being less than fifty yards across - to the exposed sandy bank opposite. In they went, oblivious to the strenuous warnings and discouragement of the assembled onlookers, and probably a few encouraging whoops as well, truth be told.

At mid-stream, the brown water erupted, vomiting its guts violently skyward, as a large Croc engulfed one kid hard across the torso. He was last seen flailing in terror and screaming for help as he was pulled under, to be drowned in a terminal death roll. His body was never recovered.

And that's just the thing about Australia; it's endlessly fascinating, intriguingly odd and occasionally very deadly...

CHAPTER 1: The Road Taken (or not...)

So, just how does one find oneself relocating halfway around the world, at mid-career, with anxious and confused family in tow? I'm sure it's different for everyone, but, in brief, here's what happened to us...

I found myself in my early fifties in need of a sea change. Oceanic, in fact... Practicing Emergency Medicine (EM) in a rural upstate New York community hospital for fourteen years, including ten as Emergency Department (ED) Director, with all the usual (and often irreconcilable) challenges; constant budget constraints, recruiting and retaining of quality staff, mentoring and encouraging any malcontents, as well as an increasing awareness of my own clinical risk exposure, were all wearing me down. What once seemed so natural and even eagerly anticipated as a younger, highly motivated and bullet-proof new FACEP (Fellow of the American College of Emergency Physicians) now just filled me with unspoken dread. I would awaken at night and remember past cases, traumas, patient deaths. Decisions made that might have turned out differently.

I was in the very front line of fire, and I was burning out, staffing a medium-sized, rural community hospital, with a 20,000-patient annual ED census and attached nursing home. We were actually a secondary receiving hospital for three smaller, even more rural EDs, tucked away in the northern Catskill Mountains. From our site, it was an additional sixty to ninety minutes in either direction to a tertiary medical center with comprehensive subspecialty services, often over icy, windy roads. Helicopters could be weathered out due to rain, fog, sleet storms hanging in the mountain valleys. Our staffing model: a single ED doc per twelve-hour shift, 24/7/365, we never closed. If you need us, we're here, taking all comers. With a Physician's Assistant (PA), hopefully, for 8-12 hours on most days. No trainees. Minimal colleague interaction, except at sign in/

sign out, for years. When the PA left for the night, you were the only doc in the entire hospital until morning, covering the fifteen-bed ED as well as ICU, floor codes and even precipitant births.

There was minimal (and highly variable) specialty backup, on-call from home and needing time to respond. Your team for a major trauma off the local interstate was you, and three harried nurses, with a single General Surgeon incoming from home, half an hour away. All the while managing the ongoing current ED flow, now suddenly at full stop. For critical cases, we operated on what we call in the ED business a "Pack and Ship" model. Indeed. I worked some amazing and terrifying cases in that setting. Looking back, it's hard to imagine that I survived for fourteen years. I should write a book... When I describe my past ED life to my Aussie physician colleagues, they just look at me in silent horror, not certain I'm being "fair dinkum". But, in reality, such a staffing model is routine in most rural American EDs. It takes its toll over the years.

Anyhow, a sea change was long overdue. I needed colleagues, backup, society... An academic post perhaps? We considered and interviewed in areas I thought desirable: Texas, Tennessee, Virginia, Massachusetts and Vermont (where I had trained), and had multiple, eager job offers. But nothing clicked - same old wine, different bottle. As this was in 2009-2010, the incoming Obama administration was just finding its feet. The already chaotic US insurance, healthcare billing and malpractice litigation environments were becoming even more unpredictable and unstable. Say what you will, and not to get overtly political, but the nascent initiative that became labeled as "Obamacare" appeared to me, as a practicing physician and ED Director, to be an utter disaster from the start. Watching the Insurance and Pharmaceutical stock prices skyrocket as the details were clarified confirmed to me that this was yet another Washington insider/ lobbyist generated pork-fest and boondoggle: one that would never contain healthcare costs or broaden provider choice as advertised. To me, it appeared more about political control of the healthcare funding stream than delivery of actual healthcare...Y'know, to actual sick people. Unfortunately, time and events have confirmed my concerns in large measure.

No, I needed an oceanic change, a frameshift - somewhere very different. As I was then entering my last decade or so of practice, I simply didn't have time for the dysfunctional US political system to finally arrive at a workable solution. As the ever-insightful Winston Churchill so well noted:

"You can always count on the Americans to do the right thing, after they've exhausted all other options..."

And there seemed to me to be a long decade, at least, of exhausted options ahead for US healthcare. I simply didn't have time to wait around. I needed to find an alternative, publicly-funded system that was already mature and functional, and English-speaking, by necessity. I sought to understand how such a system worked in actual practice. There are some things you just can't learn in a book, after all. Some may consider my approach disloyal, but in my mind I didn't leave US healthcare, it left me. I felt, rightly or not, the system was failing me, its most highly-trained and clinically knowledgeable component; the bedside, practicing physician. We'd somehow allowed the same financial alchemists who essentially destroyed our US manufacturing base for the short-term profit of company executives and connected insiders, to now have a go at the healthcare industry. I think we all need to acknowledge this evolving reality and address it somehow; as the majority of US healthcare workers I interact with feel similarly. Many feel unable to influence their own working environments; but most can't extricate themselves easily, as I was determined to do. So they carry on, disengage, drink and drug, get cynical and depressed; some consider darker options. Just look at the latest figures on US physician and nurse burnout and suicidality. We have a sick healthcare system, folks. And now being run, in large measure, by the wrong people with the wrong motivations and incentives. Just my two and a half cents here. But acceptance is the first step towards recovery. Every good doctor knows that...

So, in October 2009, I attended the annual American College of Emergency Physicians (ACEP) conference, held that year in my hometown of Boston. It's a really big deal. Of the 25,000 or so practicing EM physicians in the US, over 5,000 attended. Most everyone who's anyone in pre-hospital/ emergency services/ academia is there, and readily approachable at the various parties and "meet and greets" that happen nightly over the week. All the international recruiters and equipment/ tech manufacturers send teams to highlight their latest gadgets and offerings. It's networking central for my specialty. The entire convention center exhibit floor is filled with hundreds of exhibitors. While wandering through, I was attracted to a very large corner display: vivid red outback, azure coral seas, even a large paper windmill silhouetted against a warm ochre sunset. "Work for Us: Queensland" proclaimed a colorful banner. Intriguing...what's Queensland...? I strolled over.

Queensland, whatever that was, seems to have come over in force: a team of ten or so, including three American Fellows of the American College of...etc. (FACEPs) who'd made the jump and were living testimony to how wonderful EM life was Down Under. It sounded amazing...I needed to hear more. I accepted the invitation to a wine and cheese party that evening. What are usually pretty meager affairs turned out to be a full-on, multimedia presentation. Videos streamed in full color of said US FACEPs cruising motorcycles down open Aussie backroads under flawless skies, 4-wheeling in Utes across copper-colored rivers, snorkeling under crystalline, fish-filled seas. The wines were all Australian and uniformly excellent, as were the bountiful Tasmanian cheese platters. All three US FACEPs reassured me that yes, life was really that good for EM physicians Down Under. It was here that I first became acquainted with my future mentor, the good Dr. B. Well, I'll admit it, they had me from the first "G'day mate, how ahh ya..?"

Australia? I'd never even considered it. Several older American docs, alums from a past stint in Australia, were also in attendance, reminiscing about carefree antipodean days; and to a man (I met no women), all stated their wish to return, if it were not for the realities of seniority, tenure, mortgages, kids in school.

"If you can do it, just go, you won't regret it." offered an earnest, senior internist from Seattle. He was still dreaming of returning one day to work again in Australia. Ah, but for life, work, responsibility...

Emails and phone numbers of colleagues and references were exchanged, and I left the party in a glowing, Aussie alcohol-induced haze. Australia...Really...Australia...?

I hadn't given a thought about the place since I'd last heard that Men at Work song, "Down Under" sometime in the 1980's at college back in

Burlington, Vermont. But I sure do love that song. Doesn't everyone?

Stephanie reacted with surprise and slight alarm as I detailed my Australian epiphany in Boston, back at our farm in rural upstate New York. We'd been ensconced there for fifteen years, on a sprawling property - circa 1820 farmhouse with barns, outbuildings, pond, cabin, the whole kahuna. Not a shut-the-door-and-take-off type of arrangement. Plus, we had five school-aged kids, ages three to twelve, and large, extended families on both sides scattered throughout the Northeast. Dogs, cats, chickens, pheasants. No cloven-hoofed beasts at least. But Australia? No thanks - it simply wasn't possible, or even imaginable.

But the possibility and the lifestyle on offer intrigued me and wouldn't fade. I cold called several of the docs referred to me at the party, now scattered all over the USA. Every one had positive memories of their medical experiences in Australia and/ or New Zealand. Each was unequivocal, "If you can do it, just go..." Several expressed regret for ever having come back to practice in the USA. In fact, the prior ED Director at my current hospital had, soon after stepping down, left our staff for a six-month sabbatical working EM in New Zealand. He remained for seven years, and even renewed his fraying marriage vows there in a Maori ceremony; finally returning Stateside, regretfully, for family reasons. He noted my intensity in questioning him and said, "You're going to go, I know it, and you won't regret it. I'll follow your progress by email."

So, the courtship commenced. Queensland, Australia wanted me, and I wanted Queensland; more than badly. That mutual attraction was the easy part, as it turned out. Australia has very strict immigration regulations, and the world's biggest moat to enforce them. Though constantly changing, here was the process for us, circa 2010-11:

To gain entry, you first need to have skills that Australia finds itself short of. There's a priority list that's updated regularly. The hiring party has to first advertise the position to all local talent and certify that no Australian has the skills or availability to take the job. They may then issue a '457', the four-year, long-stay work visa through Immigration that is job and site specific. If the job dries up, or is "made redundant" in Aussie parlance, your visa is canceled, and you go home. If the job is not as advertised and you want to leave it, you can't transfer laterally; you go home. At that time, Emergency Medicine was a critical shortage skill set. So, lucky me...

To add further complexity, in the Aussie Medical world, it turns out there are three governing bodies involved, all with different requirements and, let me diplomatically state, less than stellar communication or coordination between them. I soon became enmeshed between the offering/ hiring state government agency, Queensland Health (QLDH), the overseeing Federal medical licensing body (AHPRA) and my Australian professional college, the Australasian College for Emergency Medicine (ACEM). Chaos and confusion ensued. It went on and on...I became disheartened... months drifted past.

I found a dog-eared, out-of-date, three-inch-thick, Lonely Planet guidebook for twenty-five cents at a local church book fair, "Australia"; and took it as an encouraging sign that God wanted us in Australia. I mean, what were the odds? Stephanie just rolled her eyes and carried on. In the pre-Cam Scan era, reams of documents and certified copies of diplomas and training certificates, going all the way back to high school (1975!) were FedExed internationally, only to be followed up weeks later with requests for further documentation and clarification. I learned never to expect a reply from Australia over a vacation period, for a minimum of four weeks. Curiously, that made me yearn to immigrate even more. These Aussies must really take their time off seriously, I thought (which they certainly do!). The months dragged on... a year passed; deep winter settled again into Upstate, I was only working part-time. I needed to get out.

Fortunately, I'd found a lovely, female Kiwi (New Zealand) recruiter who knew I was serious and worked closely with me for over a year. We were in touch with every ED Director in the state of Queensland and beyond. Not knowing the lay of the land, I was (foolishly) willing to go almost anywhere..Toothless, meth-head, Bogan-ville? Fine by me. Australia...She's calling...

Ipswich, Redcliffe, Caboolture, Hervey Bay, Bundaberg, Maryborough, Nambour, Caloundra, they all knew me by name. Doctor Nolan, that crazy, desperate Yank. He must be wanted, or on the lam...the perfect candidate! Most were enthusiastic but, all that paperwork and expense... Mightn't there be a suitable local candidate?

Eventually, I resigned myself to the realization that it was all just a dream, an unachievable mid-life fantasy. I vividly recall looking at the totemic Lonely Planet Australia guidebook on my bathroom bookshelf, while taking a long piss and actually talking to it out of frustration. As my bladder drained away, likewise my spirits...

"I will never see you Australia, it's not going to happen."

More time passed, spring evolved into summer, then fall beyond. Another Upstate winter drew its deep, frigid breath and approached...

Meanwhile, Dr. B., one of the Aussie-expat FACEPs I'd met at the wine and cheese meet and greet in Boston, became a sympathetic ear and life-coach by email and long distance calls over this time period, now going on over eighteen months. I leaned on him so heavily, I'm surprised that we're still friends, but we are. You pay it forward, and I've tried...

He once told me, "Stay strong mate...You'll pound your head against the wall until you feel like your brain's becoming jelly-without making any progress. But then someone from the inside will decide they want you and will just pull you in through the system."

And that's exactly what happened...

One dark, early fall evening in November 2011, just before Thanksgiving, the phone rang in my study at the farm. It was a very familiar female voice with that distinct Kiwi accent and dry wit, fifteen hours ahead of Eastern Standard Time (EST):

"Francis, would you consider an ED in the Redland?" "Where?" I stammered; "I've never heard of it."

"It's actually a really nice farming area, very green; right on Moreton Bay, very near Brisbane," she purred reassuringly...

"Well, yeah, sure... I would look at almost anything at this point."

"They'd like to set up a phone interview with you, the ED Director,

Doctor Dennis March and the senior Admin staff."

"When?" I ventured.

"This time tomorrow..."

I was dubious, and not expecting much, but this seemed a step forward; so I agreed to proceed. Stephanie remained neutral and carried on with our busy daily schedule of kids, meals, homework, school. The phone interview was a very relaxed affair, with a few questions about my past experience and ability to function as a team leader without direct supervision. Having had almost twenty years of EM practice experience in resource-constrained settings, I must have said all the right things. The interview came to a brisk close with my being asked,

"We will arrange the 457 and airline tickets, can you start before the New Year?"

I was absolutely stunned. Having been initially recruited by QLDH at Boston ACEP in October 2009 and run around in various circles until completely exhausted by November 2011, I was now being asked to relocate my family to Australia over the Christmas holidays and be ready to start clinically in less than six weeks!

After I recovered from my initial shock, we held an emergency "Team Nolan" family meeting, as Stephanie internalized these stunning developments. The kids were all pretty excited, but essentially clueless as to the implications of what I was proposing. But I was going nowhere fast professionally, winter was inevitably advancing and somehow, we all decided it was doable - a bit of a crash deadline, but doable. Australia, here we come! I held out for a start date of February 1, 2012. That turned out to be a very wise decision. There are always more hours to work but taking adequate time to process major life changes has always been my method. I mean really, if not then, when?

The hospital agreed, and kindly offered to put us up in a three bedroom, furnished rental until we'd settled and found a more permanent home, as well as provide a complimentary temporary van. It felt somehow dream-like as we each internalized the fact that we were about to leave our home and head off to a new life in Brisbane, Australia, in less than six weeks. What would it be like? I couldn't really imagine. We really needed to pull things together, get packing and finalize our farm lives. Fortunately, I had a very good friend, an aspiring author (i.e., unemployed, penniless and living with his parents) who had previously agreed to act as farm steward and pet sitter during our potential sojourn. He was an aging bachelor who, while not likely to actually keep things moving forward, would at least be low impact on our fine, old farmhouse. In fact, he was almost the perfect candidate, impoverishment aside, as he fulfilled the prime criteria for the job: he never left home or went anywhere. A constant, if benignly lethargic, presence.

We still needed to tell friends and break the news gently to family. Stephanie and I had agreed beforehand to keep them totally in the dark until we had an offer firmly in hand. We simply didn't want others to experience the emotional ups and downs we'd endured over the past two years. This tactical decision inadvertently created some sense of betrayal between me and my in-laws; and unfortunately, as things developed, our relationship was severely tested by that fateful decision.

But another Upstate winter was steadily advancing; long, dark and hard as iron. Australia was offering the dream of an entirely fresh start - a new life under the bright, welcoming, southern sun. We merely had to acquiesce and say "Yes..."

It was an easy decision to make in some ways.

CHAPTER 2: Intent and Cast of Characters

Although my primary motivation to make the great leap Down Under was to rejuvenate my waning enthusiasm for USA-style Emergency Medicine at mid-career, I also hoped that my experience working as a physician in a fully developed, publicly-funded healthcare system would give me a practical, first-hand understanding of the actual inner workings of such a system, both pros and cons. I hoped to utilize what I learned to perhaps add a clinical voice to the growing political debate developing in the USA over healthcare access, coverage and costs.

But I didn't want to write a boring, wonky dissertation on comparative healthcare system economic modeling that no one would ever read. And that's not my area of expertise anyway. I'm a front-line, patient-focused EM clinician at heart. Thus, the comparative healthcare discussion is wrapped neatly within our lively and at times dramatic "Team Nolan" explorations of this uniquely fascinating place. Never having actually lived overseas, Stephanie and I also wanted to give our kids an early, immersive experience into another culture. Perhaps a wee bit too early, but the timing, for me, was now or possibly never; and not really open to further debate or delay. You take the offer in hand, or not...

So, what exactly is this island continent, Australia, all about? How to capture the essence of the country for an outsider? You've likely heard the superlatives; the driest, flattest, hottest island / continent on planet Earth. The oldest continuous living human culture, Aboriginal (actually hundreds of distinct cultures), tracing continuous ownership lineage back over 65,000 years, an estimate recently extended yet again, but perhaps for much longer. One of the most ancient, stable landforms on Earth. Cutoff for millennia, leaving an isolated world, containing the most unique, venomous and surprising natural phenomena, as well as the vast, desiccated "Dead Heart" at its center. A new, New World whose settlement mythology rivals even that of the mythic American West. All true, all here. And a naturalist's wet dream. Even better than Jane Hathaway in tap pants.

After six years of living, working and traveling in this constantly surprising land, I have my own set of experiences that partly define what Australia means to me. It's a journey that evolves continually. Writing this book is, in part, my own journey of discovery and trying to pull the various strands of reading, accepted mythology and personal experience into a clearer understanding of what Australia is, in my singular experience. In doing so, I speak and understand through my unique filters alone. I make no claim to any special insight or received higher wisdom. And, while one may never attain the true rooted understanding of homeland that a multi-generational local may possess as birthright, I believe it's valid and valuable to see an old, established place through the fresh eyes of a newcomer.

In writing Doc Down Under, I hope not to contradict any reader's own experiences or beliefs, especially so to my adopted family and friends, the Aussies. Any misconceptions or factual errors are mine alone. But, as a fairly well-read individual prior to embarking on this enterprise, I think back to my knowledge and understanding of Australia before heading out and am now somewhat surprised to realize that it was basically nil; or at least very minimal, and mostly in error. Sort of Crocodile Dundee + Men at Work + Bondi Baywatch, with a small side order of AC/DC... All washed down with a twacker of cold Fosters...

"Yeah....nah. Not quite, mate..."

Thus, I hope readers will forgive me for assuming nothing; except that most, like my prior self, know little about the place, and much of that is off the mark. So please, come along, it will be a right bonzer trip anyway, mates. "So stoked!"

First up - our names have not been changed in the interest of creative license, as I think they are perfectly fine as given. I also couldn't be troubled with the artifice of coming up with, and sustaining, aliases I liked through an entire book. OK? Why bother?

In brief summary, the cast of characters:

Dr Francis Nolan: Headstrong, driven, self-made, restless; a seeker. Sixth of eight kids, the one child who would've disappeared into the frontier of the old West, had it been his birth era. A physician, musician, writer, insatiable reader and lover of wilderness, wine, and song. AKA: Trouble...

Stephanie Nolan: lovely, gentle, patient. A true spirit, and Old Soul. Eldest and only daughter of a CEO; also well-traveled, adaptable, tough and highly organized. A doer, if not a dreamer. A nurse by training, and the perfect partner for such an adventure, at least for me.

Luke: 12, eldest son, with the kind heart of his mother. An easy person to love; diligent and responsible. Though a bit prone to panic on occasion... Future CEO.

Claire: 11, beloved eldest daughtie, with all her father's strengths and faults. Bright, brazen, mercurial. Child most likely to attain great heights of success and then disappear, off the grid.

Aidan: 8, second son. Active, outdoorsy, yet surprisingly emotional and tactile. Attention seeking. Our Huck Finn. A bit offbeat and unusual; future direction highly variable, but invariably successful, once he sets his mind to it.

Cate: 6, charming, lovable, quiet. A wide-eyed observer and feeler. Future super-mom and entrepreneur.

Owen: 3, Mercurial, angry then loving in rapid, unpredictable succession. So volatile his (highly appropriate) sibling nickname "Mister Skunky" will stay with him for years. Unfortunately, born handicapped with a rare intrauterine, traumatic avulsion of his cervical, brachial plexus nerve roots affecting his right shoulder and arm. The limb, shoulder and chest wall all entirely paralyzed; he spent his earliest days in the ICU at Albany Medical Center, as well as Columbia-Presbyterian in NYC. A "beautiful bird, with a broken wing" and a highly intelligent child. Voted most likely to succeed due to sheer willpower, become a biomedical engineer, and design his own artificial limb; thereby helping himself and millions of others. Also, his mother's final charge and protected cub. His health issues were a major factor in our delayed exit to Australia, and pretty nearly a deal-breaker for Stephanie; but only nearly.

Sound stressful? You have no idea...

So, Terra Australis - the great Southern land. Meet "Team Nolan", soon to be in-coming. It's like nowhere else on planet Earth. Are we really ready? Let's go!

CHAPTER 3: But I Digress... Pre-launch Jitters

December 20, 2011

DDU blog entry: Back at it briefly while packing, organizing and generally turning the farmhouse up on its head. It's already a plus to work one's way through twelve years of accumulated detritus and streamline, even if staying put. You should try it some time. The place has never felt so freshened up. So, already an unanticipated bonus. How many more await? We shall see. I got a funny note from my friendly recruiter in Auckland, New Zealand today, who noted my first blog entry mentioning that we fancy ourselves to be amateur naturalists.

"Francis, you need to be aware that down here we consider naturalists to be people who prefer to go around without any clothes on."

Uhmm, whoops...

I replied in our defense,

"In the States we prefer the more specific term, nudists."

So much for cultural competency! My first big gaffe and we haven't even left home. (I can only wonder how many more await?)

It's now less than two weeks before lift-off. I'm startled to awaken in midnight and feel that silver shock of reality settling in; keeps one up and the mind races. But then, it always seems no problem once the sun is up and the day begins again. Sort of the final big breath before the thirty-foot plunge into the waiting pool below. Steady, steady...

December 29, 2011

DDU blog entry: So, yesterday was our own version of Boxing Day here at the farm. Not the post-Christmas, gifts to the help, celebration of December 26th in the British ex-Empire. No, this was literally the Big Day, when the movers came to take our belongings away for shipment to Australia. Stephanie, now fully mobilized for the many tasks at hand, was a bit pensive. She wouldn't even pose for a picture with said boxes. "This is your thing, you pose with them," she deferred.

My contract with Queensland Health (QLDH) allowed for 6,000 lbs. of household shipping. Given that we were initially planning only a one-year sabbatical, we decided to travel (very) light, mostly hiking and outdoor gear. Eight boxes in all. A major mistake as it later turned out. We left the farm behind in some sort of suspended animation - closets and drawers full of clothes. My brother J.J. joyriding about in my Subie Outback for the year; brother Joe in Vermont happily babysitting my Kubota tractor. Just keeping the parts warm and moving. We're just stepping out a moment, be back shortly...

December 31, 2011

DDU blog entry: Life throws up all sorts of forks in the road, and in the end, there is only one of two responses allowed. "YES", or "NO". And each leads in a very different direction, with repercussions that will spin off for decades, even generations, hence. In Emergency Medicine we have a pithy saying, "You can't make perfect decisions with imperfect knowledge." We learn to live with the unknown and move forward. So, to this one I say "YES," emphatically, if imperfectly. Good decision or life catastrophe? Time alone will tell...

The kids have been keeping a countdown on our mudroom blackboard for the last month; artwork changed daily courtesy of eldest daughter Claire, age eleven. It started out at thirty days to go, and as of today, we have now arrived at Day Zero. Incoming Australia!!

We are out of time, and on the road from Fairview Farm. Godspeed and

God Bless. A wide, blue world of adventure and new experiences await.

A final, frosty walk around the upper fields with my brother J.J., the brilliant morning sunshine reflecting off a fresh dusting of snow; the landscape now exquisitely revealed through the naked, leafless trees. Time to go, who knows when to return? We crowd into the large, black, rental SUV for the ride through the Catskills south to metro-NYC. One final night staying with family in New Jersey, and then the early morning flight out of JFK, on January 1, 2012. Chosen specifically, if somewhat tongue-in-cheek, to spite the doomsayer's predictions of the end of days, as evidenced by the Mayan calendar. In retrospect, it would have been odd indeed to take off, have the world end below and have nowhere remaining on earth to land, though. The incorrect choice? I wonder sometimes how that would've worked out. This specific date chosen as well in the hope that NYC would be sleeping off the New Year's reverie, and JFK would be uncharacteristically dead quiet. End of the world? Not quite. Looks like we've made it through OK so far.

As expected, the sunrise ride across the GW Bridge from northern Jersey was wide open; the vast bulk of Manhattan lay sleeping it off under a crisp, flawless, New Year's morning. NYC as inscrutable as an urban Outback to me; JFK as windswept and vacant; our drop-off a breeze. I fondly remember our five little kids racing excitedly back and forth, up and down the empty elevators and strangely moving sidewalks. A different world to our protective farmhouse Upstate. It was touching to realize their utter trust that we adults knew exactly what we were doing and that all would be well. If only!

We got into LAX by mid-afternoon and had time to kill until the 2345 overnight across the far-flung Pacific. Outside, a damp, warm mist hung over this unknown west coast city; everything a new experience in the kids' eyes, and our own. We met a few transiting Aussie families at the Qantas gate in LAX; their broad accents and friendly banter already hinting at the many curiosities to come. Finally, it was time to board, for the giant, fourteen-hour leap across the empty expanse of the vast Pacific, and all that lay beyond...

CHAPTER 4: Night Flight to Paradise

January 2012

Looking back, I'm surprised that there was only one moment of really high anxiety - barely controlled - bordering on terror, as our adventure unfolded. I recall the moment with clear intensity even to this day. We seven were in an aluminum tube, paper-thin in the sub-zero atmosphere at 35,000 feet. Flying trans-Pacific, somewhere south of the Hawaiian Islands, in the middle of the night, Pacific Standard Time (PST). LAX (LA) to BNE (Brisbane) flights leave nightly at 2345 PST or 0245 Eastern Standard Time (EST). It's around a fourteen-hour flight, a very long time to hang in the sky. So, groggy from fitful sleep, in the pre-dawn hour of around 0500 EST, in the near-hallucinatory midnight haze of the double-legged journey out of JFK (New York), I must've slipped mentally and let long suppressed, ghostly doubts animate at last. It suddenly dawned on me: the enormity of our traveling some twelve-thousand miles towards the Australian continent to a State, town and job I'd never even visited. Totally foreign, with my wife and five kids, ages only twelve to three, sleeping restlessly in their seats surrounding me. All innocently trusting in me to make the right decisions with their lives and our fates. What had I unleashed, and what drove me to this sudden, searing moment of bottomless doubt? Long story...but now a nearly overwhelming sense of electrifying alarm ran through my entire being. This was all suddenly becoming very, very real. Stephanie vindicated!

Earlier, following my globe-trotting, CEO father-in-law's recipe for managing long overseas flights, he being a seasoned road warrior, we had boarded in LAX at 2330, gotten up to altitude and had a generous dinner. His tried-and-true method: "Finish your dinner, have a glass of wine, and pop one of these," as he handed me a couple Ambien 10 mg tabs. "You'll drift off, and hopefully wake at least eight hours closer to your destination, feeling pretty refreshed - with no hangover." Sounded like the plan. All went as scheduled until the after-dinner wine. By now it being around 0500 EST, I was REALLY groggy and drifting in and out. As I dutifully brought the Ambien tablet up to my mouth, I actually faded out and dropped it; it bounced off my chest and rolled back down the aisle towards the plane's filthy tail. Oh great! I came to, still in my deep, post-prandial haze. I calculated...should I get up and chase it down; and then what, eat it off the floor?

As I was sorting out what would constitute an acceptable level of parental unconsciousness, up ahead I noticed a commotion. Our little Cate, then a mere five, was in a blind panic outside the mid-cabin lavatories. Green at the gills. Oh-oh... I jumped up with a barf baggy open in hand. At my approach she turned wild-eyed, and literally released a solid stream of vomit, in an impressive arc; a liquid line-drive of kiddie digestive contents and macerated airline junk food, that I somehow managed to corral into the baggy, in mid-flight, with impressively little backsplash!

That performance put an end to my dreams of any Ambien-induced bliss. I was a father after all. I had a role to fulfill...

After six hours of JFK-LAX, believe me when I say the LAX-BNE leg is just interminable. Twelve to fourteen hours depending on the headwinds. That's two or three movies, several complete music CDs and still a full USA continental flight. You get up, stretch regularly, drink plenty of water and hopefully avoid a DVT (deep vein thrombosis). Fortunately, the lovely QANTAS crew, with those sexy, exotic Aussie accents, are very familiar with the drill. I was up every one to two hours doing deep knee bends in the back snack aisle without eliciting even an odd look. Just another day at the office for them.

Finally, the vast, black bulk of Moreton Island, an offshore barrier island, loomed below, surrounded by the silver-blue, metallic sheen of the Coral Sea shimmering in the growing dawn light. Land-Ho...! How exotic, how exhilarating! The cabin lights come up and the crew gets busy with their landing preps.

The captain, incongruously cheerfully states, "G'Day folks it's a beautiful morning in Brisbin, 'Stralia. Clear, sunny skies with a top of thirty-two degrees, winds light at four to six knots out of the Southeast." (What does that even mean...it's all in metric for God's sake...?!)

"Crew, prepare the cabin for landing. The local time is 0600, the third of January, 2012."

And just like that, in addition to having a thoroughly numb ass from enduring the longest sitting spell ever, we have finally arrived on the East Coast of Australia and have already lost an entire day. Just where did the second of January go again? It's been repeatedly explained to me, but I still don't get it entirely. I mean, I GET it, but not really.

After blearily transiting the fluorescent, abattoir-like flurry of Customs and Immigration, then Baggage Check, we emerge from the semi-dark, air-conditioned cocoon of the terminal into the warm wave of floral, humid heat that is Brisbane, Australia at mid-summer. Coming from a northern hemisphere mid-winter, the sunlight is blinding, the warmth enveloping and lovely against the skin. Flowers and greenery are everywhere in their full, exotic ripeness. This place is alive, but clean, calm and orderly. Everyone is minimally clothed, tanned and smiling pleasantly beneath their ubiquitous sunnies.

Exotic birds are racing raucously though the filigreed verge of the parking lots...the parking lots! We squint and stumble forward, looking for our promised pickup, but not knowing who we will be meeting. Suddenly, a fit, trimmed, salt and peppered gent with a curiously British-styled, WW1 military mustache thrusts his hand forward briskly, breaking my nauseated somnolence, and says in a broad Australian accent, "G'Day Doctor Nolan, I'm Doctor Dennis March. Welcome to 'Stralia."

And we enter into an entirely new world...

CHAPTER 5: Arrival Evolves into Awakening

January 2012

DDU Blog entry: Though we've only been in-country for one week, it feels like months have passed. I suppose that's to be expected when so many new experiences are being flashed before you at every turn. Especially after being awake thirty-six plus hours in transit, then driving from the airport on the left, British-style, with all the traffic coming at you from unexpected angles, followed by the inevitable "mega-crash" into deep sleep and a resetting of the biological clock. I still can't figure out how we lost Monday January 2, 2012. Literally... Flew out of LAX at 2345 on Sunday, New Year's Day and arrived 0730 on Tuesday Jan 3rd, after flying for 14.5 hrs. Hmmm... Can someone else figure it all out and get back to me please. Disorienting for sure; perhaps we travel less well as we age.

So, arrival, then awakening into Aussie mid-summer: hot, stunning sunshine, a plethora of strange, exotic birds with unfamiliar voices; Rainbow Lorikeets, Kookaburra, and various raucous Parrots. And of course, the exotically-scented Eucalyptus with their attendant Koalas. Surprisingly, we saw two in a local park on our first foray to do so. One was "running" along on the ground. Actually, it was more a slow ramble; apparently while moving to a cooler, shadier tree, according to a local. The kids wanted to go find Koalas as a first priority, and voila, there they were. As they sleep for some twenty-two hours of every day, we were quite lucky indeed to see them at all; much less to see one moving on the ground. One of the most sedentary thrills ever!

Cleveland, where I'll be working, is a pleasant, green, agricultural town of around 12,000, only 20 km from the Brisbane Central Business District, or CBD. Right on the coast, overlooking Moreton Bay, it's the rapidly suburbanizing county seat, or Shire. Being a Shire town, the compact, historic downtown has all the regional government offices, courthouse and local hospital. The region was named the Redland by early settlers due to the deep color of the iron-rich soils found locally. The Redland Shire, encompassing some eight townships, has a base population of around 160,000, across an area approximately 10 by 30 km. In 1970, the entire area population was only around 25,000, so it's been growing pretty rapidly since. The southern half of the Shire remains tightly zoned and resolutely agricultural, with a large local poultry industry, as well as vineyards, flower and truck vegetable farming and even some cattle grazing. But everywhere the pressure of outwardly expanding and rapidly modernizing Brisbane is felt.

Even with the generally clean, orderly and well-designed public spaces around Cleveland and greater Brisbane in general, it's obvious, and a bit disappointing truthfully to the newcomer, that it's not all paradise in reality. Very nice yes; paradise, well, not exactly. Modern Aussie sprawl, all low-set and built to ward off the drenching seasonal rains, as well as the blistering subtropical summer heat, is singularly uninspiring, and definitely an acquired taste. Older heritage buildings are often retro-fitted with blunt metal awnings, topped by flat, simply painted, strictly functional signs that appear curiously, from a distance, like a string of mini-billboards. Driving in from the airport, my initial impressions were along the lines of, "Yuck, Stephanie's going to hate this place, and maybe me too..." But then the suburban sprawl gives way to spacious public parks, heritage neighborhoods, well-designed greenways shaded by the stately, drooping Eucalypts and the stunning aqua expanse of the ever-present ocean. Overall, a very pleasant version of modern, suburban reality.

DDU blog entry: My most startling image so far; picture if you will, ninety-plus degrees F, we're flat out "baking like lizards" at the local community pool. And a family there actually had a portable doughnut maker, complete with mini-deep fat fryer, sizzling away at their poolside picnic lunch. Hmmm... It looks like I'll have my work cut out for me as a physician, here too...

The Nolan kids' first day of Aussie school!

DDU Blog entry: Our four older kids are starting today at the local Catholic primary school, fortunately all together in the same place. Owen, only three, stayed behind with Mum. Surprisingly, about half of all Aussie kids attend non-public schools, many Catholic, and the Government subsidizes the choice. Uniforms mandatory, including sun hats and dress skirts or shorts, even in the State (public) schools. Individual uniform colors and patterns identify school affiliation. Very Brit... definitely a change from fashion-conscious American school dress and a big relief to busy parents, who only need to make two choices here: sport uniform or standard? We were entertained by the sight of our four American kids all kitted-out in their Aussie school uniforms, complete with broad, dorky sun hats. We lined them up by height and took photos as they chattered excitedly; each bravely heading off onto their own foreign adventures Down Under.

Curiously, on the kids' returning home after school's very first day, in a warm summer rain, we found a six -foot Carpet Python sprawled out in the front garden. Initially, uncertain as to its lethality, we were cautious in our approach. Forearm thick, brilliantly colored and quite exotic, it's not rare to find Carpet Pythons around suburban homes, gutters and especially chicken coops. Though they will strike, they're non-venomous, killing by constriction and suffocation, then swallowing their prey whole. Many locals have a favorite "pet" Python that they tolerate on their premises to keep away opossums and small rodents. So, a good-luck omen for the school year, or perhaps a sign of something slightly more sinister? Claire's eleven-year-old classmate was rather blasé on hearing the news. "Oh yeah, you'll see them around the house, but not usually when it's raining."

We are temporarily housed in a tidy, three-bedroom rental, paid for by the hospital; to assist us while settling into Cleveland. Located on a quiet cul-de-sac, with a lovely park just around the corner. We take evening walks through the stately groves of large Eucalyptus or Gum Trees. They seem strange trees to us, as their leaves remain evergreen, while the bark peels off as they mature; revealing smooth, ghost-white trunks that reflect the intense summer heat. Their aromatic bouquet is unforgettable, being slightly reminiscent of a cough lozenge.

The local bird life is stunning and quite raucous, as hundreds fly in and out to roost of an evening. Stark white Cockatoos with large yellow crests, Crimson Rosellas, Galahs - medium-sized, handsomely rose-colored, ground-feeding parrots with a pale gray top knot, and most animated of all, the swift-flying squadrons of multi-colored Rainbow Lorikeets, a smaller, nectar-eating parakeet. In large roosting trees, their evening chatter of thousands is near deafening; so loud, in fact, you need to go indoors to have a phone conversation! Small family groups of Kookaburra, actually the world's largest kingfisher, laugh maniacally in the warm, settling dusk. Thus, the wild music of the Australian bush, right here in our suburban backyard, adds an almost surreal element that contributes much to our sense of being adrift in a very foreign environment.

The weather continues hot and humid at mid-summer. Heavy afternoon thunderstorms build regularly into the darkening evening, and the rain, when it comes, pours down in sudden torrents; thunderous and deafening on the metal verandah rooftops, gushing out of the downspouts and overflowing drains. A different world altogether than back home in rural New York. Everyone remains in good spirits, trying to make sense of so many new experiences coming so suddenly at us all. We bond and share stories and first impressions as Team Nolan; our kinship tightened by our common sense of being outsiders looking in. The kids are already quite skilled at mimicking the tricky Australian accents of their schoolmates, especially adorable little Cate, now six and a budding Aussie Chick, who loves to fool her classmates into thinking she's a local, and then switching effortlessly into an exotic, American accent.

CHAPTER 6: Beauty and Danger... It's a Very Fine Line

February 2012

DDU Blog entry: Out and about in a vast, surprising country. In the weeks after landing and adjusting to life in the Southern Hemisphere, we've begun to get out and about a bit more within a few hours of Brisbane. Queensland is blessed with an extensive, 2000 km coastline, including the Great Barrier Reef, fronting a fertile coastal plain and backed up by the forested mountains of the Great Dividing Range. These mountains catch most of the moisture coming in off the Coral Sea and are spectacularly lush and diverse. Over the Range, the dry, western side stretches on for hundreds of kilometers, gradually transitioning from drier, open eucalypt and pine forest, through grazing rangelands and finally opening out into the truly arid outback of lore and legend. In short, a complex series of environments, many of which have been preserved in an array of parks and preserves. Queensland alone contains some seventy-five National Parks. We've already been to several, including the Springbrook plateau and the Glass House Mountains, both remnants of Australia's volcanic past, some 20 million years ago, and seemingly right out of the Lost World.

Brisbane, the capital of Queensland, sits in the rapidly growing southeast corner of this vast state. At roughly three times the size of Texas, Queensland has a population of only around 5 million people. Half of these live in the southeast corner; ~2 million between greater Brisbane and the Gold Coast, south to the border with New South Wales. Otherwise, it's a raw, sprawling, sparsely populated state. Geographically, a mosaic of sub-tropical transitioning to full-tropical coastline north above Cairns, a vast interior of savannah grasslands separated from the coast by the spine of the verdant, richly forested, 3,000-foot Great Dividing Range that runs, north to south along the length of the state, and actually, onward down the entire Australian east coast. West of the range, the beef and sheep producing grazing lands eventually give way to the true red-dirt Outback of Australian lore. Queensland also happens to contain the 1500 km Great Barrier Reef, running just offshore. So, in addition to being Australia's water sports playground, Queensland is one of Australia's major food-producing regions, giving forth a year-round bounty of fresh and varied produce. Everything from strawberries to mangoes, avocados, carrots, lettuce and other truck vegetables, even coffee and tea. It's also a major producer and exporter of beef, lamb, fresh seafood and shellfish. Occupying the entire Northeast quadrant of the continent, it's essentially a giant, Australian combination of Florida and Texas, with a bit of southern California and Polynesia thrown into the mix. Further out in the remotest west, it's also a major producer and exporter of coal and natural gas. All in all, it's a very lucky country indeed!

DDU Blog entry: Southeast Queensland is much more lush and diverse than we'd imagined. The contrasts can be truly startling. Malevolent appearing spiders give way to fragrant blossoms, only yards apart. A most intriguing region to explore, but you really must watch your step!

We decided to take a short twenty-minute ferry hop over to Coochiemudlo Island on Moreton Bay, noted for its beautiful sand beaches. And it was beautiful; hot, sunny and laid back. Seemingly a world away from the busy mainland, visible just across the strait. The kids were all eager for a swim, only not so fast... It seems an unusual combination of wind and tide had washed a large blossom of stinging jellyfish into the shallows. Not the truly deadly Box Jellyfish (the graphically named "sea wasps") of far northern Queensland and the true tropics beyond, but creatures capable of delivering a sharp sting from the sea nonetheless. Yikes!

The local lads were having a fine challenge trying to scoop them in their hands and throw them up onto the beach but were getting more than a few stings that they gamely laughed off. The trick was to grab them by their mushroom-shaped heads and flick fast, avoiding the short, trailing tentacles, which are apparently the business end of this business. The local Surf Lifesaver Club was netting them into gelatinous piles of the softest blue, trying in vain to keep the waters clear for swimming.

Of course, sons Luke and Aidan began immediately spearing and shredding them apart with sticks, "This is way better than swimming, Dad!" they shouted gleefully.

Predictably, within minutes Luke flung one ashore in a spray of wet sand and jellyfish particles, hitting three-year old Owen square in the face and eyes. He, quite understandably, erupted into a howling tirade that promptly alarmed the Surf Lifesaver crew. We suddenly got their full attention with ice packs and an ice- cold, bottled-water eye irrigation, performed by yours truly, Doctor Nolan, right there on the placid beach. Thanks boys, very much appreciated...

After an hour or so, the screaming wound down into a piteous, fatigued weeping and finally, blessed sleep. We all settled back into our tropical idyll. She'll be right, mate...

Following that drama, in a misguided act of brotherly revenge, Aidan thought it a funny idea to drop a live jellyfish into the genital end of Luke's bathing suit, or "togs", in Aussie parlance. I'm not kidding here, though he insists it was one of the less toxic clear ones, and not a "Blue Blubber". Luke spent fifteen frantic minutes howling dramatically, while rinsing off his "nerds" under the public water fountain, just there, in the local park; observed by all passers-by with some mildly shocked reactions!

As our blissful afternoon slipped away, another unexpected danger made its presence felt, in the unrelenting intensity of the southern sun at midsummer. Wonderful to bask in initially, but very soon overwhelming at the height of day. It really is a physical force to respect. In the Emergency Department, as Cleveland is a well-established retirement area, I see the almost unimaginable skin damage done over a lifetime of pale Caucasian meets the Sun King in the pre-SPF 50 era. These guys and gals got grilled and peeled, over and over and over again, plain and simple. The angry raised furuncle of a Basal Cell Carcinoma (BCC) is common in these climes, as are the many partially resected, truly dog-eared, ear and nose tips from multiple past similar excisions. Australia, unsurprisingly, has the world's highest incidence of skin cancers, and to be in private practice as a Dermatology Consultant here is literally a license to print money. So, slather up, people. Or as the Aussies teach their kids about sunscreen use,

"Slip, Slap and Slop"!

Back on the mainland, that very same evening, the boys and I went out fishing on Cleveland Point. There's a beautiful old wooden lighthouse, a small, manicured picnic park and the Lighthouse Restaurant that serves wonderful homemade Sorbet and Gelato. As we were walking into the shadowy park, happily licking, a man's voice interrupted,

"Excuse me mate, if you're walking across the park, watch out, there's a snake just over there..."

He came over with a small flashlight and seemed rather authoritative about such things.

"That's no Python (common, large, but harmless), I think she's a Brownie," he exclaimed, meaning an Eastern Brown Snake (nondescript, but extremely toxic, aggressive and potentially deadly).

Well, that caught me totally by surprise and suddenly burst my sunshine-gelato state of mind! I tried to get a few quick cell phone shots in the semi-dark by light of flash, while keeping my distance somewhat, as the boys warned me to beware. Even creepier, the five-foot serpent then slithered over to one of the small picnic pavilions and was last seen by us curled up at the base of a BBQ grill. We told a few people, but left feeling like we should have set off the nuclear snake alarm or something. An especially scary encounter, as this wasn't way out in the bush, but right in a heavily trafficked town park area. So, beauty and danger; close cousins and subtle role-shifters here in the land Down Under. It pays to keep a sharp eye and a quick step!

Deadly Neighbors:

Reading the above entries from my more seasoned vantage point of today, in 2022, it brings to mind the most frequent reaction to our telling people that we've been living in Australia for some years:

"Oh my God, isn't the place full of things that will attack and kill you?!"

Well, in my personal experience, "Yes, and... no, not really...It's complicated..."

Australia is home to some of the deadliest critters on the planet. Very true. You may be familiar with sayings like, "Of the world's top ten deadliest snakes, nine of them live in Australia." Well, that depends on how you define deadly. It turns out there are actually international point grading systems devised that take into account, not just lethality, but metrics such as aggressiveness, rarity, strength and volume of venom (which vary considerably over time in the same snake), frequency of dry bites (in some species up to thirty percent) and especially, local population densities of both humans and snakes, to come up with an overall likelihood ratio of encountering, being bitten by and then succumbing to said bite. By these metrics, Indian Cobras, while having venom one hundred times less lethal than some Aussie snakes, are far deadlier, due to frequency of contact, bites and the lack of readily available anti-venom. Australian Inland Taipans, in contrast, have by far the most potent venom of any snake worldwide, but they're nocturnal, underground desert dwellers; and so are rarely encountered even when out in their Outback habitat. Make sense?

Still, some Australian creatures, like the common Blue-Ringed Octopus, have neurotoxins that are so over-the-top deadly (it's reportedly the deadliest natural neurotoxin ever discovered on the planet) that it leaves scientists scratching their heads as to the evolutionary advantage of producing such a powerful substance. Apocryphal stories abound. I like the one of the foreign tourists who found a dead Blue-Ring on a beach in northern Queensland. While goofing around taking photos, one put the critter on a mate's shoulder, whereupon it promptly re-animated, bit him and he died right there on the beach. Fair dinkum? I have no idea, but I do know a fellow ED physician and friend, originally Czech, who was scuba diving and found this cute little octopus in the rocks. He couldn't resist hassling it with his hands...especially when doing so caused it to display these fascinating bright blue rings all over its body. Luckily, he happened to be wearing diving gloves, as it was only later that he learned he was messing with one of the deadliest creatures in all the seven seas!

So many good stories! To keep things on track, I've rounded up the bad actors into species, and will relate personal experiences I've had, or stories I've heard during my time here that seem at least plausible. The Brisbane Times, a free daily online newspaper, is very good in this regard. I like the local focus, and they have cracker Travel and Food sections as well. Every couple of weeks they report on the tragic stories of people, usually tourists and visitors, succumbing to wild Aussie dangers while snorkeling on the Reef, falling off of various peaks and escarpments, wandering around lost in the outback after running out of petrol, drowning in waterholes, surfers being attacked by Great Whites, Utes being swallowed whole by watery sinkholes, or rolling over off sand dunes and killing all aboard. That sort of stuff... Real News! It's always a fascinating read, one that's sure to whet your Outback adventure appetite. Have a go!

Another complicating factor is that while tourists and urbanites tend to overestimate their chances of a similarly toxic encounter, the hard-core among the large Aussie bushwalker/ greenie/ scientific outdoors community, on the other hand, tends to dismiss the odds. I'm not sure if it's a machismo, been-there-done-that sort of attitude, but in my experience it's more along the lines of, "Well mate, if you're out in the bush, ya can expect to get what the bush sends ya way. Harden up."

Snakes Rights folk...or something. A bit eccentric, really...

So, proceeding in order of currency, or likelihood that you might encounter similar:

Sharks:
No personal physical experiences, except for a few tense moments when I saw approaching fins while ocean swimming and was relieved to meet some friendly dolphins. But for surfers and ocean distance swimmers, a real and growing risk - to the point that debates around reinstituting shark culls are happening widely along the affected coastlines. Shark defenders point out that we humans are willingly entering into their habitats, and that the annual kill ratio, Humans: Sharks, is currently running around ten of us : two million of them, worldwide. But faint comfort to the victims or survivors though.

There seem to be a few hot spots; on the East Coast, especially between Byron Bay and Evans Head on the northern NSW coast (my happy place!), and in the southwest of Western Australia (WA) below Perth. A fellow ED doc and friend who's an avid surfer was recently filming his mates with an overhead drone, while sitting on their boards awaiting the perfect wave, just past the surf breaks at Lennox Heads, NSW - a really cool use of technology to improve performance. On later review of the images, they were shocked to see the shadowy form of a large Great White shark trailing behind them by less than 50m in the crystal-clear waters. They'd never even seen the shark in the water! The coastal shark patrols are now using drones in real time to watch for sharks moving along high-risk coastlines, and the images they're able to capture are stunning, if a bit spooky. We never realized what was lurking, just beyond our sight!

Another recent personal experience: Four of my senior ED Registrars (Residents), two couples newly arrived from Britain and the NHS, went down to Byron Bay for the weekend. While wading in knee deep, gin-clear water, they saw what they thought was a Dugong (Sea Manatee) floating, surrounded by seaweed, just ahead of them. As they came upon it, they were shocked to find a middle-aged male body, face down, leg raggedly ripped off above the knee, floating over a pool of freshly congealed blood! They literally pulled him ashore themselves and called for help, but he was fully exsanguinated and DOA to the beach. In this highly publicized case, the man was for years a member of a local, daily ocean swimming club, taking their routine morning swim; with his wife waiting further along the beach at their destination. Nobody in the group even realized he was missing or heard the attack. My British Registrars were quite traumatized by the experience, so I tried to offer some professional perspective and solace by stating,

"In your entire Emergency Medicine careers, what do you think the chances of your being first on-scene to a fatal Great White attack would be? You'll never see that again."

Small comfort perhaps, but highly unlikely indeed. Still, the sharks are definitely out there, and they can be deadly, or if not outright fatal, severely traumatizing, physically as well as psychologically. The book and movie "Soul Surfer" is the incredible true story of the world champion surfer Bethany Hamilton's being attacked, surviving and then re-gaining the skills and courage necessary to compete again professionally after a devastating shark attack off of Hawaii, and is highly recommended for its realism and portrayal of human courage and resilience after such an event.

But, then again, "what are the odds, mate?"

Snakes:
Everyone's deepest fear, along with spiders I suppose, see below.

I must admit to being a bit of a snake magnet during my time in Australia. Some people hike for years and never see many. But I've seen plenty, probably more than my share. Simple fact, if you spend time out in the Aussie bush, especially in summer, you can expect to encounter snakes. Sipping a coffee latte at Bondi Beach, you're unlikely to have a problem. But if you go bush and want to encounter snakes, "Oi mate, Oz has got ya covered, no worries."

It is curious that our first two snake encounters happened right in Cleveland village; the Carpet Python omen on the kids' first day of school, and the nocturnal serpent at the Cleveland Point park; that in the end, was most likely a Rough-Scaled (or Clarence River) Snake; quite toxic and aggressive, if a bit far north of prime territory, according to a snake expert I later showed the photos to. We've never seen another snake in Cleveland since our first month here! A "Welcome to 'Stralia' present" perhaps?

The Brisbane Times is, again, intriguing here. Like clockwork, as the summer weather heats up around Christmas time, the snakes become more active, on the move and looking for mates, and reports of close encounters skyrocket. Professional snake removalists (really...) are kept busy responding to wayward serpents in gutters, homes and especially suburban sheds and chicken coops. And when it gets blistering hot, the snakes will often seek a cool pool of water to get some relief, aka the nearest toilet bowl...seriously. Local EDs report more snakebites and everyone's a bit more careful walking in the parks at night. I've seen a few bites in my time, none severe, and ED management has evolved considerably over the years. We now advise a simple circumferential limb compression bandage, tight enough to impede lymphatic, but not blood flow; resting the limb and transporting said victim to the nearest ED. We'll get baseline labs and a coagulation profile, observe for deterioration after the bandage is removed; repeat the labs at twelve hours and see how you're going. Any early deterioration, and the bite is swabbed to try to ID the venom as one of five sub-family types. Valent-specific anti-venom is then given to arrest further decline. Multi-valent anti-venom, covering any and all possibilities, is avoided, if possible, due to higher rates of severe patient reactions and even anaphylaxis. With this regimen, costs are saved, unnecessary anti-venom is avoided, and it's become statistically rare to have a severe outcome or death in a monitored, 1st world patient setting. However, lack of access to effective antivenom remains a major public-health problem in poorer countries.

I've never actually had to give a patient anti-venom, as the rates of dry strikes/ bites are quite high as well. Another recommendation that's finally out, is for bystanders to attempt any strike wound (especially ass-cheek) sucking. Thankfully that; where the mate of the victim (who's often struck in the behind while sitting down, to be clear) was formerly advised to cut between the fang puncture wounds, place lips in a tight seal and suck like hell (aka the "taste and spit" method) to save erstwhile friend's life. Although an iron-clad test of true mateship, it provides no clinical benefit otherwise. Medical progress...isn't it beautiful!

But things can still go wrong, and sometimes quite dramatically so. My favorite snake story, again courtesy of the Brisbane Times, occurred up in far north Queensland a few years back. The following conversation implied by events only; some artistic license allowed if you please...

The scene: Mates practicing amateur rugby under the lights up in far north Queensland. Evening, mid-summer, full humid heat. A small nondescript snake appears in the grass, on field...

"Look out mate, she's a Brownie..." (i.e. a Brown Snake; common, aggressive and highly toxic)

"Nah mate, that's a green snake, harmless..." (As an aside, snake colors and patterns are highly variable, and even experts can't always reliably field ID snakes by appearance alone.)

"Yeah, nah mate, I don't think so..."

The one bloke, a fit, healthy thirty-five-year-old, picks up the snake by the tail, flips it off into the verge...

"Shite, she's nipped me thumb...bugger...!"

"Ok, lads, let's do a few laps 'round the oval."

Off they go, running round the oval, for twenty or thirty minutes, and suddenly the nipped bloke drops stone dead at the far end of the field. Stone... Dead....

Coincidence? Perhaps. Seems it was probably a Brownie after all...

Another fond memory from a few years back: I was hiking out of a tropical waterhole in the Daintree National Park, up in far north Queensland with Luke and Aidan, after a refreshing dip in a crystal clear, stone-bottomed pool. An entirely magical experience in the tropical heat and stifling humidity. Up ahead, commotion on the trail... A small cluster of photographers, Germans by accent, were focused intently, peering into the foliage beside the trail. Chattering excitedly, with great gear: telephoto lenses, tripods, even an overhead portable light source, crowding each other for the shot. These guys were pros. We walked up to see what was so interesting, and...

"Oh my God!" I almost "Shite me togs!"

Right off the trail, only a few feet away, within easy striking distance, was a medium-sized, dull pewter snake, moving slowly. It's a Coastal Taipan, one of the top three deadliest snakes in the world, i.e., very deadly. And known to become quite aggressive if harassed. I was certain of this, as I'd just seen an identical live specimen at the Emergency Medicine (EM) conference in Cairns a few days earlier.

And these guys had the proverbial "No Idea..."

The snake seemed unconcerned, which was lucky for them. I did warn them that their photo subject was extremely deadly, and perhaps they should move back a bit. But truth be told, I couldn't resist risking my own life to snap a few quick cell phone shots of my own. The overhead lighting was perfect... Modern problems! We walked on, and I'm not sure how their serpentine encounter ended. But I did scan the Brissie Times for a few days following, and there were no reports of any German tourists dropping off suddenly dead, at least. There are many more stories, perhaps less dramatic, but a few Aussie realities exist:

In the right season and environments, there are snakes aplenty. They are very tough to tell apart by appearance and color alone. The deadliest, and some are astonishingly deadly, are often the most drab and nondescript. And finally, some reassurance. With the right treatment, in a timely manner, deaths are now very rare.

And please do remember, ass-cheek sucking on your mate, or a complete stranger for that matter, is no longer recommended or required in any form!

There, don't we all feel better now...?

Spiders:

Arachnophobia!! Even the term sounds scary. I don't really have it, but let's face it, who's really fond of spiders? They're ugly, somewhat menacing, and their intent is never quite clear, as they stare you down with those rows of beady, black eyes. If enlarged to say, car-sized, they'd be about the freakiest creatures on the planet, for sure. The only reassurance we have is that we're so much larger, and they're squishy. They're crushable... So, while I don't have a visceral hatred of spiders, there's no particular fondness. And certainly, no love. How about you?

There are lots of spiders in Australia...really big and fast ones. They make massive webs overnight across paths and trails, or right in your home garden, that I always seem to be walking into. These webs are thick, sticky and tenacious. They feel truly awful across your face first thing on a muggy morning.

Luckily, one Aussie spider truism is, as a local friend cheerfully told me about bushwalking, "Oi mate, me Mum always told us as kids, don't worry about the ones who build webs across the trails. It's the ones that live in holes underground that will kill ya..."

And that's a pretty decent summary actually. The large, golden-orbs and web-building garden variety spiders, while fearsome to encounter, are generally pretty harmless. But they do have this species called a Funnel-Web Spider down south of here, common in backyards all over the Sydney area, that is a nasty little actor, and can, indeed, deliver a fatal bite. I'm not sure how you raise kids in such an environment, but trust me, teach your children... If you see a neat little spun-silken tunnel entering a hole in the ground, about a dime sized in diameter, do not ever stick your finger or any living member into it!

Another bad actor, common to the Brisbane area is the Huntsman Spider. It's dirty brown, hairy and almost salad-plate sized; as big as your outstretched palm, when fully grown. If you hate spiders, these fellows are your biggest nightmare. Luckily, although they can bite, they are non-venomous. If venomous, they'd be widely considered the worst creature on earth, because of the following combination of traits: 1) they're common, 2) love closets, bedding, stored blankets, i.e., cozy human living spaces and 3) they're blindingly fast and will even jump to escape your flying fist, foot or folded newspaper. They just appear, like something out of Alien Invaders. Surprising and terrifying to confront as you enter a closet or whatever darkened space your mind might imagine. On several occasions when I'd hear sudden, high-pitched screams of sheer terror coming from Claire or Cate's bedrooms, I'd get up, grab a magazine and just assume, "Huntsman..." Most of the time they'll actually out-maneuver me and get away, perhaps leaving behind a few shattered, twitching legs...

My favorite Huntsman memory was Claire's near drowning (Huntsmans at Sea; pretty rare but hear me out...). She and Cate, at ages twelve and eight, were showing great initiative, rolling the kayaks off the dock and going in for a paddle, all by themselves. I suddenly heard a familiar panicked screaming down at the canal. Serious screaming... It seems a Huntsman had taken up residence behind one sun-warmed kayak's seat back. Once the girls were underway, it appeared on the gunnel, to Claire's absolute terror! She began screaming and swinging her paddle, which only agitated the spider, who, now surrounded by a sudden moat, began rapid, evasive maneuvers by running all over the kayak, from side to side and back and forth; blindingly fast, avoiding both the drink and the paddle. Claire, by the time I got to her, was nearly flipping the boat and trying to self-eject, come hell or high water! It was a most unusual scene and very, very funny, to this onlooker at least. I managed to grab her paddle and pull her in, whereupon she sprang from the kayak in completely adrenalized

40

"fight or flight" terror, moving almost as fast as the Huntsman...Wow!!
She's been very unenthusiastic about kayaking ever since, and insists I flip
and inspect the craft thoroughly before even considering any such trip.

So, that's Sharks, Snakes and Spiders, in brief. We opened with
Crocodiles, but could re-visit in detail... Had enough? I could go on and on
about poisonous Cane Toads, Stonefish, Sea Snakes and myriad marine
nasties. Stingrays anyone? RIP, Steve Irwin. Perhaps Cone Shells ("If it's a
cone, leave it alone..."). Why, you might ask? Just.leave.it.alone...

Oh **Jellyfish**!

I almost forgot the Jellies. It's a big subject and very varied. Briefly, a
few tips: if it's hot weather, and you are north of Gladstone on the east
coast, and there are no locals swimming in that shimmering, aquamarine
sea - just stay out. Seriously, don't go in! There are likely seasonal jellyfish
around. Either the barely visible Irukandji, whose sting you'll hardly feel
until you have a hyper-sympathetic, nervous system discharge on the beach
some twenty to ninety minutes later. Severe nausea, vomiting, diarrhea,
cramps, muscle rigidity... maybe even a hypertensive crisis, aka the
"Irukandji Syndrome". All the fun stuff, but fortunately, rarely fatal. It will
ruin your day at the beach for certain though. Or, if you're unlucky enough
to encounter a Box Jellyfish, the colorfully named "Sea Wasp;" a much
larger and tropical seasonal visitor, well, the pain is said to be beyond
intense. Victims beg to have the affected limb cut off. and these stings can
be fatal. So please, follow the local's advice on any planned tropical sea-
bathing.

I personally survived being stung by the common Man-O-War, or
"Bluebottle", while body surfing out on Stradbroke Island. It was literally
the only damn one out there that day; a friend called out...

"Look out mate, a Bluey...!"

I turned and saw its little blue-bubble sail, cresting a wave around ten
feet from me, and made for the opposite direction, pronto. Just when I
thought I was all in the clear, I felt the sudden, wispy embrace of its long
trailing tentacles wrap AROUND my entire naked torso. Before I could
finish thinking..."Oh, Shi..." BAM, I was jolted by a sudden. blinding
electrical shock of pain. Zowie!! It hurt like hell! I made it to shore and got

under a warm beach shower, which did nothing to quell the linear welts that were blossoming around my feverishly burning body. So, I simply hardened up... no tears, mate. The net effect was like being horse-whipped, repeatedly, for a good hour or so. But, hey, at least I'm still alive. Note to self: assiduously avoid Bluebottles in future.

When the strong onshore Northerlies are blowing, Blueys will sometimes wash up in large numbers, literally lining the water's edge with a soft, azure thread of bubbles as far as you can see. Deathly beautiful...Wise folk then stay well and truly out of the water. One such afternoon, while strictly beach walking on Cylinder Beach, I could hear the occasional kid-yelp of sea-bathers chirping over the breaking surf; their harried mothers rushing sandpiper-like over to comfort them and saw many swimmers heading up to the Surf Lifesaver's tent for ice. I wasn't going in, no way. When I casually walked up to the iconic red and yellow tent and inquired if they'd been busy with Bluebottle stings over the weekend, the surf lifeguard just grinned and said, "Oh, hundreds, mate..."

Anyway, I hope you get the idea. Australia's a pretty hazardous place, but not really THAT hazardous. There are things you can do to minimize the risks; like stay well and truly indoors. Otherwise, stay alert, stay alive; enjoy the spectacular scenery and natural beauty. And if things don't exactly go your way, harden up mate..!

CHAPTER 7: Back to the Pit, Aussie Emergency Medicine Adventures

February 2012

DDU Blog entry: Eventually, I had to begin work again in the Emergency Department (ED). This being "Doc" Down Under, there is a significant medical component involved. I'll be using ED medical shorthand somewhat when discussing particulars, just in the interest of getting through it all. So, Emergency Medicine (EM, is the discipline, not the place; we practice EM in the ED. Everyone got it? Good...carry on...) in Australia.

I just finished my first round of four ten-hour shifts as a Senior EM Consultant. The ED is well-equipped and modern. Very well-staffed by US standards, but busy. I round regularly with the charge nurse and keep things flowing, beds turning over and transfers/ admits all heading in their appropriate directions. Beyond the clinical, or medical component, patient bed flow management is an art in itself. The charge nurses here know the system and get it done. I mostly tag along and add my two cents now and then. Junior doctors run cases by me and I advise and teach procedures like complex suture repairs, fracture reductions and procedural sedation.

On my third shift I was running a twenty-bed acute side with a team of six junior docs. My "mentor" is Yogesh, an affable, Fijian-Indian EM doc who's been in this ED all of one week longer than me. Everyone else senior seems to have left town. So, basically, the blind leading the naked. And it was busy; trial by fire, jump right off the deep end, whatever... Thank God for senior nurses! Anyway, we're EM docs, we adapt and make do. In the end, we got through the shifts without a serious hitch.

Mid-evening on my last shift we had a 65-year-old female come in by private car having a big heart attack (Inferior-Lateral STEMI, Q'ing out, for you medical folks...). Really sick and unstable. I hadn't even had a chance to review the STEMI protocol yet, but there I was, talking to the Cardiac Interventionalist at our tertiary center, the Princess Alexandra Hospital (PAH), thirty minutes away in downtown Brisbane. We thrombolysed her with tPA and loaded her onto a waiting ambulance. The ED staff then looked at me... "OK Doctor Nolan, are you riding along with her?" "Excuse me, Whaaat...?"

It turns out that, unlike the US emergency routine, the paramedics here don't transfer really sick patients without a doc on board, and the drug box doesn't travel with the ambulance, but with the Attending Physician (a fine time to tell me all this...). Scrambling ensued to grab an EMS/ACLS mobile pack, complete with airway management gear and ACLS meds (that I also hadn't had time to review). " No worries, mate...she'll be right...Off yas go..." At critical times like these, being out in a community hospital, on the periphery of a Metro area, can really seem like Fort Apache. You're on your own, with an unstable, critical patient.

So, for the first time in my twenty-plus year EM career, I found myself in the back of a foreign ambulance, adjusting a Nitro drip and setting up the pacer/defibrillator for action, as we careened through the darkened streets of outer Brisbane, lights and sirens wailing, slow-rolling through red-lighted intersections; getting to the PAH stat!

It was all very exciting; the patient went into an accelerated junctional rhythm (bad) and her vital signs began to deteriorate on our arrival at the PAH. Met there at the door by the assembled Cath lab team and off she went for definitive Cardiac care. I got a very nice tour of our upstream tertiary ED by an Aussie EM Consultant named James, and then got left standing alone out on the sidewalk by the ambulance squad, who had other places to be. So, I called a cab for a ride back out to Cleveland, gave the driver a voucher and finished up just as my shift ended at 2300. Gee, some things sure are different down here! By comparison, in the US, ED docs never transport patients. We stay put with our other patients in the ED and EMS provides transport, perhaps with an ED Nurse on board, if required for running IV medications. But it all went very well, a textbook emergency response with a good outcome in the end. Though I do wish someone had given me a heads up beforehand! So, a real life saved, a quick tour of inner Brisbane by ambulance, and a night ride back out to the country. All in all, a pretty exciting day's work. It's going to be an interesting year, that much is certain.

For all you Medical Systems geeks out there; our local public hospital has a dedicated ED Radiology suite, a 64-slice GE CT scanner, with a Fuji Synapse PACS just being implemented. Tres cool, as it's the same PACS system I'd been using in New York for the last eight years. Lab is minimal after hours, with basic I-Stat bedside Point-Of-Care testing done overnight for simple stuff. Critical labs are still car-couriered as needed into Brisbane after hours, a three-hour turn-around! As in many non-tertiary hospitals, sub-specialty coverage is spotty, to non-existent, and limited after hours. We have general surgery for elective stuff, but no real after-hours or weekend emergency surgery. No ICU, and almost zero medical sub-specialists. So, less sub-specialty coverage than in the US overall; and this in a large, regional community hospital, ED census of almost sixty-thousand visits annually.

While the quality of care is generally high, as in the US, the Aussie healthcare system is straining under almost unlimited clinical demand, lack of capacity, fragmented healthcare coordination and largely paper medical records. Being a primarily government-funded system, though with a surprisingly large component of privately insured patients, and lacking the aggressive cost-containment and billing documentation demands of a US-style private insurance industry, Australia seems at least a decade behind the US in terms of implementation of robust electronic medical records (EMR) and charge capture. As in the US, caring for an aging, more chronically ill, patient population is consuming an ever-larger portion of healthcare spending. There's a commonly quoted figure, that "15% of your patients consume 85% of healthcare resources" and that's likely pretty accurate. When discussing the future of EM care delivery with the junior Registrars (or Residents), I stick with the wizened Dr. Nolan's pithy, four-word adage, "Older, sicker, poorer, fatter..." Our grim mutual medical future, worldwide.

Which causes me to fondly recall one of my very first Aussie patients, seen on day one in the ED; the well-nicknamed "Big Steve". So called because he was so obese, that when lying on his back, the belly was as protuberant as when standing upright. Curiously, so tense with intra-abdominal fat, it literally had nowhere else to go and arched impressively ceiling-ward, an almost rigid mass. A hundred and fifty kilos (330 lbs.) easy, three chins. Hmmm, fun....

I reviewed his bedside chart quickly: 60's male, morbidly obese, metabolic syndrome, Diabetes Type 2, Hypertension, chronic EtOH (alcoholic), and oh joy, still an active smoker, one pack per day, over an 80 pack-year history. Lovely... now with increasing shortness of breath... (No shit, Sherlock...). I cheerfully enter the cubicle,

"Good morning Mr. Lawton, I understand you're not feeling your best..."

Steve is sprawled supine over the disheveled ED gurney, unshaven, naked except for dingy boxers, dusky belly arching impressively. He doesn't open his eyes or move, silent.... Dead perhaps? I should be so lucky... No, Normal Sinus Rhythm at 70 bpm on the monitor... breathing rapid and shallow...

"Mr. Lawton...?" I probe...

Big Steve smirks slightly, eyes closed, and lazily extends his left arm vertically at the elbow, extending his tobacco-stained middle finger directly at me. Nice touch...

In the end, Big Steve turned out to be quite a personable larrikin; funny as hell and delivered with a broad ocker-Aussie accent that made it hard not to enjoy. But a complete train-wreck; a chronic train-wreck, if you follow me...

"Oi, not feelin' me best doc. Do whatever ya need to make me right..."

Certainly Steve, I'm on it... Have you considered a nicotine patch, losing 60 kilos, going vegan and taking up hot yoga? No, I thought not...

The Big Steves of our world frankly just don't give that much of a shit. At least not most of them; otherwise, they wouldn't be in the condition they are. They are who they are, and we medics can just deal with it.

Amazingly, I saw Big Steve back in the ED a couple of years later. He looked exactly the same, right down to his tobacco-stained fingers; still kicking though...

To me he illustrates our societal quandary perfectly. A train-wreck physically, but actually a decent person, who isn't going to change behaviors dramatically, as he ages deeper into his multiple chronic diseases. Medically, there is no cure, no dramatic answers. Just the steady drain on healthcare resources as the Big Steves of our world dwindle gradually away. Drip, drip, drip...

"Older, sicker, poorer, fatter..." my mantra, and a neat encapsulation of the future healthcare challenges ahead for all advanced societies.

The other immediately surprising observation about the Australian public healthcare workforce was how international it is. Physicians and nurses are here from seemingly all corners of the globe, especially the old British empire countries: UK, Ireland, Canada, South Africa, and New Zealand. But also, Asia: especially India, Iran, Singapore and Hong Kong. It seemed to me that half the English NHS workforce was in Brisbane, and in fact, the medical brain drain from the NHS to Australia has become an issue of some concern to the British government of late. The Aussies are happy to poach the talent and appear to provide a much better quality of working life, according to the NHS 3rd and 4th year Registrars we were getting regularly through our ED. Curiously, I was the only American at the hospital, not only as a physician, but no American nurses, techs, nada...and so, was something of a curiosity. After my long years of solitary toiling in EDs, while squirreled away in rural, upstate NY, the breadth of experience and interesting life stories of virtually all of my colleagues was highly refreshing and the interaction stimulating. "Say, I think I like it here, kids..."

It often felt, to me, like we Aussie medics were all shipwrecked together on some distant pirate island; where the talk during lulls and late nights invariably turned to visa status, permanent residency and citizenship hassles, training progress updates and the sharing of advice, disappointments or little private victories. There were several categories of staffers; newcomers who were still disoriented and just trying to find their feet; committed folk who were fully engaged in trying to not get kicked off the island, often by scrambling to find serial temporary gigs at various sites; and the secure crew, who had Permanent Residency (PR) or Australian Citizenship status well and truly in hand. There was only a small minority who were planning on returning to their home countries to work after their rotations were complete; but even these were going back for family, community and personal reasons. Or perhaps if they'd landed an absolute plumb training slot in London or such. Almost no one was going home for the lifestyle. This seemingly endless cycle of arrivals, temporary transfers and returns, made us all feel members of a vagabond medical community; adrift and conspiring against the reality of the outside world together. There were many parties, reunions, even wedding engagements celebrated; and in large measure this clinical fraternity became my social network in our new world.

One unfortunate contrast was that Stephanie could not get licensed as a nurse in Australia, having been out of active practice for over ten years while having our babies, and so missed out on this professional network of peers to help her feel grounded by common training and mission. Australian nursing wanted her to essentially go back to square one and repeat nursing school, a complete non-starter. As time passed, this loss of professional community would become more acute, as I got further absorbed into actually running the ED. She was able to compensate partially by getting very involved as a volunteer at the kid's schools; but it was only a temporary solution. She was becoming professionally isolated in paradise...

In contrast, I was getting rapidly and fully integrated professionally, felt valued and respected; being drawn increasingly into teaching and helping to expand the clinical and operational functions of our Emergency Department. It was an enormous relief to have survived the initial entry and transition. Now, I felt we were really moving forward.

It certainly wasn't the easiest route, but it was very satisfying professionally, rewarding personally and always challenging.

CHAPTER 8: Harmonic Convergences (and increasingly good vibrations)

February 2012

DDU Blog entry: OK, so a bit of an aside in tonight's musings. Confession: I'm an avid guitar player; a semi-serious, gradually improving, never gonna be a Rock Star - but just love it anyway - kind of player... I love all guitars, even really crappy ones, as they each have a distinct voice and maybe something to teach you, if you give them a chance. Like people in a way. So heading down into the humid semi-tropics, I left all my good guitars back at the farm in New York. Such humidity can be hard on guitars and other delicate objects. We hit the Aussie coastline, set some stuff up, and my next priority was to find a guitar. Anything to get my finger-jones worked out. All you musicians know what I'm referring to here. It's like an itch...and I was getting itchy. I tried Craig's List, it was almost a ghost town. Somehow I linked up with this alternative site Gumtree.com, and that's where everybody was. Who knew? After a few non-starters, I linked up with some guy in a nondescript, working-class suburb of Brisbane; tired, but not exactly seedy. He pulled out this musty, dusty old Yamaha 12 string with strings so old you could literally feel the rust. Last changed sometime in the mid-1970's. Weird thing was, the thing weighed a ton, a proverbial brick shithouse. The woods were of amazingly high quality; very fine-grained solid spruce top, full grain rosewood back and sides. Woods that are almost unavailable today at any cost. No loose braces or joints, straight neck. I tried to play a bit; the thing sounded like shit. $250 Australian, no case and no dickering. So, I bought it, not wanting to visit any more such neighborhoods in a strange land. Mission accomplished!

I took it home, gave the fingerboard a nice drink of mineral oil, cleaned 'er up, brand new set of strings. Oh, by the way, in thirty years of playing, I'd never changed an entire set of 12 strings. A real organizational and tuning challenge. You should really try it, it's a life-list sort of experience, seriously. Now a funny thing began to happen, and it's happening still. On our first session, the guitar seemed stiff and tentative, the strings all sproingy and overly resonant. As any player knows, new strings slip out of tune and stretch a lot before they settle down. I just tuned it back up to standard and let it rest. The next day... better, more resonant and warmer, but still stiff and lacking focus. Now, almost a week into daily play, an amazing thing has happened; something discussed a fair amount, but that I've not witnessed so starkly myself. This well-built instrument, after lying fallow for some thirty years, but with its structure intact, is waking up and coming back to life under my fingertips. I'm learning its ways, and its subtle strengths; it, in turn, is responding to my explorations. Our harmonics are converging, and we are aligning our frequencies...or something. I know this may sound all hippy-Zeny and even ridiculous to a non-player, but it is happening. I am listening to its voice, and it is leading me. It's not remotely the same instrument it was just one week ago. It has regained its voice and it is singing. The perfect channel and metaphor for my own state of mind...

CHAPTER 9: Stradbroke Island and a Life Attuned to the Sea

March 2012

DDU Blog entry: We take the ferry right out of Cleveland center, only a mile from home. Head ten miles east across Moreton Bay, to arrive at Stradbroke Island, or "Straddie", as it's affectionately known to the locals. Ancestral home to the local Quandamooka aboriginal people, it's one of several massive sand barrier islands offshore that protect the entire Brisbane region from direct blows by the open ocean. The outer reaches are famous for having miles of sweeping, pure sand beaches, and excellent surf breaks around the rocky headlands. With only two thousand or so full-time residents, it's also heavily wooded, and feels like you've stepped fifty years back in time on disembarking. It's very beautiful and laid-back, even by Aussie standards, which means very...

Point Lookout, at the very northeastern tip of Stradbroke Island, is a magical, storm-swept place; and worlds apart from placid Moreton Bay, lying just to the west, around the Point on the inner side of the island. It's a very popular weekend surfing, fishing and camping destination for Brisbanites. As the ferry terminal is so close to home, we spend many weekends enjoying Straddie. On our very first trip over, we were lucky in seeing dolphins, sea turtles and a manta ray, all on a single day excursion.

It's remarkable how attuned to a life around the sea these coastal Aussies are. Every beach has weekend Surf Lifesaver clubs, and at Main Beach on Straddie, we got a close-up glimpse into their training and upbringing through the ranks to attain full Surf-Lifesaver status. To emphasize, these outer beaches are what they call "high-energy coastlines" here, and as a life-long New Englander/ Bostonian I thought I had a pretty good idea of what that meant. Not really... On a typical hot afternoon in summer, the inland heat rises, and these beaches develop steady, convective, onshore breezes of 10-15 mph, pulled in off the relatively cooler water and driving 5–8-foot waves into surf that can get choppy and disorganized. The waves build fast and break quickly, aka "dumpy" waves. Not the long rolling, evenly spaced crests that are ideal for surfing; those generally occur dependably only at very specific points around headlands, termed "surf breaks". And all that in-rushing water has to get back seaward in a hurry, which it does by creating a series of rapidly reversing, powerful rips that flow outwards from these same beaches. It takes a seasoned eye to read the water and identify the danger spots. Something that the average tourist is very inept at doing. Sea-bathing at these beaches can be somewhat more akin to "Maytag: Spin-Cycle"; and you can get badly thrashed if you're clueless, or drunk, or otherwise not paying attention. They rescue lots of folks, all the time.

DDU Blog entry: The Nolan kids were very impressed while watching the brave, little Aussie lifesavers in action. Beginning before age five, the first rung of training is by joining the "Green Caps", so named for their bright green swimming caps. Working up through the ranks, the next level are "Nippers", beginner Surf Lifesavers, ages five to thirteen, and suited up in bright orange and yellow; the iconic Surf Life Saving Australia (SLSA) colors, complete with matching, and highly visible head caps. They drill regularly on these outer beaches, swimming relays out fifty or so yards from shore through the surging breakers and around a temporary buoy, then racing back to shore. After several years of regular drills, they might advance; continuing their training for additional years to become full-fledged adult Surf Lifesavers. As these drills are playing out, the older teens are patrolling just offshore on jet-skis and Zodiacs to pluck up anyone caught in a rip. They ride the surf like rodeo cowboys, even catching air off the wave crests. Meanwhile, Mums and Dads socialize at the tide line; while toddlers, two- to four-year-olds, are being tossed around by breaking foam like so many scrambling sandpipers. Just another Saturday morning at the beach... Truly, a life defined by and very deeply attuned to the sea.

We signed the kids up for Nippers at the first instance that first summer. If not perhaps as an early career move, at least to give them a better understanding of the wild and dangerous environment of these open, high-energy coastlines. As we warned, "The life you save may be your own, or each other's." We also wanted them to be involved in an Aussie activity that would give them a deeper appreciation of Aussie culture; but we didn't want to spend weekends baking on bleachers watching amateur cricket, soccer or rugby under the blistering, hot sun. So, they all agreed to Surf Lifesaving. Surf Life Saving Australia (SLSA), founded in 1907, is an Aussie institution, run by volunteers and donations. It's also a legacy social organization that has numerous social activities and even restaurants in some singular oceanside locations all over Australia. Please stop in and check them out; and consider a donation to a most worthy cause. The life you save may be your own.

So, dedicated Mom, Stephanie, would get everyone up at the crack of dawn, every Saturday morning in season, and take the kids over to Straddie on the ferry, for their weekly Nippers work-out. I'd go as often as possible but was often on-duty in the ED or recovering from a late Friday night on-call. It's a very fun, active (and tiring) Saturday at the beach for the kids. And they sleep very well after Nipper days; every parent's goal accomplished.

It seems a long time ago that we first arrived and were marveling at the courage of the little Nippers against the vast, turgid ocean. The Nolan kids were now a part of the team and getting right in there too. It was a big accomplishment for five young Yanks to become fully accepted into the Surf Lifesaver ranks by their Aussie peers - even our brave little Green-Cap, Owen, with his paralyzed right arm. Our "tough little battler," gaining much admiration for his "never quit" spirit during the beach drills.

We're very open about Owen's handicap, which he takes right in stride. His siblings cut him very little slack. To us, it's just a part of him being Owen. But he was constantly being asked why his right arm was held in a protective sling by the friendly, well-meaning Aussies,

"Oi mate, did ya fall and break ya arm?"

They'd ask with genuine concern; to which he'd matter-of-factly reply, "No, it's been paralyzed since birth," leaving an awkward, stunned silence; which we would always wave off. "No worries, thanks for asking," to the great relief of the concerned questioner. Owen once memorably added,

"It got tangled up in my extension (umbilical) cord..."

Straddie is one of five massive, sand barrier islands of great beauty and diversity stretching along the southeastern Queensland coastline. It's the largest sand barrier island complex on earth, culminating with the iconic Fraser Island in the north, and a truly unique environment. These islands host over two hundred and thirty identified bird species (most of which you've never seen before), kangaroos, wallabies and fruit bat colonies. Surrounded by the Coral Sea, with whales, dolphins, mantas and sea turtles close offshore. Any trip out to Straddie feels as if you are somewhere lushly exotic and thousands of miles away, after only a forty-five-minute ferry trip from the mainland. Sublime, and exciting...

One weekend, we took a trip out to Brown Lake on Straddie, so named because of the tannin-stained, but pristine waters. Very brown indeed, like a clear root beer. As I was wading about, knee-deep in a flooded Melaleuca stand, glassing Iridescent Kingfishers bottle-rocketing through the bush, I was startled to see a large, black, very toxic looking snake slither right by my bare legs, just underwater! At first, I thought it must be a fresh-water eel. It then surfaced, only ten feet in front of me, turned and stared me down with lifeless, coal-black eyes... Coiling on the surface; no eel, that! It then alarmed me by swimming directly back in my direction, slicing through the water at a brisk pace; deviating to the sandy shore when only several feet away, where it came to rest. A terrifying serpent; forearm thick, coal-black with a bright red belly. Neither of us moved a muscle... It sure didn't look like any innocent garden variety snake I'd ever encountered. Everything about it screamed caution, keep away! I later learned that it was a Red-bellied Black snake. Not lethal on the nuclear scale of a Taipan or Brown snake, but quite venomous indeed - around ten times as venomous as an Eastern Diamondback, but generally docile if undisturbed. It could've easily bitten me as it swam from unseen cover, right past my legs.

Still another reminder, that whenever you are out and about in this splendidly beautiful country, real danger may lurk very close under foot. Steady... Stay alert, stay alive!

CHAPTER 10: Moving Day, a Housewarming and Koalas

March 2012

In general, Queensland Health was very straightforward about the employment offer. Which was good enough to tempt me all the way from America, and they didn't play any games. Given all the other stressors involved in such an undertaking, that was most appreciated. Well, the one area where they may have fudged a bit was in regard to housing.

"No worries, mate. At your salary ya can get about anything ya want - fully furnished, big house in a canal estate. Easy as. Even a boat if ya want it." according to the hospital's convivial physician recruiter.

Well, "Yeah, nah", as the Aussies say. On hearing we could get a fully furnished lease no problem, and anticipating only a 12-18 month stay, we came down from the USA with literally nothing except clothes and camping gear. Not even pots and pans. Of our 6,000 lbs shipping allowance from the States, we used about 400 lbs. We were "value for money" for the Queensland government, you might say.

On arrival, Queensland Health kindly put us up temporarily in a three-bedroom ranch-style house while we found our feet and more permanent housing. It was a bit of a shock then to realize that there were virtually no furnished leases available, and that rents here were almost weekly what you'd expect to pay monthly in the USA. Up in the $1000-1400 per week range for that big place on the water! Per week... plus utilities. Crikey mate!

We'd been looking for a (relatively) affordable and acceptable rental in the Raby Bay canal community, it being right on the Bay and close to the village center and hospital. But things were pretty tight. We'd been in the loaner ranch house for several weeks and were running short on time. We needed to settle soon. On the "be kind to all animals" karmic scale, a small miracle then occurred. I was out walking at the Raby Bay foreshore park one afternoon, weighing options. Perhaps we'd need to move into a more crowded, less desirable inland neighborhood? As I contemplated, a fit, petite woman in oversized sunnies and tennis-wear strolled by; being led by an older, slightly ratty-looking Jack Russell Terrier... "Nice dog," I offered, somewhat half-heartedly. "Oh, are you an American? I'm from Ontario, Canada," she offered cheerfully. Candi turned out to be one of those hyper-socially connected women, who knew all about everyone and everything related to the area; a Canadian expat for over twenty years, married with grown kids and a genuine Raby Bay doyenne. I'd inadvertently struck a goldmine of helpful community-mindedness. An hour later, we were still talking and making connections; and miraculously, I got the phone number of a hot lead to a house, just purchased by friends of Candi's, that might be available for rent, and was just around the corner. So, karma...not always a bitch, after all. Say nice things about other people's pets. Even if you may not exactly mean it.

DDU Blog entry: As rentals and homes in general are very expensive in Australia, we figured we may as well try to live by the water. If not now, when? Stephanie and I wanted the kids to become fully immersed in their new, exotic environment. It's been really satisfying to watch them fishing off our dock in the pre-dawn light; learning all about tides, boats and sea critters of all sorts; baiting, setting and checking crab pots daily. A very different world than our Fairview Farm in New York state. Most rentals are unfurnished, however. They even remove the appliances here. When it became evident that we'd have to outfit an entire household for seven, from scratch, on top of everything else, Stephanie nearly broke down into tears. It was all simply too much... Luckily, the local residents, following Candi's lead, took us in as the Raby Bay charity cases of the year, and with their incredibly generous help and hard work, we furnished most of a four-bedroom home, almost entirely on donations, over a single weekend! Salvos (the Salvation Army) was also a boon in the transient furniture and cheap, but oddly satisfying, artworks department. My unvarnished joy that we were "living like college roomies" really annoyed Stephanie, for some reason. Now, we had only to lease a washer/dryer and fridge; but that's so common here we accomplished it all within a few days; delivery, set-up and all set to go. In fact, they came and went without me even knowing they'd been here and gone. You pay monthly or risk repossession, I suppose. Voila, a new beginning!

We were soon set up in a neat, bungalow-style pad, right on an outer canal, with unobstructed views overlooking the broad expanse of Moreton Bay stretching away to the north from the shady back verandah and including a small lawn and pool. We even had a private boat dock with a constantly re-calibrating aluminum gangway that marked the changing tides. But no boat, just our patio at sea...

In the southern hemisphere, a northerly outlook is most desirable, like southern exposure up north, if you follow me. This provides direct sunshine through the winter months when the sun sits lower in the sky. So, to say I was "stoked", as the Aussies would declare, was a mild understatement. We had landed and were now getting truly settled. Living a bit like hippy gypsies, or college roommates, again. It was a perfect, low commitment environment in which to live, work and create; and a place where we ended up living for over four years. Far longer than initially anticipated, but inertia intervenes. Not cheap, but doable, and our new home away from home, Down Under.

Now, for a bit about the neighborhood. We found ourselves settling in a pretty posh development, in the worst shack on a very good block, with unobstructed Bay views even. The kind of place where people pay a million bucks Aussie for that view, and the dirt underneath a faded, modestly proportioned, but functional early 1980's house, and then do a tear-down. Some are then inspired to build a perfectly non-functional, modernist disaster-palace in its place. Architectural malpractice? It's rampant here. Just not my cup of tea, really. Different tastes, go figure.

You live across a block wall in a community like this. The waterfront land is limited and treasured. The houses are generally oversized for the lots. The boat mooring on the ocean-fed canal out back is the escape everyone's seeking. One of our next-door neighbors was a retired stockbroker from Sydney, headed soon for the blessed boneyard. He simply tried his best to ignore us, because we were just too rambunctious and alive, I suppose. Or obnoxious, perhaps? He once actually complained that the kids had disturbed his sleep, while playing with friends in the pool, at three o'clock in the afternoon. Yeah, sorry mate, it's called life. I tried to sympathize, but he rarely ever spoke to us again. In contrast, Rob and Libby, our lovely elderly neighbors just on the opposite side, embraced our five kids and welcomed us warmly; and spent the next four years enjoying their energy, love and attention, including homemade birthday cards and Christmas goodies. Aidan would disappear around the seaward end of the wall, over the jetty rocks, to mooch homemade cookies on a regular basis, while supposedly out fishing. The Nolan kids thus became surrogate grandchildren for theirs, now living far away in Canberra. A stark, illuminating contrast, and probably a life lesson for us all. Take the time to engage with the young, it's contagious!

Just as I was beginning to think that our move into this neighborhood had been a big mistake, a self-exile into the land of the highly solvent, but nearly dead, a stranger walked into the open garage one afternoon. I was refinishing an ornate teak Indonesian sideboard I'd picked up at Salvos. He was wearing a tattered Wallabies singlet, and nylon footie shorts, in beat up thongs (flip-flops). Honestly, I thought he was the gardener. Late 50's, short and paunchy, a dyed off-orange, comb-over in the Donald Trump style, and with a curiously soft, rather posh for an Aussie, accent. He introduced himself,

"Hello mate, I'm Peter Jamieson, welcome to the neighborhood. I live just across the way; my friends call me PJ..."

And just like that, I had met not only my future best mate in Australia, but had found an unlikely brother from another mother, and an anchor into this new world. Funny how fate intervenes sometimes. So, an unexpected housewarming of sorts.

It turns out PJ was a salt-of-the-earth kind of bloke, what the Aussies call a real battler. Grew up tough and semi-deprived in the outer suburbs of western Sydney; was even a pro-wrestling impresario at one point, if you can believe that. Anything to get ahead, make some cash and feed his three growing kids. He should write a book...

Eventually, he made his way north to Brisbane in the early 1980s, looking for any opportunity; and through hard work, guile and perfect timing, had made an absolute fortune in the burgeoning Brisbane real-estate market. But, as is true with most self-made men, PJ never forgot his roots, and the struggles he'd overcome. In short, a brother, and a soulmate. Over the years, PJ became my closest friend in Australia, and we've shared many great times together. Lots of family Christmases, and even his 60th birthday family dinner. Down home and unaffected, the two things he really values, besides family, are mateship, in its best sense, and good Aussie wines. I think he found this wandering American doc to be a fascinating oddity and took us all under his wing. He's certainly introduced me to a wide range of top-shelf Aussie drops. A very pleasant education indeed! It's a major step forward to make a genuine, local friend in a foreign country. I'm ever grateful that PJ helped to open doors and make us feel part of the larger community. Brothers in arms...

As we finally began to feel settled in Cleveland, we took some time to see more of greater Brisbane.

DDU Blog entry: Further exploring greater Brisbane, we made it out to the Lone Pine Koala Sanctuary; a world-renowned Koala rehab center and open-air zoo since the 1920's, that's located on the Brisbane River, a few kilometers southwest of the CBD. Koalas are an iconic symbol of wild Australia worldwide, although their historic range is only on the east coast of Oz; centered in the Brisbane region. Their numbers are declining rapidly, mostly due to suburban sprawl, habitat loss, cars and pet dog kills. They can still be seen in the wild, but only in forests and parks containing their specific eucalyptus food trees, but it's becoming less common than even in the recent past.

The Sanctuary does a great job of educating the public on the plight of Koalas and advocating for their future survival. LPKS has over one hundred residents at any given time, living in open air enclosures and dining exclusively on fresh cut eucalyptus leaves, served daily. A nursery for mums and bubs, a bachelor pad, a medical clinic, even a retirement home. The Guinness Book of Records for oldest Koala ever was clinched here (really, where else?) One female here lived to the ripe old age of twenty-seven. Koalas, besides being super cute, are yet another oddity from Down Under. Not a bear at all, but another marsupial that gives birth to a single, bare, inch-long baby that crawls up into its mother's pouch to further gestate. They are one of the few animals in the world that can eat eucalyptus leaves. Unfortunately, these leaves are so low in nutritional value and hard to digest, that the little guys sleep around twenty hours a day just to save energy. They live solitary, sleepy lives and communicate via a low rumbling bellow or "roar".

The Sanctuary also has a wide range of other Australian wildlife on view, including a popular open-air park where you can get up close and personal with kangaroos, wallabies, emus, lizards and the like. The kids absolutely loved it, except for Owen perhaps! He was then only three, and a bit afraid of the koalas and larger animals. But enjoyed hand feeding a tiny little wallaby joey very much. More his speed and size.

In Brisbane, it seems every visitor gets their portrait taken with a live Koala, and I mean EVERYONE. The walls here are covered with glossy photos of Pope John Paul, Eric Clapton, Ed Sheeran and Taylor Swift, and of course those pesky Nolans. Queensland is the only place in Australia where it's legal to handle a live Koala, and they have strict rules on how they engage with the public. The Koalas get a bit nervous if they are over-handled, and they do have impressively long, and sharp claws. The staff rotates the young, healthy Koalas for the tourist photos and strictly limit each one's exposure time. The Koalas used thus are actually doing their part for Koala research and rehab, as the portraits are a big money maker, and all proceeds go back to the Sanctuary's work. So, good on you, little Koalas!

We dutifully lined up and did our part for Koala research and preservation too. It was an early Aussie highlight for us all, and each kid's solo photo holding a live Koala is a treasured memory. As I held my koala, I must have scared her (him?) a bit, as it kindly deposited a single, very soft, very green koala poop right into my supporting palm. Thanks for that... I couldn't resist taking a whiff, and yes, I can attest, that it smelled rather like a eucalyptus cough drop; maybe a bit earthier. Perhaps like a Hall's Down Underneath?! I did the field research, and so now you know...

CHAPTER 11: First Aussie Road Trip - the New England Tablelands

April 2012

DDU Blog entry: So, it turns out there really is a region of Australia called New England. As a proud Bostonian, and multi-generational New England Yankee, I had to check it out as soon as possible. Who would've guessed?

Settled by English, Scots and Irish in the 1820-40's, it's a high, broad plateau region, up to 3000-4000 feet in elevation, and running for several hundred miles north to south in northern New South Wales. Austerely beautiful, stone-riddled, and cooler, it feels reminiscent of the Scottish Highlands; and is mostly given over to grazing large herds of cattle and sheep. This area was the hideout for numerous Australian "Bush-rangers", Jesse James-styled outlaws, in the early days of settlement. The villages are sparsely settled and tiny. The area is also renowned in Australia for actually having light snows and an annual foliage display of sorts, but it's not exactly Vermont. There's even a University of New England at Armidale, and the center for Australian country music further south at Tamworth. Yet another surprising discovery in Australia, and a unique area to visit.

The boys and I did a four-night, 1300 km road trip southwest of Brisbane, up through the impressive Cunningham's Gap and into the mountainous Great Dividing Range. In a trip filled with superlatives, we hiked the largest Granite dome in the southern hemisphere at Bald Rock N.P near Tenterfield. It looked and felt very similar to Enchanted Rock outside of Fredericksburg, Texas, for those readers with Texas roots. It's geologically similar, being an exfoliating granite dome, with wonderful views of the Granite Belt country below.

We camped at Girraween National Park, on a higher, drier plateau, but not real Outback desert. The rock formations here are outstanding; it's like a mini-Yosemite of sorts. We didn't encounter any snakes, which are reportedly plentiful here in the warmer months. We did see plenty of sunning lizards though, which makes me think the snakes were out and about too...

Heading further south, we then hiked up to the highest point on the plateau, at a remote place called Cathedral Rock National Park near Ebor. It was a real Lord of the Rings experience, as the lower elevation cool fern and lichen-encrusted eucalypt forest transitioned into a stunted cypress and beech mini-Bonsai landscape. Moving ever higher, in a most unexpected turn, the forest trees suddenly became filled with vast flocks of raucous lorikeets and parrots, flying rapidly in tight clusters. The wind-shear noise of their hundreds of wings slicing through the silence in unison, just above the stunted treetops, was startling and unforgettable. We christened this place The Valley of Parrots; a magical hidden oasis. Looming above, out of the mists, a boulder-strewn series of false summits rose overhead. Aidan, who has quite a height phobia, was really challenged to dig deep, as we scrambled finally onto the jumbled summit. The views across the broad plateau were panoramic through the ragged and rapidly shifting cloud breaks. Definitely a worthy, if somewhat obscure hiking destination; unlike anywhere I'd ever hiked before.

While camped at nearby Wollomombi Falls, the second highest in Australia, with a drop of 220 meters, (over 700 feet), where we were treated to the stunning mating display of the male Lyrebird, kitted-out in full regalia, and so named because the complex tail feathers resemble an ancient Greek harp or Lyre, when outstretched and shaken over his head during the male's primordial mating display. He was quick and highly evasive as we followed after him to get a few fleeting photos.

Turning then east, at Armidale the following day, we drove down the "Waterfall Way", named for its many beautiful waterfalls that surge eastward over the great escarpment ridges here. Numerous streams flow across the unexpectedly rich and moist, dairying uplands, before dropping thousands of feet through the Eastern Escarpment rainforests and onto the lush coastal plain around Coffs Harbor and mid-north coastal NSW. This *is yet another very surprising and seemingly "un-Australian" landscape to explore. We finished up by traveling north through the lovely, dreamswept surf and beach towns of Lennox and Broken Heads and Byron Bay, and stood at the easternmost point on the Australian Continent at Cape Byron; so named by Lieutenant (and future Captain) James Cook for one of his ship's officers in 1770, who also happened to be the future grandfather of the romantic English poet Lord Byron. A different word entirely here than the uplands only a few hours away; a sun-stunned seascape filled with friendly, laid-back locals and fantastically heaving, mesmerizing surf breaks.*

Oftentimes, a landscape gives clues as to where you might be. I like to play the mental game of, "If I was blindfolded, and dropped off here, how precisely could I figure out where I was?" Even within the indigenous Eucalypt forest, memories of hill-country Texas, western Montana, Maui or the Big Island of Hawaii, and mid-coast California come easily to mind. A curious and intriguing blend of verdant, sheep-filled Scottish Highlands, ranchy American west, and the languid US west coastlines of Big Sur all exist in close proximity in this part of Australia, a landscape that inspires dreams of further leisurely exploration. I suppose it's only human nature to try to categorize a new experience by referencing the familiar. But then a mob of kangaroos hops into view and that strange sense of the exotic is stirred, and you could only be standing out in the Australian bush.

CHAPTER 12: Further Coastal Adventures

May 2012

It's an open secret of sorts in Queensland that Brisbane, while surrounded by world class beaches to both the north and south, has no actual beaches of its own. The city was founded as a penal colony in the early 1800s, and actually sits several miles upriver and inland from the sheltered, calm waters of Moreton Bay, alongside the Brisbane River. The west side of the bay's marine environment is typically mangrove- lined shallows, evolving to exposed mudflats at low tide. The early settlers were much more concerned with eating what they could grow than surfing it seems. Good choice...

DDU Blog entry: We finally got the time to head down the coast, the whole Nolan family this time, driving a few hours south to visit the world-famous surf breaks of northern New South Wales (NSW) at Byron Bay. We spent a few wonderful nights in a holiday cabin, in the sleepy beach town of Brunswick Heads. All over Australia they rent these fully kitted-out cabins, sleeping all seven, for $200 / night. It's a perfect way to go with active kids; just book in advance, if possible, as they fill up quickly.

We are now heading into winter in the Southern Hemisphere (just add six months). The weather is cooler, and much drier, the afternoon onshore breezes, driven by the convective heat rising off the land in summer, calm and die away. The ocean water on the beaches gets crystal clear now due to less rain and run-off turbidity from the rivers in this Northern Rivers area of NSW.

The kids were all psyched to learn to surf, so a quick call got us linked up with Gary at Style Surfing in Byron. A very chilled-out and capable Aussie surf instructor. His crew helped the kids feel confident and comfortable in a whole new environment. "So stoked!" as they say here. Style Surfing made sure each kid caught several small rollers while staying very safe and secure. Even on a calm day, the surf breaks here have an uncanny, widely spaced regularity and long rolling pattern. It's very surprising how far an average surfer can ride a little three-foot roller, 75-100 yards!

They surf here year-round but use a wet suit top in winter; even though the water feels balmy if you are from the Northern Hemisphere. After a few hours in the surf, you can get a bit chilled. Then, just step out onto the beach and wait five minutes.

As advertised, everybody got up on a board and rode the waves. It was a real accomplishment for the kids and a window into the very foreign, but very cool and technically complex world that defines "surf culture." Yes, there really is such a thing, and it would be very tempting to perhaps spend my final few decades here on the east coast of Australia, working on my master's degree.

Noosa and the Sunshine Coast Adventures:

DDU Blog entry: We also visited the Sunshine Coast - a one hundred mile stretch of beautiful beaches running north from Brisbane. You first pass through the ancient, volcanic landscape of the Glasshouse Mountains, so named by Lieutenant James Cook, due to their similarity to the glass-making kilns he remembered back home in England during his epic journey of discovery in 1770. They are the sheer cinder cones of ancient volcanoes and create an other-worldly Jurassic backdrop to the landscape. The Sunshine coast culminates north at the high-end resort town of Noosa, famous for its excellent surf breaks and beaches, stunning headland National Park and, in season, the holidaying Australian glitterati set.

The four km hike out around the headland was really exceptional, with sightings of sea turtles and dolphins off the tip at Hell's Gate, a large, open, fractured gorge in the headland that channels thunderous surf into billows of seafoam hundreds of feet below. Watch your footing out there *though - no fencing!*

The next morning, Claire (11) had an appointment to ride horseback at Equathon Stables across the river in North Noosa. She's been waiting months for this opportunity and had even packed her jodhpurs all the way from NY! We had to take a short cable ferry across the Noosa River, which was fun and interesting. Locals fought off a threatened connecting bridge for years to preserve their piece of paradise, and once across you understand why. A locally well-known, but little advertised neighbor, Richard Branson of Virgin fame, owns a luxury estate comprising the whole of Makepeace Island, in the middle of the Noosa River. Yes, it really is that nice up here.

Because it was the quiet off-season, Claire got the added bonus of a one-on-one ride with her instructor Bree, through the bush and out onto the undeveloped beach. Having had three years of previous riding experience, she got to canter through the surf on a full-sized horse. Bree was very complimentary on Claire's confidence, poise, and ability to control such a large animal. Needless to say, Claire was over the moon, and fulfilled one of her Aussie dream wishes.

When it was time to leave Noosa, we turned west and headed inland, into the Sunshine Coast hinterlands, an area of mountainous ridges, small country towns such as Maleny, Montville and Mapleton, and still more impressive escarpment waterfalls. It's a popular weekend getaway for Brisbanites, full of high-end country B&Bs and fine restaurants. We returned to Brisbane by the inland route and made a wonderful long weekend of it. The wide contrast between the languid beaches of Noosa and the organic, green hill towns of the hinterlands is remarkable, being only an hour or two apart; but it makes for an irresistibly memorable combination adventure.

Gifts from the Sea:

DDU Blog entry: Luke and Aidan have been really diligent, spending hours fishing and crabbing. They take fishing mags out of the town library; they talk with classmates, learning the local tides and ocean environments of Moreton Bay. All fishing is local after all, and their hard work is beginning to pay off. Not only have they caught a few keepers that provided us wonderful fish dinners, but by using the freshly cleaned fish heads n' guts in our crab pot, we have also landed some impressively large, legal-size mud crabs. Their prosaic name aside, these are the sweetest, cleanest crabs I've ever had, easily on par with the famous Dungeness crab of the Pacific northwest. Gory bits aside, we are keen cooks, and enjoy turning our catches into memorable meals.

Aidan recently had a major success, catching a large and highly prized Flathead right off our local beach. The other adult fishermen were stunned at "the little bloke's big catch." Called a "lizard" locally, due to its somewhat reptilian appearance, its meat is surprisingly clean, white, chewy and mild - similar to a fine lobster tail. I remarked to Aidan that catching a fish like that should keep him interested in fishing for a little while longer yet. Staring out over the smooth expanse of Moreton Bay, he intently cast again and replied dreamily:

"For the rest of my life, Dad."

CHAPTER 13: Tales from the "Big Smoke" - Emergency Medicine in Brisbane

July 2012

Once we arrived in Australia, and I was working in Emergency Medicine, it was expected by Queensland Health that I would eventually attain my FACEM, or Fellowship in the Australasian College for Emergency Medicine. This is a training and certification process that can take many years. But, as I was already a Fellow in the American College of Emergency Physicians (FACEP), I was (relatively) fast-tracked. It still took me over two years of close mentoring and supervision, so it wasn't exactly a walk-on. As a condition for gaining my FACEM, I was required to do a six-month, part-time stint in a Level One, tertiary Trauma Center Emergency Department (ED); supervised and formally evaluated by my fellow FACEMs. Serious stuff. "Put on ya game face, Doctor Nolan."

As scary as that sounds, I spent three years training in a much higher-acuity ED environment at Boston City Hospital in the early 1990's, working through the first wave of the urban crack wars. It was blood and gore, penetrating trauma central. So, this was a homecoming of sorts. It's hard to know exactly how decisions made years ago will dictate your life's pathway, but mine has led me into the somewhat arcane, and highly specialized world of modern Emergency Medicine - a place where even many seasoned physicians find themselves uncomfortable.

But it's my world, and these are my people. I get the jokes, understand the veneer of fatalistic cynicism that ultimately shields one's inner core; and I feel strangely at home, sometimes even enlivened, by the steady stream of the bizarre, the grotesque and the tragic that's played out daily, and most especially nightly, in every sizable ED worldwide. It's simply humanity at its most visceral, raw and real. Bleeding, crying, shitting, swearing; many of them higher than hell...a truly Dickensian cast of characters, but rarely dull and routine. And I'm good with that, as are my colleagues, or else we wouldn't be here.

DDU Blog entry: An old Australian expression for any large city is the "Big Smoke", and the Princess Alexandra Hospital is every bit that. As the Level One Trauma Center for the entire southern half of greater Brisbane, a service area population of roughly one million souls, it takes in all the critically ill, trauma and multi-system organ failure patients from southeastern Queensland: around 65,000 patients a year. It has full USA-style, multi-specialty backup, and is one of the major teaching hospitals in Australia.

Of course, on my very first clinical shift, I walk in at 0745 and see that everyone on duty is packed into one of the five trauma rooms. Never a good sign... What's up, let me have a stickybeak mate? A 40's male, bicycle rider vs moving truck, or "Pushbike vs lorry" in Oz ED parlance; complex tragedies de-personalized and reduced to their pith, for everyone's protection. Helmeted, but he hit face first; and his face, now badly swollen, is erythematous and weeping plasma like a battered watermelon. Truck wins, every time. I don't wish to upset anyone with the really graphic details, but I spent my morning lead-gowned as an observer in the Interventional Radiology suite, watching the trauma team coiling hemorrhaging mid-facial arteries via angiogram. Though I was a complete stranger, the Aussie crew couldn't have been more professional or accommodating. And what a privilege; to be allowed a glimpse inside their fascinating work environment, and as a foreign guest no less.

This chronic unpredictability is a feature somewhat unique to a career in Emergency Medicine, and contributes greatly to the fact that emergency personnel, at all levels, experience some of the highest rates of burnout in Medicine. There aren't many careers where you can simply fall flat on your face, or have multiple disasters on your hands, on any given shift. Even with many years' experience, it's an endlessly complex challenge. We are mere actors in the play of human existence. This daily drama of medical misadventure continues around the clock, every day of the year, every year...

We walk on, play our parts, then walk away, back towards normalcy, if only temporarily. But there's always another block of shifts ahead. The play continues, with ebb and flow, but unceasingly. When coming on shift, you never quite know what you'll be walking into. Pre-shift, you're taking a mind-clearing stroll through a leafy park, watching kids laugh and play; getting centered mentally, silently gearing up. The next, you enter through the ED doors and may walk straight into a multi-trauma situation or a violent, agitated-delirium patient requiring immediate, and hazardous, physical restraint, aka a "takedown". We all learn to navigate through this uncertainty, but it steadily and stealthily drains us of our reserves. Each at a different rate perhaps, but ultimately the cardinal hallmarks of burnout; emotional exhaustion, loss of empathy (depersonalization) and a sense of personal failure, or at least impotence, become nearly universal. When you begin to see your patients as the adversary, you're pretty far down the path. And you'd be surprised at how prevalent such attitudes can become; particularly in a department lacking pro-active leadership and compassionately focused staff interventions.

Maintaining true resilience over the years becomes a personal struggle for many. Having a holistic, even spiritual, sense of mission and service helps a lot, as does a healthy, balanced lifestyle and creative outlets. Supportive family and friends become vital harbors. Drinking doesn't really help, but it's sometimes worth a try, and very popular among my peer group. Avoiding professional isolation is also a balm, and something that I found very attractive about the Queensland Health staffing model.

DDU Blog entry: It's been a wonderful and humbling experience to be back in the tertiary world after fifteen years practicing solo community Emergency Medicine. Too much time alone! Colleagues, students, interns are now everywhere; someone to talk to! Apparently, I'm now one of the "senior" ED team members, every one of my almost entirely silvered hairs having been earned during some stressful overnight shift in an ED somewhere. Everyone here has been extremely accommodating and helpful; and luckily, they aren't expecting me to run the team. Unless I want to, of course. Teaching Residents, here termed Registrars, once again has been very rewarding; I've seen a lot over my many EM years and seem to have become something of a mentor by virtue of my persistent longevity, if nothing else...!

Emergency Medicine is the ultimate team sport; believe it. You wouldn't want to run a critical resuscitation without highly coordinated team input. The urban clinical conditions here are fairly similar to those in the USA - except for the lack of copious penetrating gunshot trauma. That's a pleasant relief. And EM case management has evolved somewhat over the years. We are using lots of IV pressors, Adrenaline and Noradrenaline (no "Epi/ Nor-Epi" Down Under!), Propofol infusions, lots of Procedural Sedation using Ketamine, even in adults. But no IV Dilaudid, Benadryl, Lorazepam or Quinolones available here in Oz. Ultrasound-guided everything: central lines, arterial lines, Arthro/ Thora/ Paracentesis and bladder taps. Fiberoptic-assisted intubations. "No worries mates, it's all good, I can adapt. I'm an ED doc, that's what we do..."

When I trained at Boston City Hospital (now Boston Medical Center) in the early 1990's, an 8-slice CT scanner was state of the art; one that took seemingly forever to capture basic, and grainy CT images. On really busy shifts, we'd even have to hold trauma patients in the ED to allow the scanner to cool down between cases! We now have 64-slice scanners with rapid, futuristic 3-D image reconstruction; add angiography with the push of a button. Instant gratification! ED docs simply love that. It seems like the dark ages today, thinking back all of twenty-five years ago. So, patient management has rapidly evolved technologically, but is still the same as it ever was in the most important, hands-on, caring and humanistic ways.

DDU Blog entry: I 've seen some unique and odd cases in Australia already, many diagnostic and injury patterns being fairly regional. You just don't see many toxic snake bites and jellyfish envenomations in upstate New York. Or hypothermia and frostbite cases in Australia, for that matter. But the critical human element - giving hope and reassurance, or breaking bad news and comforting grieving family members - is universal and very familiar to me. That's where the art and soft human touch meet the hard science of Emergency Medicine: a challenging, often frustrating, yet endlessly fascinating way to spend your professional career. At least it's worked out pretty well for me so far.

I hope you've enjoyed this whirlwind tour through a major part of our Aussie adventure. I trust it's also reassuring for you to know that throughout the world, there are emergency professionals standing by to assist those in need 24/7/365 - in fact, right now, in every major town and city. Not generally recognized or even acknowledged by the public but standing ready all the same. My world, my people. Give them a thumbs up for me, please.

CHAPTER 14: Far North QLD: Cairns, Great Barrier Reef and Daintree Rainforest

August 2012

I traveled with Luke and Aidan to an EM conference up in Cairns (pronounced "cans" in Strine, as in beer cans), about 1200 km north of Brisbane. This is the true tropics, now in the cooler and drier winter months. It was our first flight away from Brisbane in the eight months we've been in Australia.

I'm a pretty keen "twitcher", or birdwatcher; and one Aussie bucket-list experience I secretly held out hope for was to one day encounter a Southern Cassowary in the wild. Essentially a six-foot, rainforest dwelling, flightless ostrich species that dates back to prehistoric times, they are solitary and wary. One of the rarest birds in the world, by the late 1990's, only ~1500 adults were estimated to survive in far northern Queensland. We were now heading up into the northern coastal forests that are one of their last wild refuges. But the odds of a wild encounter were slim. Listed as Endangered in Australia, the only other place they are found is in Papua New Guinea, still further north, across the Torres Strait. They exist contiguously over what was once a land bridge connecting the two land masses. It's now been flooded by rising seas for an estimated ten thousand years, submerged into a series of small islands and treacherous, shallow shoals. This infamous strait was, once again, first navigated and mapped by none other than the ubiquitous Lieutenant James Cook.

Torres Strait was later famously traversed in an open 23-foot skiff, by Captain William Bligh and crew, on their epic 48 day, 3,618-mile ocean survival journey west to Timor after the mutiny on HMS Bounty in 1789.

This incredible accomplishment is still considered the greatest feat of seamanship and maritime command in the entire history of the British navy, and well worth reading about in further detail.

The flight north over the extensive Great Barrier Reef offshore felt wildly exotic and filled us all with anticipation. The reefs stretched out below like an endless, aquamarine jigsaw puzzle. Lost in tropical daydreams, I began to work mentally on a new song about this stunning expanse of ocean unfolding below as we headed due north; "Deep Pacific Blue" indeed...

DDU Blog entry: The conference was a real swanky affair with rich local food, good Aussie wines, a few poisonous reptiles and disaster management, all rolled into one. We took a day trip out to Green Island, on an excursion right from Cairns, to snorkel the Great Barrier Reef, or GBR as it's called, just in case we got weathered out further north later in the trip. It can be windy and rough out on the Reef any time of year, and we didn't want to be so close and get shut out. It does happen. Green Island is a heavily visited tourist island, only an hour's ferry ride east of town, but the coral and marine life were still much better than I expected.

We had a snake expert from the Cairns Zoo at the conference, discussing poisonous snakes of Australia, said to be the home of nine out of ten of the world's deadliest snakes, and around twenty of the top twenty-five. We had a live python handling session, that Luke and Aidan eagerly participated in; and our expert even brought along a live Coastal Taipan, the third deadliest snake in the world (luckily in a glass case) - some fifty times more venomous than a King Cobra, and endemic to the Cairns region. Hold that thought...The boys loved it of course, but the hotel staff seemed a bit on edge. Alas, the conference had to end, and it was time to leave the easy life behind. Road Trip!

We headed north up the east coast on the Captain Cook Highway, said to be one of the best coastal drives on the planet. It sure seemed it to us, as bay after bay of beautiful coastal headland opened up under the bright tropical sunshine. Lieutenant (later Captain) Cook discovered and mapped this coastline of Australia during his third Voyage of Discovery in 1770. His ship, the Endeavour, was wrecked on the reef here and barely survived to journey further onward. They limped the crippled ship into what is now Cooktown, Queensland, well north of Cairns; and after seven weeks of repairs, sailed away, never to return and lucky to be alive. He was later killed by angry natives on the Big Island of Hawaii over a purloined skiff; an ignoble end to one of the greatest maritime navigators and explorers in history. Look him up, read a bit on his three Pacific Voyages of Discovery; it's fascinating stuff! He left indelible names to mark the high points of the trip, names that still remain to this day: Cape Tribulation, Mount Sorrow, Cape Disappointment, Mount Misery. Sounds like it was a real hoot, sorry to have missed out. Still today, many of his given place names persist throughout Australia, New Zealand and the South Pacific Islands.

After you cross the Daintree River, on a tiny cable ferry, the windy road passes over a steep mountain ridge and you enter a world removed. The vegetation changes dramatically to full tropical rainforest. As on the Noosa River farther south, the locals here fought pitched battles in the 1970's to prevent a bridge being built across the Daintree and opening up the then still virgin forests of Cape Tribulation. In a sort of legal compromise, the coastal road, paved only since the 1980's, ends at Cape Trib; then becoming a gravel track north of Cape Trib for the remaining 30 km into Cooktown. It's nearly impassable during the summer "Wet." The main paved highway circles the entire area miles inland to the west. This is also the only place on earth where two World Biosphere Reserves adjoin: the Daintree Rainforest and the Great Barrier Reef. It's a truly spectacular, unique environment to explore. You'll immediately notice road signs you've never seen anywhere else in your travels. Lots of Crocodile warnings, as well as jellyfish, and even Cassowary crossing signs.

The Daintree Rainforest is among the oldest on earth, at around two hundred million years. Now a mere remnant of the ancient primordial forest, it covers less than 0.5 % of the Australian landmass today, but contains over 30% of the bird species, 25% of the reptiles, innumerable flowering plants and prehistoric ferns. A living Eden, from a lost age, it's a true wonder of the natural world.

We had previously arranged a fishing and nature charter on the Daintree River in a private, medium-sized tinnie (metal boat), with a local skipper. I'd found him online and just called from Brisbane beforehand. Just me and the boys. The weather was favorable, so we crossed the powerfully rolling

Daintree River bar out into the Coral Sea and fished on the reefs around Snapper Island. Tiny ten-foot open skiffs were hand-lining for Spanish Mackerel off to the northeast, so we joined them. It was amazing to watch them bob and roll in the heaving swells. We saw a few large fish landed but came up empty-handed. Switching from hand-trolling to bottom gear, we did manage to catch a variety of smaller reef fish, and even a few Coral Trout keepers for dinner.

As the day drew on, we returned upriver and spotted Saltwater Crocodiles, aka "Salties." The skipper pulled the twenty-four-foot aluminum catamaran right up alongside the deeply cut mud bank, getting us to within ten feet of a large, sunning male. Prehistoric, deeply fissured and very impressive up close - definitely an apex predator and potential man-eater. You can't imagine how formidable and ancient they appear until you see them up close, in the wild. This large male was around sixteen feet long, over a thousand pounds, and looked to be several million years old. Truly a living fossil. The boys also got the chance to take the wheel and pilot the boat further upriver, which thrilled them completely. All in all, a fascinating outing, full of fresh, exotic experiences. It was wonderful to have the boat and locally knowledgeable skipper to ourselves, compared to booking in with a larger, crowded charter. It's a highly recommended way to explore the region, and no more costly than going with a commercial tour operator.

One curious aspect to the Daintree region is the gravel and boulder base of the streambeds. The rivers are ice cold, weed-free and crystal clear, where you might expect roiled, muddy water. Inviting pools turn deeper shades of green and aqua with increasing depth. The deepest holes, over ten feet, hold jungle perch, long-tailed catfish and freshwater eels. A natural aquarium; and a refreshing and welcome contrast to coffee-colored, muddy streams of most tropics. Swim-time! Climbing out of one such swimming hole, we encountered a four-foot, slender, pewter snake, right off the trail. This was the uncomfortable moment with the German photographers referred to earlier. It looked somewhat familiar. Oh yeah, it's actually a Coastal Taipan... Remember that one from the conference in Cairns, boys? Only the third most poisonous snake on the planet, and it's right at our feet. But without a glass barrier this time. Still, I couldn't resist risking everything to get a few quick snaps with my cellphone for the DDU blog. The overhead lighting was perfect, and after all, what were the odds?

The boys hovered in the background, nervously warning, "Careful Dad. What will we tell Mom...?" What, indeed? Well, at least I know they still care...

The following morning, we were hurriedly heading still further north at 0700 to go snorkeling on the GBR, right off Cape Tribulation. Something caught my sleepy eye, and to my left I saw this shaggy, brown object moving at the forest edge. Sudden, hard braking and a quick reversal ensued, then a frantic fumbling for the cell-phone camera....and voila! A Southern Cassowary, the rarest bird I will ever encounter; shot within ten seconds, while leaning over Luke in the passenger seat. Taken through the rolled-down window of a rental car. Isn't life sometimes strange that way?

This bird was a juvenile, under three years old, and already over four feet tall, but yet to develop the striking sky-blue head coloration and bony "Casque" protuberance of an adult of either sex.

Rare and solitary, if seen at all, they often appear like this; in the early morning along the roadside verge, where they sometimes exit the dense forests to feed. A major cause of Cassowary mortality today is car strikes. Encountering such an exotic creature was a memorable, if unexpected gift. It's encouraging that there are younger birds coming along, a hopeful sign for their future survival. Likely a once in a lifetime encounter, and an early morning stroke of pure good fortune! Perhaps under less than pristine circumstances, but unforgettable still.

After shaking off our astonishment at encountering a live Cassowary, it was time to link up with Ocean Safari, the only Reef boat operating out of Cape Trib. Look them up, they're highly recommended. With a single, tiny Zodiac-style boat, twenty passengers maximum and only a twenty-five-minute ride out to the pristine Maclay Reef, they're a topnotch way to experience the GBR. It's very relaxed and intimate, unlike the large commercial operators out of Cairns, who can have several hundred passengers on one trip. Cape Tribulation is the closest the main GBR comes to mainland Australia, beginning only minutes offshore. In other areas, it's a several hour boat ride just to get to the inner reefs, the outer edges being even further hours offshore. It's a huge reef, fronting a truly massive continent. Consider that in your trip planning. The Ocean Safari crew is informative, young, fun and energetic. They pull the boat right up onto the beach. You climb aboard over the inflatable gunnel and take off at high speed. Wetsuit recommended, and provided, as it is midwinter in Oz in August, and the water is surprisingly cool. But then, in winter, the winds slacken and the water clarifies. An Aussie friend, who was an underwater photographer and scuba guide for years in the Whitsunday Islands off MacKay, recommends July and August as the best season to visit the reef overall. Perhaps something to keep in mind when planning a trip.

As for snorkeling this more remote section of the GBR, all I can say is that it fully met and surpassed all my expectations, which were very high. You drift silently over entangled forests of healthy, vividly interlocked Staghorn corals, each branch tip shimmering with an iridescent pink or purple terminal bud. Multi-hued, living Brain and Shelf corals shelter schools of swaying reef fish in Technicolor... Suddenly, the sun breaks through the light cloud cover overhead, and your entire visual field opens up in a mesmerizing display of shifting shadows and light. Rapidly evolving colors that stretch 360 degrees, far beyond the limits of the water clarity, and change subtly as you fin forward. It's a seemingly endless, living coral garden. No Scuba gear required, as you are only snorkeling in two to ten feet of water; and at times become alarmed that you may be deposited prone on the corals by the falling swells and tide...as they sway enticingly, just inches below your chest.

The truly magical, pure peak moment for me was my hovering over a slowly swimming, three-foot diameter Green sea turtle in only six feet of water. It wasn't alarmed, as I maneuvered gently from above, without touching; and so, continued along its stately way, now only a foot or so below my prone chest. I synchronized my arm strokes with the fore flippers, and we swam along together, in harmonious flowing rhythm, for several surreal minutes. Absolutely sublime...and an experience that left indelible memories of a most amazing day afield in pristine nature with my two eldest sons.

Finally, it was time to head back south, towards Cairns and the flight home. But not before a final night in the hip resort town of Port Douglas, and an early morning trip into Mossman Gorge, one of the most well-known, and photographed, gorges in all the tropics. Mossman Gorge was indeed being loved to death, getting ~300K visitors a year - so some crowd control was needed. The Queensland government had just opened a beautiful, multi-million-dollar visitor's center, only eight weeks before we arrived. Operated by the local Aboriginal people, it provides jobs, education and protection for the area. As in most Australian parks, the facilities are world class and not too intrusive. Private cars are now limited to keep the area well-tended. You pay a small fee to be driven into the Gorge on a shuttle bus, but are still free to hike, wander, and to swim in the magical, pristine pools. Strangely, the large boulders and cold, clear waters reminded me somehow of the Kancamagus Highway in the White Mountains of New Hampshire back home, and now half a world away. It really is a magnificent setting and well worth a visit.

CHAPTER 15: Sydney! A Girl's Road Trip

October 2012

DDU Blog entry: After many Aussie hiking adventures and road trips with the boys, the accusations of favoritism and neglect had reached a deafening crescendo from Claire and Cate. The girls wanted their own special trip with Mom and Dad. And not camping in the rough or dodging snakes either. The girls wanted bright lights, soft pillows, great food; a little luxury... SYDNEY!

We found a couple of beautiful heritage-listed B&B's in Sydney on Trip Advisor that were of an acceptable level of comfort for our dear daughters, though they didn't really appreciate the "no pool" concept. These provided the perfect bases for exploring all that Sydney has to offer: a vast, teeming working harbor, world class botanic garden and zoo, leafy restored neighborhoods, and of course the iconic Opera House and Harbour Bridge.

The extensive Royal Botanic Garden of Sydney sits on a scenic cove in the center of downtown, on the site of the original convict settlement's farm. It's nearly two hundred years old, beautifully maintained and free to the public. The vegetation is interlaced with graceful walkways and lawns. It's the most impressive Botanic Garden I've yet seen; and I generally make a beeline to the Botanic Garden when visiting any new city for the first time. I find them to be dependable and calm green oases in the midst of the tiring urban maelstrom. The semi-outdoor Fernery here is an especially nice spot to sit and contemplate life under a primordial green canopy.

As the walkways lead you down to the water's edge, the view of the fabled Opera House is revealed - surely one of the world's great urban-designed landscapes. Much has been written about the Opera House, but as a newcomer to Sydney a few immediate impressions came to mind. It's much larger and more complex than anticipated, and is set precisely, even intimately, within this setting. It also feels unexpectedly organic and "right" for such an astounding structure.

A bit more about its difficult creation. The project took almost fifteen years to complete and went over budget by some fifteen times the initial estimated cost. Jorn Utzon, the Danish lead architect, quit in disgust before its completion and never returned to Australia to see his completed accomplishment. So, a difficult birth for a remarkably singular structure. That said, as a non-architect, and from a layman's point of view, when you see the genius of the conception up close, almost every other building you have experienced looks somewhat more humble and prosaic - just another in an endless series of boring boxes and rectangles, however cleverly gilded. To compare in musical terms, this structure is a John Coltrane "sheets of sound" free-flight solo compared to the average high-school marching band. Both musical, yes, but on vastly different planes of creativity and execution. It's simply stunning.

Another intriguing aspect to the Opera House is its outer skin. I always assumed it was encased in white clad aluminum (or possibly even vinyl?) siding. Not so. The skin is actually composed of almost one million ceramic tiles, computer designed to lay perfectly flat in a subtle mosaic pattern. This gives the structure a creamy, earthen warmth that reflects light with a soft, subtle glow - never harsh - a magical trick of the light. It's perfectly understandable that it was granted World-Heritage cultural status as a singular creative achievement of the highest order. So, please come back Jorn, all is forgiven...even the budgetary blowout! One day, I hope many of my readers have the opportunity to travel to Sydney and see it for yourselves. Although that's hardly the only trick that Sydney has up its antipodean sleeve.

Oh, there's that word, "antipodean" again. What's up with that anyway? Pretty simple actually. It seems long before any European had ever traveled into the South Pacific, some very intelligent astronomers and geologists postulated that there must be, by necessity, a large landmass in the southern hemisphere, if in fact the earth was a spinning globe, to keep things in balance. They called this imagined landmass Terra Australis, or roughly the "Southern Land" in Latin. This hypothesis, around since antiquity, was later proven entirely correct. The associated term, "antipodean" comes from the Greek, as far back as Plato, referring to an opposite point to anywhere on the globe. Literally translated as opposite foot; "anti" or opposite and, "podean" in reference to the foot, i.e., as a podiatrist is a foot doctor. Thus, "antipodean" refers to Australia as being this counterbalancing landmass in the southern hemisphere, the opposite foot... Antipodean to points in Europe, and I suppose to all the feet in the northern hemisphere, of which there are very many, I can assure you.

DDU Blog entry: Next morning, we were up early, walking across the Botanic Garden again from our B&B in Pott's Point to catch the ferry across Sydney harbor, leaving from Circular Quay, out to the north arm of the harbor headlands and Manly Beach. The ferries are fast, regular and cheap, and a wonderful way to see one of the finest natural harbors on the planet; actually, a vast estuary containing multiple sizable harbors within. The stroll across the Corso commercial district to the outer beach at Manly maintains an air of faded Victorian elegance and is lined with nice shops and cafes. And the beach is a superb sand crescent that feels miles away from the busy Sydney CBD just upriver. The name Manly is said to pay tribute to the manly physique of the original Aboriginal inhabitants as noted by the early British sailors.

A peak Australian experience for me occurred while sitting on the upper bow deck of the pitching ferry as we returned upriver, into the Sydney Central Business District, or "CBD" in Oz parlance, coming on sunset. A sharply freshening sea breeze kept most everyone indoors. Alone on the upper deck, rolling with the swells between the impressive North and South Heads, and lost in my thoughts. A shimmering, golden sunset sank behind the Opera House and Harbour Bridge, leaving them and the entire Sydney CBD indelibly etched in black silhouette; cut in sharp relief as if from sheet metal, while the lights outlining Sydney harbor blinked on into the gathering dusk. It was a solitary hour to relax and marvel at this new, New World city, and to contemplate the surprising journey that got me to this seat, in this settling city, at this very moment in life. It was an unforgettable, life-affirming experience. And, perhaps, a silent affirmation that we had made a wise, if sometimes difficult, decision in embarking on this Australian odyssey. "Nothing ventured, nothing gained," as the ancient sage advises...

We then moved over to the Rocks, the oldest part of Sydney, dating to the 1820s, and so named for the rocky peninsula that convict laborers spent decades hacking apart with hand tools to build the original stone buildings of the nascent city. It's an interesting neighborhood of restored heritage buildings, warehouses and high-end cafes and bars. Located in a lively section of central Sydney, right on Circular Quay, and by the docks where international cruise ships berth. They are too massive to go further upriver under the Harbour Bridge, and so terminate here. A large portion of this area was razed when the Harbour Bridge was built in the 1920s and 30s; and incredibly, the entire Rocks district was slated for complete demolition during the urban renewal craze of the 1960s. It was only saved when the construction workers' unions went on strike and refused to do the work. This was the first such "Green" strike in urban history, and a watershed moment in the development of a heritage preservation mindset worldwide. So much for listening to "expert" guidance. The next day's journey took us again across the harbor by ferry to experience the Taronga Zoo, another Sydney landmark with excellent hilltop views of the city CBD from the north shore. It's a vast, well-designed park, and well worth an entire day, especially for those traveling with kids.

The other Sydney landmark that dominates the skyline down at the Rocks is the Harbour Bridge. Impressively massive, its southern footings and buttresses are anchored here, and the industrial, metallic superstructure looms right overhead. We hiked up onto the pedestrian walkway two nights in a row to watch the lights of the entire Sydney metro area come alive. Home to some 4 million people, strung out along the undulating waterlines, inlets and islands of the variegated harbor that stretches for miles towards the east and the open sea. The entire, vast harbor scene was illuminated like a massive, filigreed Christmas display below. It was breathtaking to behold. We even witnessed a free fireworks display over the Opera House and harbor below on Saturday night. A sublime, shared memory for us all.

Finally, all trips have to end, and it was time to say farewell to the Rocks and Sydney. It was perfect planning to spend three nights exploring right in town and on the harbor. We were glad to have canceled a proposed side trip into the Blue Mountains, two hours west. That's a whole 'nother adventure. Exploring Sydney was a wonderful opportunity to spend time bonding with our rapidly growing-up young ladies. In retrospect, I could certainly get used to the way these girls travel, pretty deluxe indeed! Maybe they'll agree to invite Dad along on the next girls' road trip. And finally, here's DDU's closing wish that you may also have the time and some means to get away and travel with your kids and teach them the "rules of the road" wherever and whenever you can. They are growing up so quickly now, in the blink of an eye...

CHAPTER 16: Aussie / Pub Cultcha

Let's face it, no one travels to Australia for high culture. Fact, and common sense. Excellent museums you can get anywhere, Europe's chockers with them, and I do enjoy them occasionally. But Australia has natural magic: live Koalas to snuggle, Uluru standing sentinel in the vast, timeless Outback, the aquamarine world of the Great Barrier Reef to dive and snorkel. Visit a museum? When it's so warm, bright n' breezy? "Yeah, nah, mate, maybe tomorrow..."

A recent poll of international visitors to Australia clearly bears this out. Australia contains amazing landscapes and entirely unique flora, fauna, Aboriginal and Colonial history. This is the reason people are willing to travel all the way Down Under. It's like nowhere else on Earth.

So, we're not comparing Australian galleries with the Louvre here; Sydney isn't trying to compete with Paris; it doesn't have to. Very few Aussies that I've met seem to have any concern that their homeland's not considered to be a highly cultured place. They're too busy sailing, fishing and hitting the excellent surf breaks under flawless skies, year-round, to give it much thought.

But yes, there are art openings and galleries, dance recitals and classical music concerts occurring regularly, and they're actually pretty good; though I haven't spent much time there. In actual fact, the very best of Australian culture combines both elements, tending towards outdoor visual art displays like Sculpture by the Sea, on the eastern Sydney beaches Cliff Top Walk; the Vivid Fest, again in Sydney; or the indescribable, but wildly creative and family-friendly Woodford Folk Fest in rural Queensland. Young, hip, multimedia experiences with fantastic music. The weather's great, the vibe is chilled out. Hey, if you've got it, flaunt it!

So, leaving any pretensions to high culture aside, everyday Aussie culture is still pretty fascinating and at times downright bewildering to outsiders. As an American, you are perhaps a few steps ahead of, say, Asian or European visitors, for a few reasons - primarily that Australia has, for better or worse, since WW2 been heavily influenced by US mass media culture and language. Plus, the language is common, though meanings can vary considerably. Finally, an American accent immediately identifies you as being from, not the "mother" country, England, but even better; from the "big brother" country, America. It's almost assumed, "You're fun and easy going, just like us, we'll be right." Instant mateship...

It's history now lost on most Americans that, in WW2, the US basically saved Australia's bacon from the Imperial Japanese forces marauding down through southeast Asia from the north. They got as close as Papua New Guinea, only some forty km across the Torres Strait from the northern tip of Queensland. General MacArthur's legendary Pacific campaign was actually headquartered in downtown Brisbane for almost two years, and a little-known museum in an older high-rise right downtown is left as a perfectly preserved time capsule of the day the War ended and they closed up shop. In all, almost one million US servicemen transitioned through Australia between 1942-45, giving rise to some twelve thousand marriages between US GIs and Australian women. Believe me though, the Aussies well remember. Many of their Nans and Gramps, even some of their Da's, Uncles, Mums and Aunties served directly with "The Yanks." So, as an American, you will be almost universally welcomed by the Aussies as being some sort of long-lost cousin, and "Oi, did I tell yas, me Mum's sister married a Yank and lives to this day in Kentucky? I've been over several times meself. I loved it!"

Aussie culture:
It's a vast subject, like any country's would be in totality. In the interest of brevity vs boredom, I'll concentrate on a few of the more surprising aspects that I've encountered as a newcomer. And as always, it's just my take on these various topics, not unassailable truth, or "struth" in "Strine".

Strine - Australian slang:
First off, it's still a very Anglo-centric place, with all the eccentricities

of time, space and distance thrown in as a delightful seasoning of sorts. Many words, turns of phrase and ingrained habits are probably more familiar to a Brit than a Yank, due to common cultural roots that are still closely shared, compared with the USA and Britain. Somewhat similar to Canada, I suppose, Australia only gained complete sovereignty from Great Britain in 1986, and is still technically a Constitutional Monarchy with representation of the Queen by the Australian Governor General. Australian English is considered a separate regional dialect similarly to American English. As in the States, the more rural you get, the broader the accents and the more archaic and colorful the usage. For shorthand it's termed "Strine". To speak Strine is to speak real, authentic Australian. Strine...True Blue...While many terms are widely used nationally, Queenslanders (being from a relatively insular, homogeneous area originally settled as a penal outpost (1830-1870s) and spread over a vast, rural state), are particularly noted for their colorful turns of phrase. A few of the more common ones visitors may encounter:

Bogan - Pejorative, insulting. An uncouth, uneducated lout. A redneck.

Larrikin - complementary. A charming rogue, funny and good with the ladies. Crocodile Dundee was a prototype.

Drongo - a stupid or incompetent person, often proceeded by bloody, i.e., "Piss off, ya bloody drongo!"

Ocker - Adjective and a noun - an uncouth person who speaks 'Strine. Can be a compliment of authenticity, i.e., "That Bruce is such an ocker Aussie, mate, fair dinkum..."

Pom or Pommy - a British person; mildly ribbing. Origins unclear, perhaps referencing the new settler's fair, orange-rose complexion, like a Pomegranate? Not likely in reference to "Poor Old/ Property of Mother England", as is commonly assumed.

Grommet/Ratbag - A pre-teen skater/surfer weasel. Grommet more surf specific.

Dag - noun- an affectionate insult for someone lacking self-awareness regarding being goofy, unsophisticated, unfashionable. "He's such a dag..."

Daggy - adjective- unfashionable, eccentric, i.e., daggy trousers.

Wanker/ Tosser - a jerk, i.e., "dickhead". To "toss off" is Aussie slang to masturbate.

Ta - a casual "thanks".

Whinge - to whine or complain.

Havin' a blue - having a heated argument, a row.

Naf - something in poor taste, awful.

Sook - noun - a crybaby; verb- To have a sook- have a good cry, feel sorry for oneself.

Rabbit on - to talk too much.

Stickybeak - noun or verb. You can be a stickybeak or have one. Noun - "She's a real stickybeak", i.e., innocently nosey. Verb - To have a look at or into something in a non-threatening, even helpful way, i.e., "Let me have a stickybeak at that, mate."

Barmy - crazy, mad.

Cark it - To "cark it" is to die or break down, usually suddenly or unexpectedly. Perhaps to become a carcass?

Spit the dummy (kid's pacifier) - to totally freak out, lose control.

Struth/Strewth - a mild oath or expression of surprise. For real? Truth?

Shout - to buy the round/ meal, often used when drinking. Can be used when paying for a meal, i.e., taking the check, "I'll shout, mate..."

Your shout - a polite way of saying "Your turn to buy the round, ya cheap bastard." (Do not ignore this suggestion, if directed at you).

Goon - cheap box wine, as in: "Mate, I sure spewed after eight cups a' goon...."

Goon bag - the poly liner inside the wine box. Carried by young Aussies to parties on the beach or in the bush. Creative minimalism y'might say...

Plonk - poorly structured, sub-standard wine, but one with higher expectations (and price) than goon. Such disappointing wine might be referred to as tasting "Plonky."

Tinnie - a can of beer or a small metal skiff.

Ute - a pickup/work truck. Utility vehicle.

Esky - ice cooler. For Eskimo?

Dunny - an outdoor toilet, latrine, as opposed to Loo- an indoor toilet.

Avo - avocado.

Arvo - afternoon.

Aggro - to get, or be, aggressive, i.e., " Give me some of ya avos this arvo, or I'll get aggro, mate..." (I've never actually heard all three strung together thus, but anything's possible I suppose)

Snag - an inexpensive (generally beef) sausage, ubiquitous at casual backyard Barbecues or "Barbies." Classically served on cheap, diagonally folded white bread, perhaps with grilled onions and "Tomato Sauce", or Ketchup. That's it. Mustard or Relish, rare; BBQ sauce, possible, but unlikely. Grilled green and red peppers would be entirely alien, or radically on the culinary cutting-edge, depending on your perspective.

Prawn - never a shrimp on the barbie! Never a "shrimp" in Oz at all, for that matter...

Fang - fetch me, i.e., "Fang me a snag mate..."

Thongs - flip flops, not lingerie.

Swimmers/Cozzies/Togs - bathing suits, all; use dependent on location.

Ripper - really good, i.e., a ripper party.

Stonkin' - really great, i.e., "She's a stonkin' snapper mate."

On the piss - drinking heavily, as in: "If it's Friday night, Bruce'll be on the piss with his mates..."

Taking the piss - ribbing a friend affectionately. Bullshitting. None of my mates has been able to explain why the phrase isn't "giving the piss." No, "taking" the piss... As in, "We're just takin' the piss with ya, mate..."

Bludger - lazy, a shirker.

Knackered - tired out.

Feelin' crook - sick.

Chuck a sickie - call in sick to work, typically when actually well.

Yakka - Physical work, hard labor. As in, "We sure put in the hard yakka today, mate."

Chockers - really full, crowded.

Root - to have sex. Never, ever say you will "root for the home team" in Oz!

Pash - make out heavily, passionately.

Crack on - to hit up on somebody, flirt.

Fanny - a vagina, not a bum.

And finally, some often heard, but mostly misunderstood, Aussie standards:

Bloody oath?! - A question or a statement. When used to end a sentence with a question similar to "For real?" Or, "Are you shitting me?" Also can be added as a statement, implying emphatic agreement, like "Damn right..!"

Fair Dinkum - Also used as a question or a statement. Someone or something truthful, genuine, real. "That Bruce is fair dinkum, I tell ya." As a question, similar to "Are you putting me on?", or "Are you being straight with me?" "Fair dinkum?"

Mate - used casually and commonly, i.e., buddy; but in a deeper sense mateship is an ill-defined sense of unquestionable responsibility for, and loyalty to, one's friends. Particularly male-male. Mateship is earned over time and through bonding experiences, good and bad. Casual acquaintances might be off-handedly referred to as mates, but they aren't really, in the deeper sense. In USA terms, similar to buddies vs. blood brothers.

Aussies seem to love to curse and swear. You might be surprised at what you hear come out of a toddler's mouth around here, but always with such a charming accent! A classmate of Luke's summed it up this way, " 'Stralia's the only country where ya call perfect strangers mates, and yer best mates cunts." True that; and if they're really great guys, and I mean just simply the best, you might even call them "mad cunts..." Sigh, it's just the way it is down here, folks.

As my best mate PJ says, "Doc, ya know we like ya if we're takin' the piss with ya. If we're too polite, we're not sure yet..."

My current favorite was casually offered up by a senior nurse while in the ED on patient teaching rounds. "Well, that's as obvious as dog's balls..." she replied, to the whole group, without even a smirk.

So many odd colloquialisms from this strange, far-removed culture that developed in fairly profound isolation over two centuries. And believe me, when you are with a group of Aussie mates, and they're going off in full-on, rapid-fire Strine, you will really feel they are speaking a foreign language; one full of asides, gentle put downs, and indecipherable inside jokes. Sharp, fast-moving and witty; not for the faint of heart. You sip your beer, smile silently and think, Wha...?!?!

Pub Culture:

Likely derived from their Anglo-Saxon roots, the strongest Aussie cultural institution is arguably still the pub. More than one in every town, popular and central to the community, a place to gather and "take the piss" (bullshit), watch "the footie" and bet on horses, keno etc.

By US standards, these pubs are fairly utilitarian affairs, not fern, brick and brass, more lino and tile. The beer's always served ice-cold and preferably draft. The pubs also generally have the gambling and retail liquor licenses, so serve threefold community duties. In general, it's a drinking culture; lots of beer and liquor, increasingly wine, especially among the women. And getting blotto, bluted, shit-faced, is fairly well tolerated and accepted as normal, as long as you don't drive. A minor curiosity is the lack of single urinals in the men's rooms. Instead, they have what I call "the wall of stainless." These, in larger, busy pubs, can be entire walls, or even two meeting in a corner, of chest high stainless steel, auto flushed (and rarely, judging by the stench...) urine-guzzling monsters, approached over industrial, stainless grates in the hazy need to "drain the main vein." You simply approach, from almost any angle, and let fly... Efficient no doubt, minimal accuracy required; but I would sure hate to lose footing and fall into one during some drinking session!

In Queensland, they serve draft beer in a confusing array of glass sizes, either a Pot: a half beer, around 8 oz; a Schooner: a long thinner glass, around 12-14 oz; or a Pint: a full beer - actually an Imperial pint or 20 oz. Schooners seem most popular, likely due to being finished before it's warming and flat in the Aussie heat. "There's always a freshie on tap mate, no worries." So, thus prepped, if you now step up to the bar confidently and say something like "A schooner of Four X Gold, mate" your accent will be noted, and they'll assume you're a Yank who's been around a while. If sounding confused, they'll start asking gregariously,

"Where ya from mate, and did I tell ya about me Auntie in Kentucky?" It's your choice...

It's also a wildly enthusiastic sporting culture; especially Football, aka Soccer, and Rugby, all three types (who knew...?). They play Union, AFL and NRL (also called "League"). Popularity of each is dependent on where you are located on the Continent. Confused yet? I still have trouble telling them apart after six years, forget understanding all the various rules and strategies! Suffice it to say, the locals are into it...very... No snide comments please. Aussies are great folks, really friendly and outgoing. But they are also pretty straight-forward, physical and proud. Irony is generally lost on the pub crowd. As a non-local, being a wise ass, acting like a wanker (dipshit), or cracking on somebody's girlfriend ("Mates don't mess with other mate's Sheilas") is a sure-fire way to get your ass kicked thoroughly. So, be funny, be respectful, keep it straight-forward and "No worries mate, too easy." Cheers!

One very dark side of Aussie pub culture, that I'm exposed to by the nature of my work, is the concept of the King Hit. I just don't get it at all, but it's basically a sucker punch, thrown without warning to some poor sap, who may or may not have asked for it. Generally, it happens late at night, inside or just outside a pub, involving the Hitter - generally a 40-ish, beefy, strong but gone to pot, ex-rugby player who gets a bug up his ass about life in general or something - and takes it out in a single blinding King Hit on the poor Hitee, and "whack" down the poor fellow goes. This is always followed by an arrest, as the Hitter generally never even runs off. The Hitee often awakens days later in an ICU somewhere far away with a closed head/brain injury with assorted facial fractures, if they are lucky. Unfortunately, these blows are sometimes fatal, and highly publicized, events.

In my time working in Aussie EDs, I've seen more than a few facial injuries due to King Hits; luckily mostly orbital rim and floor fractures or broken Zygomatic arches. I've spent numerous late hours, meticulously repairing the injuries and commiserating with the sobering victim and his intoxicated friends. It now occurs to me, at least I've never had a female patient who's been King Hit; and no fatalities yet, thank God.

Incredibly, when the case goes to trial a few months later, the Hitter appears before the Magistrate invariably all teary-eyed, suited-up and appropriately contrite. The wife and kids are brought out, crying for the cameras, and his best mates saying what a good community-minded bloke he really is, and that it was just an argument that got a little out of control... A true tragedy for all involved... And incredibly, oftentimes these guys, instead of being strung up, end up getting a very short sentence or even probation/ parole/ community service, by my reading. The King Hit, an awful, and to me inexplicable, Aussie reality. Well, I guess nowhere is perfect after all...

Pub Grub:

To a much greater extent than in the US, pub food is a widespread institution in Australia. Though sometimes said with a derisive tone, pub grub is actually a reasonably priced, dependable and surprisingly good dining option. A few helpful hints: stake out your table early, it's always a big rush around 5:30 - 9 PM if the food's any good. Don't expect table service, you'll sit a long time! The etiquette is to line up at the counter, order ya grub, get drinks ordered at the bar (separately), go off to the side tables and grab cutlery, serviettes (napkins), sauces, etc. and go back to your table and socialize while awaiting your buzzer to activate, which can be over an hour later if it's full-on dinner rush. In some places they bring the food to you, but that's highly variable. You won't get a buzzer if that's the case. The menu runs towards burgers, chicken parmie and deep-fried pork schnitzels, served in huge portions with hot chips and green salad included. Aussie comfort food.

The fresh local seafood specials are always beautifully cooked, and delicious, but are somewhat pricier. Meals run from $20-30 for mains. It might seem steep, but the quality is uniformly high, and the portions are enormous generally. If you're traveling light on money, it's pretty easy to split a single main (or entree as called in the States) and feel fully satisfied. On that note, the ordering terminology seems backwards to an American. There are no appetizers (or apps). They're called entrees. What Americans refer to as entrees are called mains. We once ordered dinner, and the waitress paused and asked charmingly, "Wouldn't you like to order entrees?" It was a clumsy, silent moment before we got it...

Many pubs have gotten on the worldwide foodie/locavore train and are upping their game considerably of late. Often the finer dining can be enjoyed in a quieter upstairs room or verandah at the same pub, or you can still have it down in the mosh-pit with the kids, either way; the locals don't care. The dress code in general is "Yes", clothed, please. Aussie casual includes nearly anything except full frontal nudity it seems. And maybe shoes; footwear or thongs (flip-flops) at least.

I recently had one of the best steaks I've had in six years in Australia, including urban fine dining, upstairs at a beach-side surf club. Sitting at the outer rail, overlooking the thumping surf; generous aged, bone-in porterhouse, rare, sides of mashed, glazed carrots and Béarnaise sauce. Well-handled and professionally, if casually, delivered. It was top-notch, and I thought a great value at $50 AU. The Aussie food scene has exploded in recent years. They have an awesome bounty of fresh local ingredients year-round, extremely diverse and wonderful regional wines and intelligent people who care. And these improvements have indeed filtered down to the realm of the lowly pub grub. Definitely indulge, it's where the real Aussie community life is happening, and you will be made to feel right at home.

A final point is that there's no tipping involved. Aussies are baffled by US tipping culture, until you point out that it might incentivize better service in general. They'll understand you from that angle, as service in Australia can be casual to the point that the staff might almost sit down and share your hot chips, "So mate, did I tell ya about my Auntie in Kentucky?" Minimum wage runs around $15/hour, so staff are fairly compensated for their labor straight away. All in all, I think it's a better system than in the USA, above-board and streamlined. Prices in Oz, even though apparently steep, are all in, including a 10% GST, service, everything. You choose yer poison, I guess.

Pub Music:
To me, as an avid guitarist, a great pub, in addition to having colorful locals and decent food, should also have a lively local music scene. Luckily, Australia has a vast, varied and very exuberant music scene, centered on its pubs. Everything from acoustic neo-folk, to full on AC/DC and INXS cover bands, it's all out there. Though sometimes competing with the sports screens, generally they're multi-purpose spaces. When the band starts, the screens go off and it's showtime! It's always a great experience, people watching as the band finds its groove and the booze kicks in. Aussies are, on the whole, very unaffected and fun-loving. Things can get pretty rambunctious with ease, and the dancing can be spectacularly wild.

At my favorite hidey-hole pub, one with live music under the Poinciana trees, on an open-air brick patio, tucked away on the northern NSW coast, I once witnessed a muscular sixty-something bloke, head shaven like Mr. Clean, seductively peeling his tee-shirt off in time to the music, while dancing with a much younger woman. Flexing his muscles to the beat, he then, with great fanfare, and to the boisterous cheers of the crowd and fellow dancers, actually lit his copious chest hairs on fire! They incinerated in seconds, with a pretty impressive flame, followed by an acrid cloud of smoke. It was simply awesome! Epic, in fact, but I bet he felt that one the next morning... Aussies are a very musical bunch - check a local entertainment rag, and just show up, however you like. It's pretty hard to attract too much notice. Memorable weekend experiences are pretty much guaranteed, although flaming chest hairs and live dwarf tossing are actually pretty infrequent occurrences, unfortunately.

So, that's a quick primer on Aussie pub culture, which isn't exactly synonymous with Aussie culture, but close enough for our purposes. So, don't be shy. Get out there and mingle at your local...You will perhaps create lifetime memories, monumental hangovers or, at least, have a very good time. "Cheers mates, too easy..."

CHAPTER 17: Tas-mania!
Australia's Wild Island State

Tasmania - the name conjures up strange images of howling, dervish Devils, remote rock-strewn beaches, filthy escaped convicts crossing dank, peaty bogs, finally resorting to cannibalism to survive in the wilds. Or, just as likely, draws a total blank, except for vague name recognition...

As Australia's only island state, the "Apple Isle" remains something of an enigma, even to Australians, many of whom have likely never been there.

First the basics: it's larger and wilder than you'd think; about the size of Switzerland (pop. 8 mil.) or Ireland (pop. 4 mil.) with a static population of only five-hundred thousand. For an American perspective, roughly equal to the land area of Vermont and New Hampshire combined (pop. ~2 mil.). So, one-quarter as populous as those two rural, northern New England states combined. There are only two significant cities, Hobart to the south on the Derwent River, and Launceston to the north on the Tamar. Topographically, it's wildly diverse, from broad, sunny, fine sand beaches on the East coast, intimate rocky coves in the North, to the deeply variegated, Maine-like coastlines of the South. The entire southwest quarter of the island is preserved in stunning National Parks and World-Heritage reserves that protect vast, ruggedly inhospitable mountain ranges and the largest intact stands of temperate rain forest remaining in the Southern Hemisphere. These are the damp, gloomy haunts of the Tasmanian Devil and the now (likely) extinct Thylacine - both large, carnivorous marsupials! This landscape is best symbolized in the popular imagination by the iconic image of jagged Cradle Mountain mirrored across the placid face of Dove Lake below, though this is really just the tiniest tip of a vast wilderness iceberg.

It's very old, Hobart being the second oldest city in Australia, founded in 1804, and Launceston in 1806. This curious fact is accounted for by early navigators' use of the "Roaring Forties" - the sub-Antarctic, circumpolar winds blowing to the east across the Southern Atlantic: to blow them along the 40th parallel, under Tasmania; then pushing them north into the Tasman Sea, separating Australia and New Zealand; and finally up the east coast of Australia to the early penal settlements of Port Jackson/Sydney Harbor. Due to its extensive forests of fine timber, suitable lumber for building homes and ships, Southern Tasmania was colonized very early.

Tasmania's colonial history was very dark and bloody indeed. Following the little-discussed "Black Wars" of near total extermination of the native Aboriginals, who were never present in large numbers, the colony became the harshest of the British penal colonies, which thrived from 1804-1850s. An inescapable island fortress for the worst of the recidivist prisoners, Port Arthur, on the southeast coast was notoriously brutal. Extensive ruins remain there today as a memorial shrine to this era of inhuman subjugation.

It's also remarkably intact. As remote colonial outposts, many of the cities, towns and villages have extensive, intact collections of early architecture that escaped the ill-considered, urban renewal holocausts of the 1960s and 70s. To many travelers, parts of Tasmania appear "more British than Britain", and some sixty-five percent of today's Tasmanians can trace their ancestry directly back to the original ten-thousand or so "First Family" settlers.

Modern-day Tasmania has a vibrant and growing arts, handicraft and gastronomic reputation. The local food, wines, dairy and seafood on offer are world class, coming from such a pristine environment, and are skillfully handled. It's a surprising and intriguing place to travel. I've since returned three times, for the sheer adventure, and to work as an Emergency Consultant in various Emergency Departments there. It's a wonderful window into the real Tasmania, and I find the people witty, interesting and without pretense. Helping out great people in a beautiful part of the world - what could be more satisfying? Our first exposure to Tasmania was early in our Oz adventure, way back in 2012, as recorded in the Doc Down Under blog:

December 2012

DDU Blog entry: Stephanie and I finally found the right nanny, mature, middle-aged and seemingly capable; and got us away for an eight-day trip alone to Tasmania. There was a four-day Emergency Medicine conference in Hobart, the tidy southern capital; then a three-night road trip up the east coast was planned. It was our first trip away alone in ten years. And it was a wonderful break. Blessed silence!

Tasmania, though very remote, has a long history by Australian standards. Hobart, the state capital, is the second oldest Aussie city, founded in 1804 as the second colony after Sydney. The initial settlement was only 262 people, 178 of whom were convicts. The colony grew rapidly, and became infamous as the most feared penal colony in the British Empire between the 1820-1850's.

Tasmania is considered a sort of Vermont of Australia-Vermont being considered sort of the Switzerland of the USA, if you follow me. It's bucolic, fertile and agricultural in the north and east, becoming wilder, more remote and mountainous in the west and south. Nicknamed the "Apple Isle," it has a highly developed, artisanal food culture; famous for its pastured lamb, fruit, fine cool-climate wines, rich cheeses and dairy and especially fresh seafood. Foodie heaven. There's lots of open space and wilderness to explore, for those so inclined. Tasmania also has one of the largest collections of stone heritage buildings in Australia, many convict designed and built.

Hobart is a compact, walkable city of 150k with great architectural diversity. It began as a fine inland port on the Derwent River on the island's southern coast. The place has a remote, sub-polar vibe; much like towns I've known in coastal Alaska. Temperate, with cold winter winds blowing in from Antarctica instead of the Arctic. We arrived in November, late spring, so the evening light was long and lustrous; and flowers were at their brief peak of bloom. Hobart maintains one of the oldest Botanic Gardens in Australia. Like Sydney and Brisbane, it started as the early colony's farm and is said to have the largest specimen collection of conifers in the southern hemisphere. One day, we took a drive to the top of Mount Wellington for panoramic views of the city and southern coast. It's a stunning vantage point, with the entire ragged coastline of southwestern Tassie spreading out below.

On the way down, we stopped in at the Cascade Brewery, Australia's oldest, sitting hard under the very foot of brooding, austere Mount Wellington, towering high overhead.

Behind the bar at the brewery, they have a life-sized model of another Tassie oddity, the Thylacine, a now extinct (?) large, striped, carnivorous wild dog that, bizarrely, is also a marsupial; carrying its live young in a pouch. Called a Tasmanian Tiger, the last known specimen died in captivity at the Launceston, Tasmania Zoo in 1937. There exist early black and white movies of it while still alive. The Thylacine is the very symbol of wild Tasmania. Even today there are regular unconfirmed sightings of living Thylacines in the wild, mountainous wilderness of southwestern Tasmania. Could they still be out there, lurking...?

If they could exist undiscovered anywhere on earth, it would be in the vast, trackless forests of southwestern Tasmania. There are regular expeditions to re-discover Thylacines in the wild, and lately even serious discussions about the possibility of cloning them back into existence! But currently, no actual confirmation that they still exist.

DDU Blog entry: The local Tasmanian ACEM Chapter put on a wildly diverse social program that blended Art and Science, including a private party with open bar for four hundred or so at the Museum of Old and New, or MONA. This is a private museum and winery recently built overlooking the Derwent River by a local internet gaming billionaire. It revolves around his conception that all great art is created out of the fear of death or the desire for sex.

Personally, I thought it was a bit of a freak show, but a half dozen or so cocktails got me through the thing intact. It's wildly popular, and a major tourist draw for the Hobart region. It's a must do, at least once in your life, if only to witness the highly complex and disgusting poop-making machine, or the electrically-wired inner brain, the blank book library or the actual M.C.Escher-style Penrose stairway to infinity, or nowhere at all. You try navigating that stairway after a couple of stiff cockies - it's a real challenge! Yup, the MONA, some seriously weird shit, that, but all in good fun...

The next night there was a five-course degustation meal with matching wines at the old Hobart Town Hall. A very swish affair, all highlighting the very best of Tassie produce, wines and live music. During dinner, a very anorexic, bare-chested bloke actually contortioned himself through an unstrung tennis racket, from head to toe. Wouldn't believe it if I hadn't seen it during my entrée, or maybe it was the wine flight. Odd perhaps, but aids the digestion I'm told.

These guys party like rock stars down here. The food was amazing, especially the local oysters and cool-climate wines, both of which were plentiful to the practical point of being unlimited. Sublime, entertaining, just plain unforgettable all, but we had to get out of this town and preserve my liver!

So, the conference was attended and survived intact, and we hit the road up the east coast. We avoided the western mountains because Tassie friends in Brisbane had warned us that the weather could be really touch and go up in the high country at this time of year. And it had been windy and freezing up on Mt. Wellington, so we opted for the mellow route, traveling through a bucolic landscape that reminded one of the English countryside, to the village of Richmond, site of the famous, convict-designed and built stone bridge. It's the oldest stone bridge in Australia, c 1823, still in use and aging gracefully with the gently undulating sags that only great age can impart, and overlooked by Australia's oldest Catholic church, c 1836. All in all, a decidedly un-Australian scene, somehow more reminiscent of a misplaced 19th century agricultural English village, ignoring the Eucalypts and Lorikeets of course. It's said that Tasmania is more English than the English countryside these days. A preserved time capsule, protected by its isolation. Having never been to Britain, I can't judge the veracity of this observation, but it seems reasonable. As we headed northeast, the landscape flattened, becoming luxuriantly emerald and densely sheep-flecked. It appeared suddenly, and curiously, Irish to me, with sheep grazing right down to the edge of the cobalt sea. Ahead, still further to the northeast, over the flat ocean bay from Swansea, in the far distance, rose incongruously, the rounded granite masses of The Hazards on the

Freycinet Peninsula, our destination for a few days of coastal hiking.

This is the location of iconic Wineglass Bay, and the landscape here is a very fetching combination of small, sheer, rugged peaks, verdant pastures and pristine estuary seascapes. The vast Moulting Lagoon that backs up the Freycinet Peninsula is a world-renowned refuge for migratory waterfowl in the Southern Hemisphere, and the source of the highly prized, local oysters and farm-raised scallops.

The weather was perfect, and the long-evening, summer months twilight burned amber on the bare stone summits of the Hazards from our waterside B&B in tiny Cole's Bay. The following morning, we hiked the easy one km trail up to the Wineglass Bay overlook- even more stunning that the thousand or so calendar pictures you've seen. Having plenty of time, we then hiked over the pass and down onto the broad, sandy arc of the beach at Wineglass Bay. This steep, rocky jaunt eliminated ninety-five percent of the tourist traffic, now left far behind. There are several options from this lovely, undeveloped beach. We chose the twelve km route across the boggy isthmus which, we were warned by Rangers, was prime Tiger Snake habitat; and returned to Cole's Bay along a remote headland. The trail was generally broad and sandy, and we didn't encounter any snakes. This was a relief, as I've become a bit of a snake magnet over my years of bushwalking Down Under.

DDU Blog entry: The bay waters were crystal clear, azure; like the Caribbean, although definitely not tropical this far south. The sea rocks are painted at the tide line with the curious, narrow band of brilliant tangerine lichen that's endemic to this region and appears as a linear citrus-colored slash across a distance. Small hidden coves unfold, awaiting exploration- a world away from modern life. We took a refreshing dip in these bracingly cold southern waters, so reminiscent of Acadia National Park in coastal Maine, USA. It was a magnificent hike, its uniqueness never forgotten. After our exertions it was time for some cool, local Riesling and fresh Freycinet scallops, harvested that same day from the bay we were overlooking. Served Tassie style - creamy orange roe-on, rich like an egg's yolk, barely sautéed in butter, on the large half shell. I was a very happy man at this moment. In fact, I felt as if a little Buddha was sitting over my right shoulder, in my perfect contentment. But perhaps it was just the combination of tired legs, energized mind, beautiful fresh scallops and chilled wine, with a bit of warm sunbeam resting upon my contentedly settled self. A Zen moment of perfect mindfulness and peaceful bliss in beautiful rural Tasmania.

The following morning, it was difficult to leave Coles Bay on the Freycinet Peninsula, an uncommonly beautiful blend of agrarian Ireland and granite encrusted Acadia N.P. in coastal Maine. Not stupendous nor grand, but something even more intriguing, pastoral, intimate, harmonious, with glorious food and sunshine beside the ever-restless ocean. A very remarkable place on the planet indeed.

Our route took us north along the coast, through Bicheno and up to Binalong Bay and the sublime, subtle beauty of the coastal Bay of Fires, so named for the multiple aboriginal settlement campfires seen by the earliest explorers from the Bay. We had excellent fish and chips made from locally caught Big-Eyed (or Blue-Eyed) Trevalla, an Antarctic Cod, considered to be among the best eating fish in these southern waters. It was delicate, firm and moist, some of the best we'd ever eaten. If I were aboriginal, I'd likely choose a place like this to live as well: well-watered and forested, on a rich, protected bay.

We only had time for a short day hike at Bay of Fires, but again, the harmonious landscape, and bright tangerine-striped granite boulders made for a unique and memorable environment. There's a longer, multi-day Bay of Fires walk, fully catered with high-end private eco-lodgings for those so inclined. I'm sure it would be a blissful retreat from our overly busy world.

Turning inland, we drove west, away from the coast, through small, but steep mountains, towards historic Launceston. At ninety thousand people, it's the second largest city in Tassie and the economic center of the northern half of the island. Along the route, the fertile valleys, interspersed with surprisingly steep and windy, rainforested mountain roads, made for slow going. We got into town two hours late for dinner reservations; a bit ragged and rumpled by our adventures on the road and shore. We changed clothes in the car in the parking lot, wandered in, and had our best meal yet in Australia at Stillwater, a locavore temple set in an old, converted flour mill.

The staff was superb, not even acknowledging our disheveled state.

Stillwater represents what I think is the future of fine dining: classy but casual, creatively handling superb local ingredients in a relaxed, even educational atmosphere. No snobby pretensions here; instead, a sharing of experiences and perspectives. The menu is innovative, but not to the point of freakishness. A robust selection where you scan down while saying to yourself, "Yes, yes, yes and yes... I could happily eat every dish on this menu." Beautiful food. I still fondly remember the stunning scallop entrée (appetizer) five years later; eight generous local scallops, lightly broiled whole, roe-on, with a whipped potato, prosciutto and lemon foam finish. A meal to savor and remember. Stillwater comes very highly recommended, a fitting finale to an amazing trip, and a deep immersion into another aspect of Tassie's plentiful offerings.

During our leisurely meal, Stephanie and I took some time to review the high and low points of the past several years, and the decisions we'd made that had gotten us to this unusual place in the world, at this moment. There was a lot to be thankful for; we'd survived, as a couple and a family, by pulling together in a strange land, and working hard as a team. Now coming up on our first anniversary in Australia, we were feeling more settled and comfortable. The kids had adapted to their new schools and were all keeping up academically. Stephanie, while aware of the opportunities this journey provided to us all, was still missing her past life and grieving the loss of regular family contact in the USA. We've always worked so well together as a couple, in an almost effortless division of labor. This trip, this evening then, was some small compensation - a well-earned reward, and a night for us to celebrate and savor our shared successes in the unlikely setting of northern Tasmania. We resolved to do everything we could to keep our romance and relationship kindled, even in the maelstrom of raising five lively kids overseas. Toasting our accomplishments, I offered, "We need to get away alone like this more often," as she smiled and nodded in contented agreement.

We flew back directly into Brisbane out of the tiny, two-gate Launceston airport, somewhat fully recharged and ready to rise once again to the many challenges of raising our wonderful, rapidly growing, and very energetic kids. But, after ten years of daily parenting, my only questions on arriving home were, "When can we get away alone again, and where to?!"

Alas, it's not quite so easy... The kids were absolutely overjoyed on our arrival at the front door. Once our slightly addled, matronly nanny left with check in hand, the chaos and litany of complaints erupted:

"Mom, she was so mean, she wouldn't even let us jump off the garden walls into the pool..." "She was a witch!" "I think she was secretly drinking while we were at school!" "Please Mom and Dad, promise you'll never leave us alone with a sitter again, it was terrible..."

They all joined in, a rare, one hundred percent agreement; the Nolan kids were adamant. And relieved to have their beloved Mother (and Dad too, I suppose) back home again.

And the feeling must've been mutual. We never heard from that nanny again...

CHAPTER 18: Fraser Island and Rainbow Beach, Queensland

March 2013

DDU Blog entry: I scheduled some time away from the ED and checked off another Aussie bucket-list item with Luke and Aidan. We drove four hours north from Brissie, camped at Rainbow Beach and took an eco-tour out onto World Heritage-listed Fraser Island. First, we veered off the M1 at Gympie and headed seventy kms east on a sparsely populated two-lane road to the hamlet of Rainbow Beach. The town's surrounded by national parkland, has a population of only around five hundred, and sits above the most stunning beach and coastline imaginable. There are over one hundred miles of continuous, protected coastline here, the largest such stretch on the Australian east coast. There were only a couple dozen people around and about, enjoying a backdrop of the highest sand dunes on the east coast of the continent, up to seven hundred feet and multi-colored. It's the lost beach town of your deepest dreams.

Rainbow Beach started life in the 1960's as a timber cutter's camp. It survives today as an end-of-the-earth beach town, and the southernmost departure point for Fraser Island. Very laid back and chilled out. At sunrise, we caught a 4WD truck with Getaway Fraser Island Adventure Tours eco-tour company and headed up onto Fraser Island. It was much wilder and rougher than we expected. Just to get started, you have to drive off road, out onto a barren sand spit at Inskip Point, onto a waiting barge, that drops its ramp right onto the beach, cross a brisk estuarial, tidal river, and then drive up the open beach on the eastern side of Fraser Island. The beach is actually designated as a public road. They also land light planes on it, and that's just to get started! Friends suggested we simply rent a 4WD vehicle and head up there ourselves. No way, it's not for the uninitiated. We counted six rigs bogged down just trying to get onto the island ferry at Inskip Point! Even our experienced tour guides travel together for safety via two custom-fitted, purpose built, four-wheel drive trucks, in pairs. On our trip we actually had to stop right on the beach to change a flat truck tire, obtained while crossing over a rocky headland separating two remote beaches. It's not a place you want to break down alone in a rental ute, trust me. Once off the beaches, the roads into the interior are atrocious - the worst I've ever driven, even in the Amazon: deep soft sand with eighteen-inch ruts, single lane, no shoulders. There are no paved roads on the whole island. Some roads were even closed to the rugged eco-tour trucks, due to their risk of getting bogged down. Lots of fish-tailing and thumping ensued, exciting but hard on the neck and lower back. Fraser Island is also enormous. At ~ 80 by 10 miles or so, it's the world's largest sand island, containing many distinct, unique and rare ecosystems. The entire island was World Heritage listed in 1992, when logging was finally halted entirely.

Fraser Island consists of pure sand, thousands of meters deep. Centuries of rain have been captured as if by a giant sponge, forming a dome-shaped aquifer that rises several hundred feet above sea level, trapped within the sand. The world's purest water leaches out from all sides of the island, filtered continuously by the purest fine silica. It's said the leach alone from Fraser Island could supply continuous fresh water for the entire Brisbane metro area of 2m people! Eli Creek is a famous leach stream that sends millions of gallons of pristine fresh water out into the ocean across a remote beach. It makes for an invigorating, ice-cold dip! Luke, Aidan and I drifted lazily on our backs down Eli Creek, through the rainforest cover and out onto the open, sun-dazzled beach. A fantastic natural memory.

Another Fraser Island superlative is the iconic Fraser Island dingo. It's thought they arrived on the island with Asian sea traders as long as 5,000 years ago and have been completely isolated from other canine species since. They're considered to be the most genetically pure strain of wild dog on the planet. They look like smallish German Shepherds. Numbers are culled to keep the population sustainable at around several hundred, and being primarily nocturnal, they're infrequently seen on day trips. We were exceptionally lucky, not just to see dingoes three separate times in broad *daylight, but to come upon a mother and pup feasting on a Wallaby carcass at the tide line on an open beach. They completely ignored the truck and carried on about their meal as we observed and shot photos. Greg, our guide, said that he'd never seen this in eighteen years of regular guiding on the island.*

The tour also takes you to the famous "perched" Lake MacKenzie. Composed entirely of raindrops, it has no inlet or outlet, is thousands of years old and pristine. A sedimentary carbon layer, built up over eons of leaf fall, seals the bottom, and it lies in splendid isolation several hundred feet above sea level, hence the name. There are also "window" lakes, so named due to their communication with the underlying water tables. Fraser Island has over forty such lakes, again, the largest number in the world. Lake MacKenzie, the subject of many calendar shoots, is a fantastic spot for lunch. Out in the middle of the bush, your Aussie guide grills you up a steak (while you take a refreshing dip in the lake), complete with salads, fresh tropical fruit and a cold Aussie beer or soda. For $100 AU, it's the only way for a Fraser Island neophyte to go. Very good value for money here. An additional plus is that the guides have encyclopedic knowledge of the area's complex flora and fauna, history, politics and logging controversies; and provide a very engaging running commentary throughout the day.

Another unique feature of Fraser Island is the presence of extensive hardwood forests, comprised of the rare, giant Satinay trees, which grow seemingly out of pure sand. Actually, there exists a shallow layer of nutrients about three feet deep that nourishes these giants; precious humus built up over the untold ages. These forests are considered to have developed over some 750,000 years to their current state. Individual mature trees can be over six hundred years old and twelve feet in diameter. The Satinay tree is unique to Fraser Island. Highly prized for its resistance to rot, the wood is said to have been used to build the London docks, and line the Suez Canal. Many pitched battles were fought to curtail their destruction by logging, which was finally stopped permanently only in the late 1980's. There are many other Eucalyptus and Melaleuca forest ecosystems on the island as well.

In sum, an eco-tour day trip onto Fraser Island should be considered by any tourist interested in natural history and unique island environments.

One could easily spend several weeks out there. There are modest eco-lodges and campgrounds on-island for those wishing to spend multiple days on Fraser. While perhaps less well known than some of the marquee Australian destinations, Fraser Island will prove to be a high point of any tour along the Queensland coastline. As an added bonus, the Gateway tour drops you off right in front of your hotel or campground at Rainbow Beach in the evening, before heading on further south to Noosa. A very full and fascinating day!

Fraser Island, while not exactly unknown, is a bit off the typical tourist track. It's certainly a unique and fascinating environment that is highly recommended for visitors to the southeast Queensland coast. You might consider going as part of an organized eco-tour group, to alleviate worries, especially if it's your first trip out there. Getaway Fraser Island Adventure Tours did an excellent job introducing us to this vast, unique and wholly remarkable landmass. It really was much wilder than I, or the boys anticipated, but that's a very good thing indeed. To reinforce the point, the local pubs have "Walls of Shame" photo collages of the numerous rescues of roll-overs and severe accidents involving off-roading on the island over the years. Not pretty... It really is a challenging environment, even for experts. I would not recommend renting an off-road ute for your first foray onto this breathtakingly wild island.

A final tip is to consider staying a few nights right at Rainbow Beach, which is a beautiful spot with a nice hotel, pub and campground an hour north of Noosa. All the Fraser Island tours that access the island from Inskip Point in the south begin and end in Noosa, an additional hour's drive to the south. Instead, they can pick you up and drop you off just south of Fraser Island at Rainbow Beach, saving you an additional hour's transfer time both ways. The alternate option is to approach Fraser Island by ferry from the northwest, leaving out of the busy port town of Hervey Bay, a few hours' drive still further north on the M1. Either way, it's an entirely unique natural history adventure not to be missed by travelers to mid-coastal Queensland.

CHAPTER 19: Deep Pacific Blue - Early Aussie Songs, 2012-2013

I've been writing creatively for over thirty years, but this is my first attempt at a real book. Looking back, my life seems always to have been rushing forward; we do what's required to survive and thrive. Fascinating, enriching and unique experiences all. But there was simply no time, the one commodity quality writing requires.

I got around this limitation, adapting as always, by melding my innate love of all things musical with the urge to record the arching, fireworks trajectory of life as it flew by. Songwriting was the perfect solution for me. At its best, a sort of shorthand haiku; the lines pared to their sharpest, suggestive intent. An entire story in sixteen lines. Over the years, I think I've improved; learning that if you can't say it on a single page; re-write, distill it down. The art is in the brevity of clear expression.

And during my many itinerant years as a student, medical student and Emergency Medicine Resident, the guitar's been a constant, dependable companion. A means to decompress and disengage from the stressful, algorithmic mindset of medicine, and enter into a world of free-flowing creativity and inner self-exploration, all without having to leave your bedroom. It's great therapy. Over the years, I think it's been a major factor in helping me maintain my resilience and longevity as an emergency doc.

As this book is, in essence, the story of our past six years in Australia from an American expat doctor's somewhat bewildered perspective; for me, by definition, this includes songwriting that was inspired by the experience. It's how I filter my life and deepest feelings. Often, I'm not sure what I'm trying to get at until long after the song's complete. As in real life, clarity and insight often unfold only over time. But it sure beats psychotherapy and is entirely portable - a fresh pen and a blank page. You simply supply all the ideas, kid.

I chose the pen name of o.g. many years ago, as a kind of insider joke. Once I knew the direction I wanted my songwriting and playing style to go, I realized I'd be an old guy by the time I ever got there, and it just stuck. So, here I am today, o.g.nolan - fully actualized. And it's been an entertaining journey every step of the way!

Music, for me, is the highest art form; an endlessly challenging process of filling silent space with sound over a specific time frame, only to conclude at inevitable silence in the end. Beautiful, melancholic, invigorating, arresting... a universe lies open at the hands of the creator. And by adding lyrics and vocals, matched to the shifting tides of the music beneath; attempting the perfect fusion of idea and energy, unspoken emotion with concrete lyric; well, you have simply entered into the realm of the magical, in my estimation. Great pop songs are simply miniature jewels, twinkling ever so seductively; touching subliminal areas we scarcely know exist. But you just feel it and understand...

The other singular attraction of music for me is its plasticity, its utter versatility. Easily adjusted to suit one's mood and state of mind, unobtrusive to enveloping - just turn it up! It enhances activity and efficiency without demanding overt attention, in fact, quite the opposite. I could never imagine having completed this book without a solid hit of my morning Mozart, Vaughan Williams or J.S. Bach. Try the Mozart "Haydn" string quartets, or Schubert's "Trout" quintet. Fleet, subtle, invigorating, but without bombast or distracting lyrics. The perfect morning brain-breakfast, just add coffee.

I also love to work to Brazilian Bossa Nova. The rhythms are stimulating but mellow, simultaneously, and because the lyrics are sung in a language I can't understand, they simply settle into the whole soulful concoction and become an integral part of the groove. I just can't write to lyrics sung in English - I'll get easily and happily distracted. Much modern neuro-scientific research confirms this link between music, brain stimulation and modulation of the emotional state. In sum, well-chosen music enhances brain activity and can make you more focused, efficient and, well... smarter. And, it has zero calories. What's not to love?

So, very long story short, relocating to Australia was a wonderful move in most respects, but coming along for the ride was the most severe case of writer's block I've ever endured. Inevitably, there was a significant period of disruption, both in leaving and then re-settling. In addition, I was wickedly busy trying to land on my feet in a busy, foreign Emergency Department and make sense of that highly complex world, all while keeping my patients from clinical misadventure. Most writers have, by necessity, a real job; it pays the bills. For me it's Emergency Medicine. It's been a good fit and a wild ride. I'm blessed to have it. But in truth, it seems that "life sometimes gets in the way of living..."

It felt like a part of me was missing or had been deeply suppressed by all the chaos. Although our arrival in Australia had been a seemingly magical immersion into a surprising and marvelous new world, it was also exhausting. We were all very relieved to finally have that period of our journey now fading behind us, and to feel a sense of order and homeostasis beginning to take hold. And then, like some subliminal life-force re-animating, I began to write again; influenced by all we'd recently experienced.

So, here are a few favorite songs from that magical early period of innocent arrival. With a bit of their back story, that I hope helps illuminate the trajectory of our family experiences and my writing journey while Down Under. A story arc within our story's arc. They form, to my mind, an integral part of this tale.

"Sailing On the Coral Sea"
Always fondly recalled as the one that broke my writer's block. Sitting, of a warm evening, under those unfamiliar southern stars, out on the back verandah, strumming and looking out over the expanse of Moreton Bay, shimmering under the moonlight. It came simply and organically, like all the best songs. A fantasy of sailing over strange, exotic waters, and leaving your known world behind. At that point I had never actually sailed the Coral Sea. A triumph of the imagination then. But I did so later, and the experience lived up to the hopes expressed in the lyrics. Often, on completing a song, I will have a specific singer's vocal range and timbre in

mind. This one was intended for a Norah Jones type singer; a smoky, late night, noir-ish vibe; all softly tinkling piano keys and string bass...

"A coral moon climbs out of the Coral Sea
and casts its pale light on the heat-kissed land..."

By this time, we had settled into our beachy bungalow, sited on a canal in a sailing community overlooking the Bay. The house, offered to us by friends of friends, was an inside deal. Simple, open-air, furnished by dowager donations and Salvos, but in a great location with daily sunrises and sunsets illuminating the surrounding waters. So diametrically opposite to our farm lives in upstate New York, but that being the whole point; a place that really inspired me, internally as well as externally. Having Stephanie and the kids settling into school and community helped provide the sense of somewhat ordered stability vital to my creativity. The songs began to flow, and change - reflecting new experiences and my growing familiarity with the wider region.

"Byron Bay Getaway"
A love song to a place: the sublime beaches and surf towns strung out along the northern coast of New South Wales, only two hours south, and another world away, from busy Brissie. Basically, Maui at the edge of a continent. The song tries to capture the sun-bleached bliss of a breezy coastal drive along that fantastic stretch of coastline. Truly, my happy place, and one of the most beautiful environments that I've experienced on planet Earth.

"Pack your bags we leave today, let the breeze blow your cares away
Well, nothing could be better, hey, a Byron Bay getaway..."

Now heading into our second year in Oz, I was feeling that things were coming together, that we had, in fact, taken a huge gamble at mid-life and career that was paying off. The hospital Administration was happy with my work and surprised me by offering to sponsor us for Permanent Residency (PR) if I agreed to stay on with them for an additional two years. I had no desire to move on at this point anyway, things were progressing well on all fronts. So, it seemed the next natural step was to take no new steps at all, but to simply carry on. Our twelve-to-eighteen-month teaching sabbatical was now evolving into something very different than we ever expected;

though that's only been clear in hindsight. It seemed we might actually build a future here, however unanticipated. Stephanie and I discussed options and agreed that staying put was the best move at this juncture. We held a Team Nolan meeting with the kids, and all decided to stay on a while longer yet - perhaps somewhat naive as to the implications of our fateful decision.

"Freedom Song"

Effortless - written in thirty minutes, tune, verses, choruses. It feels easy, even though it's rhythmically complex. It's about finding the confidence to take charge of your own fate and live the life you dream of. Go figure... I was just feelin' it and singing it too. They should all be so simple, but, alas, not.

> "Fate unfolds, no one knows the mystery your life holds
> So be bold, sing your freedom song, your own freedom song..."

Most of my formative years were spent in cooler, grayer Northern climes. Since arriving in southeast Queensland though, I've been absolutely mesmerized by the blue, oceanic environment at our very doorstep. Stephanie and I take daily three-mile walks along the local foreshore park, and I never tire of the play of light on tide. And watching the various boats coming and going or tacking in unison at their moorings. In winter, dolphins sometimes surface right alongside the rock jetties, close enough to let us hear their blustery exhalations clearly. On the offshore islands, I sit and watch surfers display their stunning aquatic acrobatics over sinusoidal, heaving waves. It's as if the very ocean is alive and breathing...ebb...flow...ebb...flow. My only attempt thus far at surfing was akin to getting a good, fierce waterboarding. I couldn't even get past the shore break! So, I'm content to simply sit and observe, to be enveloped by this alien environment, to melt away into the southern sunshine.

On the winter Bay, there are many days when the still waters actually appear bluer than the skies they reflect. On these warm, windless days, a light sea haze gradually builds until the horizon line becomes indistinct, and the sky melds with the sea, like a mirrored edge reflecting back on itself, until it becomes impossible to discern the true horizon. In all, an environment completely unlike any I've ever lived in - endlessly intriguing and full of beautiful surprises.

114

"Deep Pacific Blue"

This was my attempt to contrast our lives before and after, and to express my fascination with the light and color of the Australian coasts. There's also a strong element of longing expressed, of being pulled away, and dreaming of returning. A foreshadowing of future events? Read on, gentle reader...

> "Silver sun on water haunts your dreams,
> as you run in place, wondering what your life means..."

After deciding to stay on in Australia for some while longer, a discussion involving a lot of "campaigning" on my part, according to the kids, some pressures started to build. As I was gaining in confidence and respect at work, contributing to, and becoming fully integrated into the ED, and accepted fully by my Aussie EM colleagues (no minor accomplishment), fissures began appearing on the home front. Our lovely, eldest daughter Claire, only eleven on arrival, and now approaching fourteen, was feeling really homesick and very unchallenged by the laid-back Aussie schooling philosophy. Another subject entirely, but surprising for the lack of homework and academic rigor. I suppose I was fulfilled professionally and thrilled to be staying on in Australia, so in some denial. I papered over a lot of the kid's fears and feelings. Stephanie, as usual, was very aware, and tensions cropped up between us as well. After one frustrating attempt to communicate with my uncharacteristically sad, sullen daughter, I went into my bedroom and did what came naturally. I picked up a guitar and wrote my feelings out.

"Talking with My Daughter (for Claire)"

This is a love letter to my eldest daughtie, Claire. My attempt to explain to her my wishes and fears for our future together. A few days later I played it for her and we were both in tears. It really felt like a breakthrough for us, as I finally and openly acknowledged the challenges and sacrifices she was making too, on this now extended overseas adventure.

> "Sitting talking with my daughter, what to do and if we oughta
> stay a while in this place so far from home..."

Approaching the three-year mark in Australia, we'd reached a sort of fulcrum, a balancing point. Life was surprisingly good here; we loved the weather and exotic travel. My career was accelerating in respect and responsibility, with great pay and benefits. The question now became, "How long does the dream last, and if we end it voluntarily, then what comes next?" Every expat traveling with a family along for the ride must eventually hit this point, solo wanderers perhaps excepted. Sometimes, the costs of extrication simply begin to outweigh the inertia of staying put. I imagine this is how many well-meaning people, from a distant perspective, seem to leave home and never quite return. It just sort of happens, as "way leads on to way..."

There was nothing particularly bad about our home and life in New York, in fact many wonderful things. Especially Fairview Farm and the lifelong friends and family that simply can't be replicated by new friends in new places; there's never time for that concentrated series of formative bonding experiences later in life. But Stephanie's three younger brothers were getting married and having babies. These new cousins were suddenly turning three years old, walking and talking. People died, weddings and funerals were missed and lamented. We were living an extended family life vicariously, via Instagram and Facebook. Inevitably, we were really searching for answers as to the best way forward. Lots of prayers for guidance and lengthy late-night discussions ensued, and some awkward silences too. Balancing competing desires and concerns, the pros and the cons. With five kids, and two adults, 100% consensus on anything was almost impossible. One was loving school and making new friends, another was missing Grandma and Grandpa.

My in-laws made our situation somewhat more difficult by essentially trying to starve us out, withdrawing their emotional support. They rarely communicated via Facetime or Skype. Letters became fewer and further between. Looking back, I suppose they had their reasons for being saddened or angry, especially towards me, the instigator of all this separation and heartache. Although our staying on in Australia was never by design, this separation became increasingly difficult for Stephanie and by extension, stressful for us as a couple and family. Life was moving on. We were becoming detached, adrift from people we knew and loved back home in the USA. Living our lives on the other side of the planet, by our own choice... Tough stuff, folks.

I relate this uncomfortable side of the fairy-tale story mainly because it's the truth; but also to warn other potential expats that, as good as the sea change may be for you, you will be leaving large parts of your former lives behind, even if only temporarily. People's reactions might surprise and confound you. Relatives can become threatened and very distant. Turned silent, or even angry, by your decisions. The dark side of the Overseas Retirement Industry pitch. Well, forewarned is forearmed, I suppose. I was really surprised by the intensity of reactions, both positive and negative, that our journey sometimes elicited. On the other hand, as my sixty-year-old sister in Boston stated so bluntly:

"Stay in Australia, you'll have a better life. Why would you want to come back here to live?"

As all this was unfolding, one morning I was hit as if by a bolt out of the Queensland blue sky. I'll never forget it. It was mid-morning, bright and clear; all alone at the house. I was standing on the gangway to our dock drinking coffee, watching the sea life moving below, a regular pastime. Suddenly, I had the overwhelming urge to write. I had no title or tune, nor even words; just go, pick up a guitar... which I immediately did. My brain synapses were literally tingling as I subconsciously decided and struck the low E minor chord. And it was off to the races once more. That indescribable feeling of groping ahead in expectant discovery. Like a sculptor working in clay, a cutting away - the flux/flow state where I don't know what I'm looking for necessarily, but I know what I don't feel. Hit the G major chord, or whatever...no, not that... cut it away... shape it by exclusion. And within ten minutes, working mostly from my subconscious, an entirely new song and lyric revealed itself.

"Living On the Tides"

This is, I think, one of my finest efforts. Not to sound arrogant, let me try to explain. Success in songwriting, like most arts, is mostly internalized. Does the finished song reflect what you wanted to say or create? Has it moved your craft forward? Do you like it? A very distant concern for me is "will **they** like it?" But I'm fortunate in not having to try and earn a living at my avocation. For me, it's not exactly a hobby either. It's deeper than that; more an ongoing spiritual quest for understanding my place in the world and recording life as it unfolds. I'm blessed, I only write what and when I want to, so it's always real for me. And that's why it's usually so excellent too...lol!

Generally, I consider a song successful if it accomplishes even one of these goals. "Living On the Tides" was just a grand slam out of the park for me. It arrived fully developed. It answered affirmatively to all of these, in spades. "Ticked all the boxes..." as they say in Oz. The words are questioning, searching...seeking guidance. The music, in a minor key, provides a mood of melancholic uncertainty, even sadness. Curiously, the lyrics are nocturnal, observing the phases of the moon over the sea as a metaphor for time passing. Perfect, delicate, mysterious...though the inspiration came in broad daylight. Some years later, I still feel it's among the very best I've written. A perfectly composed examination of my own questions. Comforting, though never explicitly answering any, leaving them to linger - perhaps only resolved by the passage of time.

And that's the entirely magical aspect of music and songwriting coming to the fore. The final creation is often most surprising to its creator.

> "The moon is nearly emptied out, the waters fall and rise
> I feel the seasons passing by, living on the tides..."

It felt great to sense the creative energies rising again within me, shedding dormancy, like maple sap in springtime. I was coming back to life and beginning to feel whole again. The chaos of our departure, arrival and settling was beginning to recede, and we were no longer visiting Australia. We were becoming a living part of it, like so many immigrant pioneers before us. The noble tide of history, sweeping us along like tiny particles washing over a stony stream bed... A new life overseas gradually, but steadily, becoming our reality.

And now a note from our author:

All the DDU-associated song mp3's discussed in this book are currently available on Amazon, Spotify, etc. These hosts seem to change pretty regularly, so try Googling o.g.nolan or go to www.docdownunder.com and see what comes up. The songs correlate to the three chapters in DDU that discuss songwriting: "Deep Pacific Blue", "Settled Songs" and "Sea Change". Some twenty original o.g.nolan cuts in all. The DDU soundtrack if you will... and entirely **free** - so, bonus! And if perhaps you were kind enough to order this book or e-book, "Thank You" for your support of this effort. I hope this music moves you in some positive way and adds another dimension to the story. Please have a listen and drop me a note or a testimonial via the website, www.docdownunder.com. Cheers! Doc

CHAPTER 20: Country Queensland and the Scenic Rim

May 2013

DDU Blog entry: Even though we all imagine Australia to be a vast, under-populated continent, total population being only around 25 million, I believe most Americans tend to think of it as being all hot and dusty Outback - and sort of barren. I know I sure did. Well, there's plenty of that indeed. But there's also a vast and sprawling ranchy, beef and sheep raising aspect to Australian life, especially in Queensland, beginning just twenty miles off the palm-fringed coasts of the Coral Sea. The landscape is somehow reminiscent of the Texas or Oklahoma Hill Country. Of course, this being Australia it has to be a bit weirder than that, so the hill country has a backdrop of 3,000 foot rainforested peaks, that are the remnants of ancient volcanoes. And there are stands of eucalyptus containing koalas and cockatoos instead of blackjack oaks, with raccoons and flycatchers. But they do have real cowboys, and even cowgirls; they're called Jackeroos, and Jilleroos. So, something quite familiar to many Americans, yet somehow strange and again, intriguing. There's a vast region west and south of Brisbane called the Scenic Rim, which is a rural ranching area that backs up to the volcanic northern slopes of a series of National Parks that run over one hundred miles west, including the world heritage-listed Lamington National Park. The steep ridges remain forest-clad, but the valleys were cleared by settlers over a century ago, leaving a landscape reminiscent of the Mission Range of western Montana, complete with cattle; lots and lots of cattle, and even local Aussie country music.

As Queensland alone is roughly three times the size of Texas (!) with a population of only ~4.5 million, this area is still very rural, even though it's technically in very southeastern Queensland, on the periphery of rapidly expanding greater Brisbane. In this state, you can drive twelve hours north and still be in central Queensland! And it's a 2000 km (1,400 mile), four to five-day drive from Brisbane to the "Top End" at Torres Strait. This is a BIG country, even by USA standards. Like Texas, it's also a region of horseback riding, rodeos, bushwalking and having campfires under the strange southern stars. So vastly different than the coastal surf-scene, only a few hours away. It feels like another continent entirely.

Aidan and I played hooky for a few days of camping and hiking in the Mount Barney area of the Scenic Rim. As a father of five unique individuals, I feel it's important to keep an eye on each and every kid, to observe carefully for any subtle signs of stress or trouble adjusting. Especially so, since we'd taken the kids out of their familiar surroundings into this strange new world and life. There are positive aspects in making such a move, and challenging ones as well. Each child filters and reacts in surprisingly different ways. Aidan, our second son, is smart, quirky and charming, but also a bit of a stress internalizer. Compared to all our other kids, for me, he's sometimes the hardest to read and deeply understand. So, I had a block of time off and asked Stephanie to let him skip school, in favor of some quality solo time with Dad, doing what he loves to do, exploring the natural world. Fortunately, she and I are philosophically aligned as to the benefits of real-world, experiential learning. Sitting in a classroom and rote learning may be a necessary part of student life but can't compare to actual hands and eyes-on learning in the outdoors. So, she happily agreed. Given the choice, we'll always hit the road with our kids, and hope to see some interesting and educational things along the way.

It was mid-week and dead quiet. We camped, swam, built campfires, caught some small fish. We even saw our first Platypus feeding at dusk, something we were both keen to witness in the wild. In all, it was an awesome outdoors adventure, spending quality time together with my beloved boy. Aidan seemed perfectly content to be living the Huck Finn life for a few days. I tried to draw him out about the new school and any problems being accepted or making friends, but he reported no major adjustment issues, and reiterated his love for the fishing he was experiencing in Australia. "I miss home sometimes, but I like it here Dad." he reassured me, to my great relief.

The Platypus is one of only two egg-laying mammals in the world-if you can get your head around that one-the other being the Echidna, also found only in Oz. Locally they're fairly common, but you must locate the right type of habitat. Ideally, a deep-ish, clean flowing stream with soft earthen walls, so they can dig burrows. Active at first and last light, they appear like small electric boats breaking the still surface in whirl-a-gig patterns, as they paddle and dive incessantly in search of food, which they locate by means of their highly specialized and sensitive, sonar-equipped, duck-like bills. And the males actually have toxic spikes on their hind legs as a defense mechanism. Truly one of the oddest creatures on a continent well-known for its oddities. In fact, it's said that when the first specimens were transported to London for scientific study, the biologists involved were convinced that the entire animal must be some sort of an elaborate hoax!

DDU Blog entry: We hiked the six km round-trip to the lower rock pools below Mount Barney and were surprised at how clear and cold the deep crystalline pools were. It was a wonderful swimming hole, we had all to ourselves in the Aussie bush wilderness. It felt like being in the Green Mountains of Vermont, except for the entirely different forest, the rock wallabies, and a close encounter with a venomous, but mild-tempered, Yellow-faced Whip Snake, we encountered while crawling through a small, rock-slide cave while approaching the upper pools.

We had so much fun exploring the Scenic Rim that we booked a farm stay weekend in the area over Easter for the whole Nolan clan and invited our Tasmanian friends along for the second night. They're the only Aussies we know who are also crazy enough to have five kids. So, Easter farm stay, ten rambunctious kids, wine and bonfires - what could go wrong?!

Country Queensland, Cedar Glen Farmstay:

June 2013

DDU Blog entry: The Cedar Glen farm stay is one of the oldest eco-lodges in Australia. It sits in the middle of a 1000 acre working cattle ranch, two hours southwest of the Brisbane CBD. In the 1970's, beef prices were too low, so the family started hosting guests to help pay the bills. They have since expanded beyond the main house and have added three other heritage buildings that were either on-site or moved from surrounding ranches. Visitors now provide seventy five percent of the ranch's income. There are all sorts of outdoor activities on offer: hiking, or bushwalking, 4WD Jeep tours, horseback riding, creek dipping, birding. Even boomerang throwing and making billy tea and damper Aussie-style. The ranch sits high up in the Lost World Valley, hard against the northern slopes of the Lamington National Park, so the bushwalking, birding and wildlife watching is superb.

A really big hit was the twice daily farm-animal feeding and cow milking, including chooks, turkeys, piglets, sheep, the whole lot. Everyone got some attention and the kids loved it! Just staying in touch with their Fairview Farm roots while away in Oz. The first day the younger kids also got horseback riding lessons, which was fun and challenging for them, especially little Owen.

It was too soft and muddy to go on the 4WD tour up onto the lookout high atop Jack's Rocks, so Luke, Aidan and I hoofed it up for the views. It was a steep, tough one-hour scramble through waist-tall grass and brush, with only animal trails to guide us. The views were fantastic; the primordial Lost World Valley stretching out, richly verdant and undulating, for miles below, tapering off high on the rainforested slopes of Lamington N.P. far away to the south. Hard to believe, but this landscape was also Australian. And as an added bonus, on our return, we bushwhacked under the sheer, rocky bluffs, to explore a series of remote caves and got absolutely filthy scrambling around inside. On the way down we got caught in a soft, misting rainstorm, then took an invigorating dip in the clear, icy creek on the valley floor, rinsing off the hard-earned filth. Swimming in the rain, we couldn't get any wetter, and what a wonderful way to spend Easter morning! As we relaxed in the rain-dimpled pools, a team of horseback riders threaded through the wet trees, forded the stream and were absorbed in succession back into the dense, living forest...magical morning images. Straight out of the mythical, Australian frontier settlement past. Finally, it was off to the cottage to greet our in-coming Tasmanian friends, and work on Easter dinner for fourteen.

Earlier, I had been a bit concerned about encountering snakes, especially going off trail up onto Jack's Rocks. "Weather's too cool, no worries, mate" reassured Nigel, the gregarious ranch manager, before we set off. Of course, after the swim, while driving back down the access road leading towards Jack's Rocks, we came upon a 1.5 meter long, dusky-gray, very thick and highly poisonous Tiger Snake, basking right there on the edge of the warm gravel road under clearing weather. I drove up alongside, and it didn't bother to move, sunning comfortably right below me. At first, I thought it must be an exposed drainpipe, but apparently not... Suddenly comprehending, and seeing that frightful living serpent, I would never have set foot off the verge at all; and it would've simply ruined our otherwise splendid little adventure! So, my take-home point: ignorance is bliss, even (and perhaps especially) when the stakes are potentially deadly...

DDU Blog entry: Easter dinner was a blur of activity, and a wild kid-frenzy, all ten being aged-matched almost perfectly, from around five up to fifteen, and free to wander and get rowdy in the pastures and hedgerows surrounding the heritage cottage. They kept the bonfire well-fed, and the neighbors wide-awake! Right before dinner, the skies opened up with a thunderous roar, and we had to move the main course off the backyard grill and into the ancient gas oven in the cottage, which miraculously functioned, and didn't blow the whole lot of us to kingdom come. Imagine such a torrential rainstorm, deafening on the tin-roofed cottage, two perfectly cooked legs of lamb with complimentary sides, set out on the deep, old wooden verandah. A feast for fourteen and all washed down with copious quantities of lush Aussie Shiraz and Cab Sav. Now blend in lively conversation, acoustic guitar and assorted kid mayhem. Stir in the sense that we were all seemingly adrift together in the warm, starless, black night at the very edge of the earth - like sailors adrift on an unknown sea, the cottage a wooden life raft of sorts. The high, remote mountain ridges close-in all around, but obscured by the wall of storm. A sublime memory, perfectly timeless and unique.

And then, at the very height of the festivities, our being visited (assaulted more precisely) by a very large and aggressive panhandling opossum, who certainly knew the drill, as he demanded to be fed by yet another group of hapless visitors. Hissing furiously, with white mouth agape, he refused to leave his perch on the open rafters right above the dining table, even when threatened with a stout hiking stick. At one point, I thought he might actually leap down and abscond with a leg of lamb we'd set out below! Our ten kids responded in a chaotic uproar, organizing to drive him off and save their Easter dinner. Blurry pictures must exist somewhere of the epic battle that ensued to salvage the meal and the evening, but trust me, it was a most unique Aussie experience. Certainly, the final, bizarre feather in the cap of a perfect stormy evening, adrift in a wooden lifeboat of sorts, alone with friends and family, somewhere out in rural Country Queensland.

CHAPTER 21: The Northern Territory: Darwin, Kakadu and NT National Parks

Nolan Boys Outback Adventure, Part 1:

June 2013

After several months of careful planning, I felt finally ready to take Luke (14) and Aidan (10) on a serious boy's Outback adventure. Ten nights, nine camping rough in a two-man mountain tent. 1400 kilometers (~850 miles) into the bush of the wild Northern Territory. All heat, sweat, stink, dusty roads, snakes and Crocodiles. Add in some wild Barramundi fishing, remote gorge hiking and waterhole swimming. Throw in a nightly campfire under the vast Outback stars and some ancient Aboriginal rock art; it sounded like an absolutely epic adventure on offer. And believe me it was! The girls, on hearing the proposed itinerary, deferred. They wanted their own adventure, just one without the snakes and Crocs, and hopefully, happening again soon.

Darwin, our flight destination and jumping off point, is the capital of the vast Northern Territory, and has an area population of less than 150K. Over fifty nationalities make up the population of this small, mellow city: the Australian gateway to Indo-Asia. It sits isolated on the tropical Timor Sea, next stop to the north, Indonesia. Incredibly, it's the only population center of any size between Cairns on the far northeast coast of Queensland and Perth on the far southwestern coast of Western Australia, a distance of over 3,000 miles, across the fabled "Top End" of tropical, monsoonal Australia. An entirely different world to Brisbane and the rest of this vast continent. On arriving, it feels at the very ends of the earth too.

A classic Darwin experience is to have dinner among the Asian food stalls at the Mindil Beach markets west of downtown. Only open during the "Dry" between May and October, it's a free, tropical, open air street fair held on Thursday nights and Sunday afternoons. The fresh, diverse Asian food, tropical fruits, arts and crafts are wonderful to enjoy, until the sun begins to set. Then everyone meanders through the dunes to watch the blazing tropical sun sink like a flaming torch, until it's gradually extinguished into the tranquil Timor Sea. As twilight falls and the stars come out, the lights go on and the market pace and music picks up. It's exotic and sublime. We flew in specifically on a Thursday to make sure we got to experience it; a good call, and an experience not to be missed when in these parts. It's a wondrous, magical welcome to the "Top End", as the Aussies call this upper 1/3 of the Territory. The lower 2/3 becomes increasingly desiccated the further from the coast you ramble, becoming remote desert south of Alice Springs, aka "The Alice." This is an entire region that we never did explore.

The next day, it was up early to load up on provisions for our days in the bush. A quick bit of site-seeing around Darwin, and then we were heading off into the wilds. Darwin has a very varied and interesting history. Briefly, it was the only Australian city to be attacked by the Japanese in WW2, and was bombed sixty-four times, with pretty extensive destruction. There are old fortifications around all the strategic and coastal points outside the city, including underground storage tunnels. That, however, was only a prelude to the much greater destruction wrought by Mother Nature on Christmas Eve 1974, when Cyclone Tracy scored a direct hit and leveled 80 percent of the buildings in the area. Many of the original, classic examples of tropical architecture were wiped off the map forever; and today's downtown feels a bit more average and nondescript than one might expect. Natural calamities aside, Darwin retains a very mellow, Margaritaville-vibe; like some giant, remote Key West, that is beguiling and easy to embrace.

DDU Blog entry: Drive 40 km east of Darwin and you are already getting into the real bush. Civilization drops away quickly, and Kakadu National Park (NP) is still two hundred km away. First stop, Mary River National Park, where we had a tent site and a rental skiff awaiting. Aidan's then #1 bucket list for life was to catch a wild Aussie Barramundi: a hard-fighting, aggressive estuarine species highly esteemed by Aussie fisherman. Like

Texas bass, for some it's a religion. I think Aidan just got born-again!

As detailed in the Prologue, we were intently watching for Crocs, working our way up this tiny, remote tributary with dusk falling, when I happened to run the outboard motor up onto an underwater rock ledge and stall out, with said Crocs drifting right alongside the boat. Seriously... After a few frantic minutes, we managed to free the boat and miraculously hadn't snapped the screw or the drive shaft. We were all very relieved to be underway and heading back downriver to camp.

It might've been a very long, hot night; swatting mozzies while waiting to be rescued. And an entirely true story, no embellishment required! And occurring literally on our first night in the bush. Whew, what other unanticipated hazards await us deeper into the real bush, I wondered silently to myself. (Haven't you just gone one giant step too far on this outing, Dr. Nolan?) Maybe, but "don't tell your mother..."

Next stop, Kakadu NP, which is considered a crown-jewel of the Aussie park system, right up there with Uluru and the Great Barrier Reef by those in the know. So, it must really be something special, right?

The cynics among the locals call it "Kakadon't", the inference being it's a very long way "out bush" to see a whole lot of nothing, I suppose. And besides the waterfalls at Litchfield NP are said to be just as good and much more accessible. But I must disagree. The thing about Kakadu is that it's so vast and varied that it helps to have an overview as to what it actually is, in its totality, to guide your itinerary. One thing's for certain, it's not a sit in the comfort of your car and drive around type of experience. The more you're willing to exert and put yourself out there, the richer will be your rewards.

For starters, let's do a quick rundown of its natural features. It's vast: over 7,000 square miles. It's the largest contiguous bird-breeding area in the entire southern hemisphere. With almost 300 bird species, it contains 1/3 of all known Aussie species, and over 10,000 insect species. It has seven or eight major, unique eco-systems substantially intact within its borders; hundreds of miles of pristine, Crocodile-infested, mangrove coastline, vast seasonal tropical wetlands, open Eucalypt savannah, several entire undisturbed tropical river systems intact from headwaters to coastal estuaries and open ocean beyond. The park is bisected by an ~ 500 km long, 500-foot limestone escarpment over which fall some of the most impressive waterfalls on the planet. And to top it all off, it's the site of the oldest continuous living culture documented on earth. The local Aboriginals, 15 major distinct groups, have been living here for an uncertain eternity; most recently (announced in July 2017) proven to be at least 65,000 years, and likely much older. The tiny hamlet of Jabiru is the world's oldest known site of sophisticated seed- grinding tools, fine axe, arrow and spear head construction by some 20,000 years, and is noted for large-scale ochre production for artistic purposes. The limestone escarpments are riddled with an estimated 15-20,000 rock art and sacred sites, less than half of which have been documented. So, all in all, a pretty amazing place to spend some quality adventure time.

DDU Blog entry: Ubirr, our initial goal, is a small, geologically isolated rocky peak sitting above an easily accessible, major art rock site that's set up and well-managed for the tourist hordes; an antipodean Sistine Chapel of sorts. Unlike most of Kakadu, you can drive right up and park. The gallery is set within a stunning shallow depression, surrounded and protected by low limestone cliffs, over which Ubirr rises. Amongst its many treasures, are depictions of early explorers sailing vessels and a clear depiction of a Thylacine; providing proof that the now likely-extinct Tasmanian Tiger existed on the Australian mainland at one time. Ubirr is considered a broken-off outlier from the main escarpment ridge, some 20 miles to the south. This gives it the advantage of sitting at the edge of a vast, flat alluvial flood plain that stretches northward to the ocean, over the far horizon. A classic Aussie experience, bordering on pilgrimage, is to climb atop Ubirr and contemplate life and the passage of time as the sun sets dramatically over the floodplain, as it has done every evening for eternity. The scale of the view is truly breathtaking... It was, indeed, a peak experience in my life. You really can get a sense of the infinite, looking out over a place so long-inhabited as this; even though today you are unlikely to be entirely alone. You can still wander off over the broad, flat-topped summit, find your deep, silent space and make believe. We were there at a quiet season, so fortunately shared the summit with only a handful of fellow spiritual travelers. Entirely magical... The overall landscape feels very, very ancient, exotic, alien... With the heat even in this, the cooling season, rising to over ninety degrees Fahrenheit during the day, it's reminiscent of the Rift Valley of Africa or somewhere similar I'd imagine, though I've never been. But, should a herd of elephants come crashing out of the bush below, it would seem perfectly in keeping with the landscape, oddly enough. But no, only a few foraging kangaroos, a Wedge-Tailed Eagle silently soaring the updrafts, a mob of coarsely squawking Sulfur-Crested Cockatoos, breaking the enveloping stillness of dusk. This is deepest, soul-stirring Australian Outback indeed, and a vividly indelible memory...

Enraptured by the Ubirr experience, and not wanting to simply drive off afterwards, we foolishly, in retrospect, camped that night locally at a place called Merl. A tiny sliver of forest nearly surrounded by the vast alluvial wetland, the campground was primitive and nearly deserted. As dusk deepened, we realized why. Merl has forever since set the standard for density of mozzies in my lifetime's camping experience, including backcountry Yellowstone, Alaska and even the Amazon basin. Winged clouds so thick that we were literally eating them as we gobbled a hasty dinner around the smoky campfire before heading for the lifesaving nylon barrier of the tent. Eating them...! We later talked with a park Ranger about the extreme experience and lack of warning signs, causing him to grin wryly and offer, in broadest ocker Strine... "Oi, I see yas been Merl'ed," with a soft, knowing chuckle; and thus, turning the location into a handy verb, still used by us today, as code for it being very, very buggy. Very... Being "Merl'ed..."

But the Ubirr sunset was so superb, the next morning, all was (nearly) forgotten. We climbed back up onto Ubirr's low summit to see things in a somewhat different light. Not another soul around; the alluvial floodplains stretching out to the farthest, heat-hazed horizons... Deathly still, beautiful and timeless. Unforgettable Ubirr... popular, yet still profound. An indelible reminder of one's place in the complex tapestry of space and time, and a moving reaffirmation that we are only minute specks on the vast canvas that is Kakadu National Park.

Kakadu National Park - Outback Waterfalls, Koolpin Gorge

Nolan Boys Outback Adventure, Part 2:

DDU Blog entry: Next morning we were, again, up early and heading for the Yellow Water Billabong sunrise wetland tour. It's also popular, and an excellent way to get out on the extensive wetlands that are so much a part of Kakadu. The tour is part of a hotel and restaurant complex that's owned and operated by the local "traditional owners" or Aboriginal peoples of Kakadu. In fact, they own the entire park and lease it back to the government. This provides much needed income and local jobs, while keeping the younger generations involved in providing stewardship and working out on the traditional lands. So, win-win all around. The guides are well-versed in all the local lore, flora and fauna, so you'll also learn a lot while on vacation. Triple win!

As the sun just begins to rise, almost imperceptibly to the east, the bird life becomes fantastically active. For a brief thirty minutes, until full pre-dawn light, the air literally vibrates with the sounds of thousands of Whistling Ducks coming in waves to roost for the day. On our two-hour tour, we probably saw forty different species of birds; wetland, waterfowl and some tropical woodland species. Kingfishers, buzzing woodland jewels, glittered everywhere in the brightening morning light. The species you may encounter here at Kakadu vary tremendously with the six distinct seasons recognized by the local Aboriginals, as many are seasonal migrants.

We visited in mid-June, at the tail-end of the Wet, which seemed to provide the perfect blend of reasonable temperatures, clearing skies, residual lushness and lots of bird activity. Although true Kakadu aficionados, and there are many, will say you really must visit at the peak of the "full Wet" to experience a totally different facet of this fantastically diverse environment. The tropical heat-fueled, mid-summer lightning storms are said to be primordial on an epic, earth-trembling scale. And the seasonal flooding is epic on an almost Biblical scale.

DDU Blog entry: Having seen some of the more accessible and popular sites, it was now time to hit the 4WD tracks and get out into some serious Kakadu backcountry. Jim Jim Falls, 20 km up a corrugated, red dirt road, then an additional 10 km down a rutted goat path, was the day's destination. The rented Toyota Land-Cruiser 4-door mine truck, complete with Roo-Bar, lights and siren, that seemed so over the top on the streets of Darwin, proved itself to be the perfect ride in this wild, rough country. Atrocious roads for such a major tourist destination, but really, it's all part of the adventure...! In fairness, the falls had only been open for a few weeks due to receding high water and annual Croc surveys. Neighboring Twin Falls, ~10 km off on a Y intersection down the same road, was still closed to the public, having not yet been declared Croc-free. Out here, it seems things were just waking up for the high season.

After the wild and wooly last 10 km 4WD ride into the falls area, we parked and hiked in the last 1 km - up a rocky, narrowing canyon, with the roaring sound of the falls increasing as we approached. The cool, moist mist was blowing downstream into our faces from half a km away. It's all pretty fantastic as the canyon and thunderous falls unfold. The searing heat hovering over the desiccated, rocky uplands disappears as you enter into the darkening, moisture-laden tunnel of greenery being perpetually nourished by the explosive power of the falls up ahead. Otherworldly in fact...

The Top End has a distinct tropical, monsoonal climate, hot and dry winters (May - September) and hotter and extremely wet in the summer (October- April). In fact, the local Aboriginals recognize six distinct seasons, with the build-up and wind down of the Wet. Most of the park is closed in the full-on Wet, as roads can be under six-eight feet of water for months at a time. It was now early in the Dry and the massive torrent that flows annually over these escarpments had slowed to a safe level. The rangers had been busy putting in the temporary bridges and boardwalks that are again lifted out by helicopter before the next Wet begins.

DDU Blog entry: It's hard to fathom how large and impressive Jim-Jim Falls is from pictures. The canyon walls are sheer and 400-500 feet high, crowding in overhead on three sides. The sky narrows to a remote sliver of brightest, clear blue - a part of another world somehow. The base plunge pool is around one hundred yards across, the depths clear, coal-black and slightly eerie. With a steady, cool breeze blowing off the falls from the force of the crashing water and channeled down the canyon, the 90-degree heat dissolves and you are standing in a shady, glistening cathedral of sorts, that is among the most impressive I've ever experienced. The sound of crashing water reverberating off the high walls is tremendous. We did the obligatory plunge into the base pool, though we were suddenly no longer overheated. Looking down while nervously treading water, my shockingly blue-white toes appeared dead - drowned - ten lost sailors dangling lifelessly just above the sinister, black void... Tempting little beacons attracting any carnivore in for a blood-warm feed. It's a bit nerve-wracking to contemplate whether or not this massive reservoir of deadly, cold water is truly Croc-free after all, and the shiver you feel electrifying your spine is only partly due to the dramatic drop in body temperature. There's a real sense of relief when you get out of the main pool with limbs numb, but intact, and towel off. Having packed in masks and snorkels, moving downstream from the main plunge pool, we snorkeled among submersed boulders, some car-sized, leading into intricate grottos and fish-filled, gravel-bottomed lagoons. We were amazed to explore this intricate world of underwater boulders, timber snags and submerged sandy ridges that felt almost Caribbean in its purity, here in the remote canyons of Kakadu National Park.

Hiking up into the canyon, you see plenty of warning signs to stay Croc aware. During the Wet, these canyons are inundated with brackish water being forced upstream in ferocious flood. Estuarine Crocodiles (aka "Salties") follow inland, upriver, feeding. As the waters recede into the Dry, many are trapped high in the canyons, far from home and they get mighty hungry. The rangers have a very precise method of clearing the pools for swimming, hiking and even camping nearby, but there's no guarantee...They must do five separate night floats, shining high-powered lights into the depths from skiffs looking for eye shine. They also set baited Croc traps for several weeks. Finally, once things seem safe enough, they leave behind small buoys which the Crocs will attack to drive interlopers out of their territory; leaving tell-tale tooth marks on the buoy. Only then is a pool or stretch of river declared "Croc-free" and tourists are allowed into the area. It all makes for some very spooky pool plunging for sure, but I suppose that's another part of the thrill of this wild, remote place!

DDU Blog entry: The hike out, with a chilling breeze now at our drying backs, marks the reverse transition from the moist, mossy riparian canyon oasis back out into the desiccated, sun-stunned, dry sclerophyll eucalypt bush so prevalent elsewhere in the NT. A complete transition into a different world over only a kilometer, and a most remarkable natural juxtaposition.

Soon we were back out on the dusty, ochre backroads of Kakadu, leaving dense clouds of fine red dust settling in our wake, as we rattled and fish-tailed over the miles of rough, corrugated washboard strips of roads. The Land-Cruiser handled it all with aplomb, but we were rattled to the core, and the powdery, ferrous dust found its way into everything. We spent a few magical days heading out through the rough, stony escarpment country, exploring the various swimming holes on offer, under a flawless sky. We boys were lost in Outback heaven...

Next stop: Maguk Falls, a one-hundred-meter-long aquamarine pool headed by a gently sloping cascade. The subject of countless calendar photos, it's crystal clear, cold and full of fish; literally an Outback aquarium. The approach trail, wending one km through a lush, riparian tropical rainforest pocket in the 90-degree heat only added to the anticipation. The gorge here is much wider and shallower than at Jim-Jim, and thus much more sunlit; offering a gentler, welcoming and less-threatening vibe.

The open eucalypt savannah that dominates the uplands along the escarpment ridges here is an ecosystem that is shaped by annual bushfires. Termed a dry, sclerophyll (from the Greek – literally, hard-leaved) forest, it's perfectly adapted to enduring long seasons of unrelenting heat and meager rainfall. The Aboriginals have burnt seasonally for millennia, considering it an annual clean-up of sorts. The understory thus remains open and lush grasses thrive in season. The larger trees stand almost as a vast, inter-linked, open grove overhead, with very little brushy understory. As we drove along, snaking tendrils of slowly advancing grass fires burned, sometimes right up to the road edge - sending carbonaceous walls of rich, acrid smoke wafting across the horizon, and sometimes obscuring the road ahead. Through the walls of dense smoke, squadrons of Whistling and Black Kites, large soaring raptors, could be seen diving in groups, closely following the flame lines over the newly charred earthen remains left by the fires; feasting on suddenly exposed meals of snakes, rodents and lizards. This added greatly to our sense of alien, apocalyptic excitement in traveling through such a strange and unusual landscape.

After another cooling dip we encountered a field of Cathedral Termites and their fascinating mounds, some up to twenty feet high. They harvest and store grasses inside. These tiny insects, less than a quarter of an inch *long, but numbering in their untold millions, create colonies that last for up to a century. The shell is a hard, rough sandy consistency, strong enough for Luke to climb.*

Our camp for the next night was in the remote Koolpin Gorge, or Jarrangbarnmi, sacred to the local tribes and lying deep within the remote "Sickness Country" of southwestern Kakadu. Here the rocky land rises and trees thin out due to poor soils and less rainfall. There are many ancient legends about dangerous spirits living underground here and how you must be respectful not to disturb or anger them. Access is strictly limited by advance permit to around twenty people per day, and the final ten km is by rough, steep 4WD track, crossing several river bottoms, after a forty km dirt road approach. You need to reserve and pay ahead, and then drive to an unmanned ranger station in the southwest quadrant of the Park, where you pick up a key in your name. You then use this to open a remote gate that gives you 4-wheel drive access to the final ten km dirt track. This dead-ends near the mouth of the gorge and is your final destination at the very ends of the earth. A memorable approach! I'm not sure how I even came upon this place during my pre-trip, online research. But once considered, I couldn't get it out of my imagination. This is possibly the most remote stretch of backcountry accessible by vehicle and open to the public in Kakadu. The campground is primitive, set in a shady grove at the base of granite cliffs, some thirty miles (~fifty km) from the nearest paved road. Fantastic southern stars, with Scorpius and the Southern Cross shining much more brilliantly than I'd ever seen, in the clearest and deepest, blackly pristine atmosphere imaginable, or likely obtainable. This is a very remote place, even by Australian standards. There was space for perhaps ten fully equipped utes here, but only two others were seen during our stay.

The most amazing consideration is that this area just happens to be the site of one of the richest uranium deposits on the planet. The earth here also holds major deposits of mercury, lead, and arsenic. When scientists finally mapped these deposits in the 1960s, the boundaries were almost exactly aligned within the defined "Sickness Country" of the local Aboriginals! It seems there was a strong basis for their ancient legends after all.

DDU Blog entry: We set up a primitive tent camp under the stunted trees.

There were only two other vehicles sharing the broad, grassy site. It was a magical evening sitting beside a glowing campfire and imagining local Aboriginals doing the same for tens of thousands of years continuously. The boys loved every wilderness minute of it.

From the campsite you can't see any water, or even the gorge, just a sharply rising low mountain of tumbled boulders, forested in the ubiquitous, stunted eucalypts. That evening we explored the immediate region, under the gaze of watchful Rock Wallabies. Not a hundred meters down the sandy track, you come to a beautiful, clear pool spilling out of the gorge mouth, shielded from view by its running perpendicular to the approach road and hidden by bluffs. Heading up the gorge into the rough stone country felt a bit eerie, truth be told. There was a freshly- baited Croc trap: twelve feet long, of heavy, galvanized steel, in the lower pool; gape-mouthed, awaiting prey. And multiple Croc warning signs along the lower pools, detailing the dates that live Crocs were last spotted here; and it was not really so long past. As we climbed higher with late afternoon shadows lengthening, on high snake alert, we felt indeed alone, and a very long way from help. The rocks formed a challenging barrier to following the stream uphill; the terrain jagged and tumbled. Few birds or signs of life, everything silent, as if waiting; the very earth holding its breath at the approach of these intruders. We all shared a subliminal sense of caution and vulnerability, as if anything could go wrong at any time. And that we would be entirely on our own if so...

In the waning dry heat, we finally got to an upper pool; reportedly permanently Croc-free due to the waterfalls and impassable bluffs. It was large, deep and ominously dark. Enclosed by steep rock walls, with only a small stream outlet, it resembled a granite bowl or trap of sorts, and was a bit unsettling actually...

"What do you say boys?" I offered with strained bravado. "We came for a swim..." as I somewhat reluctantly plunged in off a ten-foot cliff and swam out a bit offshore. My bone-white toes, ten drowned sailors, hung again suspended and helpless over the bottomless, cold void. It was too easy to imagine a rogue Croc lunging up from the depths and dragging me under; uncomfortable to say the least. The boys joined in, aware that their young courage was now in question. Feeling much more vulnerable than at

Jim-Jim Falls, due to our sheer isolation; we each did the requisite single plunge to cool off but were silently relieved to be climbing out of the lifeless pool, quickly dried, clothed and heading back down into the strange gorge.

The overall effect here was the antithesis of the fertile, relaxed and welcoming feel of Maguk Falls on the previous day. We each instinctively knew; this was serious, isolated Outback. The "Sickness Country" and well named. Every caution was in order. Croc and snake central... No place for a misstep... You could just sense it. After several hours of rough down-hiking, it was a relief to be finally back at camp, in all honesty. Having two young boys in tow under my watchful protection added greatly to my sense of responsibility and unease. We had reached my outer limit here.

And they really seemed like much bigger young men to me back then. When I look back at pictures now, I shudder silently a bit. What was I thinking to have them all the way out there? So exposed, and them being unaware of just how much; trusting me implicitly to guide them safely. Bad Father!!

But the entire trip was an irreplaceable bonding experience for us, from the retrospective vantage point of no bad outcomes, at least. The calming rhythm of camp life, gathering wood, cooking dinner, setting up for the night; all felt like a true connection to the timeless continuity of a place as remote and filled with magical memory as this, so rare and remarkable in the modern world. Sleeping out under that shimmering tapestry, so far off into the Outback was truly magical. Luke and I sat up for hours beyond midnight, under the flooding river of southern stars, not wanting the spell to end in sleep. Feeding the guttering fire, talking of life, family and friends; the strange constellations turning silently overhead, reinforcing our sense of being oddly displaced and very, very far from our home back in New York.

Kakadu and Litchfield National Parks, Darwin

Nolan Boys Outback Adventure, Part 3:

DDU Blog entry: Next morning, we were, again, up early in the building heat, and hiking back into Koolpin Gorge. No one was really motivated to climb all the way back up to the third pool, due to fatigue and the general bad - Juju vibes of the place. It felt truly eerie up there, the Sickness almost palpable. And the water here in the lowest waterhole appeared calm, clear, more welcoming. Hmmm... Inviting... No Croc activity evident; the baited Croc trap at the far end of the narrow pool, a good hundred meters away, lay undisturbed. All was peaceful Outback morning serenity.

"Anyone up for a morning dip with the Salties...?" I chided. "What are the odds...?"

"Do you think it's safe Dad?" Luke queried...

"Probably a thousand times safer than the drive out here, statistically speaking, I'm sure..." I reassured them, but to myself mostly... Aidan observed all with a concerned, focused silence.

At least we couldn't say we weren't warned. As I stood sentinel atop a flat boulder, observing the calm pool for any movement in the bright, rising morning heat, Luke did a quick plunge and jumped back onto the sandbank as if scalded; hooting and laughing at fate tempted and craftily cheated...

"I'm too quick, even for Mister Saltie...!" he laughed excitedly. (yeah kid, right...)

"Well," I teased, "you survived it..."

In the clear, lime-green main pool, not a ripple stirred... I could plainly see down ten to twelve feet, all the way to the sandy bottom; though the far, boulder-strewn corners were somewhat murky in lingering shadow, to be honest. But so enticing, and easy...

"So, does anybody know how long a Saltie can hold its breath?" I questioned the boys.

"Twenty minutes, I guess," offered brave little Aidan.

"I think we've been standing here longer than that", Luke stoically replied.

Then, unable to bear the heat or the tension any longer, I set yet another bad example of sorts - and plunged in off my sentinel boulder...

"Cannonball!" The cool water felt divine, worth the risk, I thought... And out I jumped, onto the bright, sun-warmed sandbank.

"I think this is a goer boys, just be cautious..."

Then Luke, being a dripping wet, foolish, yet brave boy, standing at the very top of the sloping sandbank, suddenly dropped and rolled himself in the fine sand, which stuck and covered him like a meaty sugar doughnut.

"Look Dad, crumbed children!" he shouted, as he rolled down the bank, in a wild spray of sand, and splashed happily into the water.

"I believe that's called tempting fate son," was my innermost thought.

Younger Aidan quickly followed suit, laughing in delight; a smaller crumbed child... Rolling happily down the bank and into...??

Crumbed children indeed! "Mom would absolutely murder me, if she were here... But she's not...and it's getting hotter," I thought smugly, "Carpe diem!"

So, there we were, lost in the remote Northern Territory Outback; and me an Emergency doc no less! Happily feeding up my "crumbed children" to the stirring Crocs...

Some example of a father you turn out to be Dr. Nolan. I mean really...!

I'm not certain of the life-lesson I imparted on that remote morning, but "Crumbed Children" has become a code phrase in the family lexicon for taking seemingly outrageous, but actually measured and well-considered, risks, and living to tell the tale. Or at least that's what I think it means.

Or perhaps, "Stupid-ass tourists just asking to be eviscerated and dying horribly alone in the remote bush?" But in the end, with guards and lookouts so posted, a quick, refreshing dip was accomplished with no limbs lost, or even skinned up. Simply sublime, and a memorable morning wake-up, I can guarantee. Oh, and boys, please remember...

"Don't tell your Mother..."

Weeks later, after Luke posted (unbeknownst to me) a short "Crumbed Children" video on the internet for laughs, we got a terse, angry emailed reply to the effect:

"Yeah, and it's wankers like you who then cry out for Croc control after your kid gets eaten by one, ya wankers..." And you know, that bloke makes a very good point.

Wankers, like me...

DDU Blog entry: Thus refreshed, it was time to head back towards civilization, or at least a paved road. Miles and miles to go. On the way out we stopped and saw some aging remains of past Uranium mining, discontinued in 1964. The area is said to be riddled with unsafe mine sites and shafts - enter at your own risk. The rusting detritus of long-abandoned mining efforts leant a certain melancholic feeling; another great effort expended and ultimately exhausted, to the already lonely, remote ambiance of this unique area of Australia. I've never experienced anything similar in all my travels.

Next stop, Gunlom Falls, famous for having been the setting of the outback waterhole scene in the first Crocodile Dundee film, as well as for the much-photographed plunge pools high above the main falls cliff face. It's an easy drive up to the campground and popular on weekends, but a beautiful spot indeed. Of course, this being Australia, it then all has to get just a bit weirder. We were at the tiny beach here, on the far edge of the wide, still plunge pool and I was about to jump in from a rock ledge when, looking into the clear, curiously lime-green water to the rocky bottom around six feet down, I noticed the coiled form of a massive snake resting underwater directly below me! Five or six feet long, as thick as my forearm, OMG, ISYN! Really, the term snake understates the beast; this thing was a serpent. A marine SERPENT...! Man, I swear this country is just trying to kill me dead! Later, we learned from a ranger that it was most likely a harmless File Snake, but still. I mean REALLY..! Note to self: Look before you leap, especially in these mad lands...

So, it seemed a wiser course to climb up above the falls to swim. And it was - perfectly formed, cool pools cascading under the tropical heat, with panoramic views across the undulating, open savannah that stretched for miles away from the escarpment ridge. Another classic Kakadu setting, and absolutely unforgettable.

Later that day, after a hot six-hour drive, on macadam road at least, heading north towards Darwin, we arrived at Litchfield NP. Not nearly as remote as Kakadu, it's a popular weekend destination for Darwinians, being less than two hours south of the city. And the falls here were fantastic, as impressive as Kakadu's, if not as wild. They spill off a large central massif, which the road circumnavigates, so as you drive along you pass one major landmark falls after another. Some are strictly off limits to non-Aboriginals, however. We spent fantastic hours under tropical heat swimming and snorkeling in the aquamarine pools of Buley Rockhole - a series of intimate, interconnected pools tumbling along a swift, clear river - where strangely enough, nearly all the young adults we met were from France, of all places. They were very friendly and chilled out; apparently Kakadu and the NT is a favored exotic destination among French college-aged travelers. Who knew? Also outstanding were Wangi Falls (the busiest pool, but clean and impressively large), and Florence Falls. We spent two nights camping rough, exploring and swimming; same old, same old...

At Florence Falls, which is set in a stunning, deep, natural punchbowl, the photogenic high volume double streams drop freely forty to fifty feet, as if into a massive sink basin. We got up early, climbed down into the water-carved canyon over an extensive stair network and had the entire pool to ourselves. This punchbowl is clear, clean and very deep at its center. Another wild, natural aquarium. We snorkeled and saw prolific fish life including long-tailed catfish and freshwater eels of great size. It was an unforgettable experience!

Litchfield NP is an accessible and uniquely beautiful landscape in the Australian Northern Territory. It's a highly recommended destination for any travelers to the Darwin region, especially those without the time to explore deeper into Kakadu.

Getting closer to Darwin, driving north, we came upon a large field of Magnetic Termite mounds. A different species than the Cathedral, they actually orient their thin mounds North to South, keeping one side of the nest in the shade all day long. Internal temperature recordings confirm that this keeps the nest dramatically cooler than a random or East-West orientation. Fascinating natural history! The mounds are much thinner and more delicate than those of the conical Cathedral mounds, but perhaps even more impressive for their eerily organized orientation. A large field of Magnetic Termite mounds gives off the orderly, somber air of a great graveyard carved out of the silently brooding, olive-gray Australian bush.

After eight nights camping in the rough, and sharing so many wild, wonderful experiences, it was finally back into Darwin for a final night. At least we had local markets, fantastic Asian food, safe swimming pools and souvenir hunting as compensation. I even bought a genuine Australian Crocodile belt as a family heirloom. And no more peanut butter and jelly, at least for a while! Even after all that wilderness swimming, the boys were still dying to try out the Darwin wave pool. Due to the summertime presence of potentially deadly Stinger jellyfish in all these northern, tropical waters, municipal swimming pools are widespread and very popular. The massive one on the Darwin waterfront actually creates pretty impressive swells and waves on an automated basis. The crowds rise and fall rhythmically without fear of encountering the jellyfish and other assorted marine nasties that inhabit these climes. Personally, I thought it was just OK, not exactly Florence Falls; but the boys loved it.

On our last day, we crammed in as much sightseeing around Darwin as possible. East Point has a wonderful park with lots of preserved WW2 fortifications. The Mangrove boardwalk was interesting, especially watching the local Aboriginal kids spearfishing with homemade gigs and catching stingrays under the shady mangroves...

DDU blog entry: We had an interesting cultural experience watching barefoot Aboriginal kids, around the same ages as Luke and Aidan, hunting stingrays using homemade gig spears, fashioned from sharpened rebar, while out on a mangrove boardwalk. They excitedly scrambled through the shallow, muddy flats beneath the dense tangle of mangrove trees, as they tried to corral their elusive prey using teamwork strategies. Their dad proudly showed us their successful catch, a fresh, medium-sized stingray, which was on its way home to be cooked up for dinner. Luke and Aidan were fascinated that such a primordial scene could unfold right there within the Darwin city limits.

We also managed a quick tour of the Art Museum of the Northern Territory, which has a superlative collection of northern Aboriginal and Tiwi Island artifacts as well as a fantastic collection of local wildlife and fish specimens. And a very moving exhibit on the 1974 Darwin Cyclone Tracy. Certainly, this is one of the finest regional museums I've seen anywhere; and it's free. Don't miss it when in Darwin. The Botanical Gardens were also lovely: a shady green oasis, but somewhat more limited in scale than the world-class gardens in Sydney, Melbourne and Brisbane (also free and highly recommended).

Finally, we were out of time and winging our way back home to Brisbane. It all seemed another world after the remote and timeless silence of Kakadu, Litchfield and the Outback Northern Territory. After eleven incredible days and ten nights out, I have to admit, it felt good to contemplate sleeping in my own bed again, next to Stephanie, and getting back into a comfortable routine. But the memories of unstructured hours in the pristine remoteness of the Top End with my two rapidly growing young men will bond us forever and become the stuff of family legend and tall tales for many years hence. We are truly fortunate to have had those precious days and nights exploring together in the Aussie wilds.

So, Kaka**don't**? I certainly don't think so. Not at all... If it's your cup of tea, a well-planned trip to charming, exotic Darwin and the more remote parts of the "Top End" around Kakadu and Litchfield National Parks will certainly rank among the most unique and memorable outdoor experiences of your life. I feel we barely scratched the surface, even though we made a pretty fair dent for a single trip, and we all dream of returning again one day. Perhaps to experience the full-on, legendary Wet, as happily "Crumbed Children" frolicking wild once more in the antipodean natural world.

Kaka**do,** indeed!

CHAPTER 22: The Posh Woman on the Coin Club

So, after all my cheerleading about life in Australia, why aren't more of **you** living Down Under? Or, to resurrect the infamous words of a failed Aussie tourism promotion from several years back (one that left its intended American audience utterly mystified and probably slightly unsettled.)

"Where the bloody hell are ya...?!"

Nice huh? Sheer marketing genius. Another prime example of presumably shared cultural assumptions gone off-course and run amok. Americans just never quite got that one, but it's very typically ocker Oz banter. Go figure. I have a few theories; let's dig a bit deeper...

We got settled, most unexpectedly, out in the wild, suburban bush country (!) about twenty km east of the Brisbane CBD by Queensland Health in their bureaucratic wisdom, as I've already described. The Redland shire is an old agricultural region, not a town, on Moreton Bay, linked to downtown Brisbane by a nice, sleek, modern train system. Commutable, yet right on the glistening expanse of Moreton Bay. In short, a really nice place to live and work; comfortable, bordering on wealthy; stellar by international standards. On the outskirts of the third largest Aussie city and smack dab on the eastern Oz seaboard, it is the shortest incoming destination for international flights from the USA and Canada. And did I mention only thirty minutes from said International Airport, the Aussie "Gateway to Asia"? Sweet as, right? And for my specialty, most unexpectedly, then a designated "area of need."

The area is chockers with expats as you'd expect, especially Brits. Also, plentiful Irish, Scots, Kiwis, Canadians, South Africans, perhaps the odd Rhodesian, or Zimbabwean as they are now known. Increasingly, pan-Asian, especially from Hong Kong, Singapore and India, but strangely, no Americans... Or comparatively, very few. Hmmm, why would that be?

For example, of the fifteen-hundred or so employees at our local hospital, I am the only American on staff. Not the only American Consultant, the only American. No nurses, clerks, orderlies by marriage, zippo. The remainder of the staff is like the United Nations, however. So, why would that be, again? Per official figures, Americans make up less than one percent of foreign expats living in Australia; that's still around one in a hundred. Not here, not even close.

But it's not that Americans aren't living overseas. By US figures, there are over seven million of us living outside the Land of the Free and Home of the Brave, and we're absolutely flooding Latin America, a place I know pretty well, to the point of driving up real estate prices and alienating some locals. Physically close perhaps, but culturally on another planet at times, in my experience. While Australia, at its core a strongly Anglo culture, would feel so much more familiar, even comfortable, to the average American.

Another oddity I've encountered: a great escape, gap-year experience for young, post-college (high school) Aussies is to escape north, to snow-country and a dream job as a ski-lift operator or mountain bike coach. But seldom to Utah or Colorado. Generally, at Whistler in British Columbia, or Banff, in Alberta. That's Canada.

So, two-way, long-established travel and working arrangements, but we're not included...Well, I've thought long and hard about it, no one actually seems to discuss this down here. It's not the distance, or eastern Canadians and Irish would be near extinct, but they're as common as starlings, in fact. It's certainly not the weather. Something else then?

I call it the "Posh Woman on the Coin Club". Here, take some change out of your pocket. Have a look. An assortment of old, historic white guys, some still wearing wigs. No women, and most definitely no Queen Elizabeth. "B-I-N-G-O..." Bingo!

Yes, that must be it! It's now so obvious. All the old English Commonwealth countries, they communicate with each other. They know things... They know that Australia's a fantastic country in which to live and work. It's one of the many secrets they all share, but not with us Americans, or other outsiders.

Come visit please, "Spend yer Greenbacks and go, mates" (Where **the bloody hell are ya**...?!)   But a few at a time will do. The last thing they need is for hordes of us Yanks to be coming down here and taking over their peaceful, laid-back country.

"Well, maybe a few of you good ones can stay on, to add some spice..."

Look at it from their perspective, folks; there are over 330 million of us Americans, more or less; who really knows anymore. There are only some 25 million Aussies in existence, and around twenty percent of these, or 5 million, are expats, mostly from colonies of the former mother country. We could overrun their paradisiacal island nation over a long weekend, easy.

All those turkey-eating hordes from the North - those who call gridiron football and disrespect or misunderstand our national sport of Rugby, all three versions; they think Cricket is only played by white-suited, geriatric, time-indifferent eccentrics - and that real football, aka soccer, is played only by little girls, Europeans and sissies (and all true, that) ...

"People who can't abide the taste of good lamb for God's sake! And who drink piss for wine..."

And in terms of closer neighbors, consider that Indonesia, the country that's geographically right next door to Australia, has over 250 million residents. That's ten times the entire Australian population, in just Indonesia alone! Then there's Malaysia, and India and the biggest Kahuna of all; China, at around 1.4 billion people in 2020.

Happily for the locals, 'Straya has the world's biggest moat surrounding this, the luckiest of countries. Thousands upon thousands of miles of unbreachable ocean.

Someday, I believe, they'll surely need it.

So, remember folks, it's the "Posh Woman on the Coin Club". It reaches out worldwide. And most of us ain't in it...

CHAPTER 23: Melbourne and The Great Ocean Road

September 2013

DDU Blog entry: Life has really accelerated for us all here in Australia, with full time ED work and all five kids in school. No longer wide-eyed visitors to this remarkable continent, we are now somewhat more settled, working and living here; that's a very different experience. Recently, I was able to get away for an EM Management conference in Melbourne. Three nights right downtown in a nice hotel on Collins Street, the ritzy shopping and dining area in the center of everything. It seemed like the perfect time for "Girl's Weekend, Part 2". So, Claire (13) and Cate (8) played hooky, and off we went. It's now mid-winter in southern Australia, so a bit nippy, but nothing like mid-winter in Boston or my homeland of New England. In fact, it's a good time to visit, as lots of plants are in bloom, and you avoid the hot winds blowing in off the central deserts northwest of Melbourne that can make the city scorchingly hot at mid-summer.

Greater Melbourne, population ~4.5 million is, along with Sydney (also ~4.5 million) one of the two largest urban centers in Australia. Nearly a third of the Australian population lives within their two orbits. There's a very vigorous, friendly rivalry between the two for best-of status; think Boston vs NYC, without any other contenders nearby. With Melbourne playing the role of Boston: all arty, cool-weather cafes and hipster brick neighborhoods; and Sydney being NYC: more brash power and new money, all wrestling for attention on that stunning harbor. Or as my Kiwi recruiter so memorably stated, "Francis, you don't want to go to work in Sydney; it's all flash, flash and air-kiss, darling." Indeed...

In truth, they are very different experiences to a casual visitor. Melbourne lacks the dramatic setting of Sydney Harbour and its impressive headlands, or the iconic landmarks of the Opera House and Harbour Bridge. Instead, it's a subtle city of sweeping, graceful parks, ethnic neighborhoods and outstanding food, with a very active cafe culture. Its famous "laneways" are small dead-end streets, linked to the maze of boutique shops right downtown. They're filled with cafes and wonderfully diverse open-air street life. For what it's worth, an international poll recently and repeatedly has named Melbourne the best city worldwide for overall quality of life. Sydney-siders were not pleased, to say the least! Melbourne's a lively, safe and friendly place with plenty to intrigue a visitor for days. The climate here is much cooler and wetter than Sydney, and is famously unpredictable, lying as it is on the northern edge of the vast, flat expanse of Port Phillip Bay and directly exposed to the winter Southerlies coming straight off Antarctica. The Melbourne-based band Crowded House sang about "Four Seasons in One Day" from their local experience. Even though they're mostly Kiwis, they're considered "true blue" Aussies by default. Check them out if you're unfamiliar. They were unjustly overlooked in the USA but are a cultural institution Down Under.

I think it's this bracing, temperate climate that contributes to the city's rich cultural tapestry and focus. It's hard to build a vibrant cultural community when the weather's perfect and the beaches are beckoning, a la Brisbane. If you want great arts culture, I say, look first where the weather's crappy. NYC vs LA, or Northern Europe vs Club Med. Sometimes you just need lots of quality indoor time. Anyway, being a proud Bostonian, I felt the strongest sense of being in a "real" city here more than anywhere else in Australia. Melbourne has old, established Italian and Greek communities, and up north on Lygon Street, their own version of Little Italy, an antipodean Old North End complete with excellent and authentic pizza and calzones, a rarity in Australia, trust me. Melbourne's said to have one of the largest Greek communities in the world outside of Athens, the surprising product of the initial post-war immigration wave of the 1950s and 60s. The Italian and Greek immigrants brought with them such strangely exotic treats as garlic, haloumi, coffee - espresso even! These food cultures took root, enlivening the old, standard Anglo Sunday roast and veg, and are now a vital, celebrated part of the fabric of Australian culture, merely some sixty years later. And it's nowhere more strongly evident than in Melbourne. It was mid-winter, the cafes were packed; it sometimes seemed that's what this entire town is all about, as well as a few quality museums perhaps. Melbournians are very serious about their food and coffee, which we heartily support!

DDU Blog entry: The Queen Victoria Market is a Melbourne institution dating back to the 1850's. Right downtown, it runs thrice-weekly and provides a mind-boggling array of fresh produce, meats, seafood, almost everything imaginable really. Truly foodie-heaven, it was even featured on Anthony Bourdain's "No Reservations". For anyone ever in town on a market day, it's a must do. Melbourne is also considered the cutting-edge fashion and shopping mecca of Australia. Lots of interesting things to see and buy. If that's your bag, baby...the sky's the limit!

The Shrine of Remembrance is a very moving tribute to the Australian war dead of WW1. It sits just beside the Botanic Garden on a hilltop overlooking the city CBD. There's a second story overlook that wraps around the medieval-like structure and allows for unobstructed 360-degree views of the entire region. Made entirely of hand cut local stone, it's oriented so that on the exact annual date and time the Armistice was announced, a beam of sunlight enters the room and crosses silently overhead, moving slowly across the tomb of the unknown soldier, centered on the floor far below, for fifteen contemplative minutes. Curiously, the monument creates a very Indiana Jones-like ambiance; like an ancient tomb, it retains a powerfully timeless and melancholy quality. They do a daily simulation on the hour, which we respectfully observed. It was quiet off-season, so cooler and silent within the dun-filtered light of the Shrine, and very moving to witness. Certainly, a high point of any trip to Melbourne; we were told it can become much busier and less meditative in the summer season, and may lose that ephemeral wistfulness, especially on holidays.

It's then an easy, relaxing stroll from there directly into the Botanic Gardens, and at this season, so thankfully quiet, a very meditative and beautiful way to process the full impact of the Shrine of Remembrance, which will stay with you for longer than you might expect. These are among the finest Botanic Gardens I've seen in all my travels, the full equal of Sydney's, if perhaps lacking the dramatic setting of the Harbour. And as always, a quaint cafe awaits nearby for a "hot cuppa and a bikkie" break, sheltered from the raw Melbourne weather. This singular combination is again, an iconic, if subtle and melancholic, Australian experience. Both are free and open to the public without requiring reservations and are not to be missed by any visitor to gracefully aging, vibrant yet elegant, Melbourne.

As you might have gathered by now, we are not really urban-focused folk. We love to get that city vibe for a few days, but then it's always "Let's hit the open road and see what lies just ahead, over that next rise..." So, the plan was perfectly laid, three nights in downtown Melbourne and then head out along the southern coast to visit the seaside summer resort town of Lorne via the Great Ocean Road (GOR). Quiet off-season and one of the world's great oceanside drives beckoning our exploration - let's go..!

The Great Ocean Road (GOR) has a fascinating history. It began as a jobs project for returning WW1 veterans and took over twenty years to complete. It runs for over a hundred miles, along some of the most remote and rugged coastline in Australia, previously trackless. There's a string of tiny old fishing and resort settlements strung along this coast and backed by the temperate, rain-forested Otway Mountain ranges, now all preserved as National Park. In summer season, it's booked-out a year in advance; off-season you'll have the place to yourselves. Per-fect! The low Otway Ranges are remote, rain-swept, and steep right down to the ocean. Similar in ambience to Big Sur perhaps; only, totally different. Numerous creeks run off southward to the sea, carving tight canyons full of locally indigenous plants, birds and wildlife. A unique environment, even within Australia; and seemingly a world apart. We were surprised at how many large waterfalls and accessible hiking trails exist right off the Road. Stopping at any creek outlet and heading inland leads into an impressive stone canyon within a few hundred yards. Or, turning in the opposite direction takes you out onto wild, windswept, driftwood-piled beaches, enclosed by tight, rocky headlands. It's all very dramatic and fetching. We chose a 6 km day hike into She Oak Canyon, hiking around and over the dramatic waterfalls on excellent, maintained trails, which culminated in our exploring a large open cave high above the main falls. The girls were very animated by the cooler weather, running happily though this strange fantasy-world of misted tree-ferns and mysterious, gnarled forest, like woodland Sprites. It was a dreamlike, Tolkienesque, and fantastically diverse hike over only a couple kilometers.

DDU Blog entry: We stayed two nights in the well-known summer resort town of Lorne, now completely dead off-season. Got a great winter escape package online: a modern condo, complete with a full kitchen and two bedrooms. Of two hundred or so units, there were perhaps six occupied. The girls were over the moon in finding that we had the extensive indoor heated-pool complex, with space for hundreds, entirely to ourselves, including the hot tubs. It's a convenient base for exploring the GOR and taking the long day trip out to see the iconic Twelve Apostles near Port Campbell, our agenda for the next day. The girls were a bit apprehensive about the long, twisting road ahead, being worried about car sickness. But, in the end, were brave and cheerful travelers.

As we drove west, down out of the undulating Otway ranges, the weather cleared and we basked in a filtered, winter sunlight, lying low in the northern sky. The day glimmered hopefully over extensive, dusky heath moors that unfolded as we approached the Twelve Apostles, yet another iconic Australian landscape, three twisty-turny hours later. As you arrive, past the excellent visitor's center, towards the very cliff edge, the bracing, onshore ocean breeze builds anticipation, and the overall effect does not disappoint. You are standing at the ragged and storm-battered southern edge of the continent and could be nowhere else on earth. As the sunlight and clouds shadow play on the breeze, the limestone formations change rapidly in depth and distance. The effect is simply mesmerizing; a different scene and mood unfolds every few moments, as the famous sentinels magically shift, suddenly close, then distant; and vary dramatically in color and shade under the fleeting, wind-driven light. This great Southern Ocean, driven by the crisp Southerlies blowing sharply off frozen Antarctica, is ever restless; and the incessant roar of its rising and falling adds greatly to the raw ambiance. By all reports, we were most fortunate, as in mid-winter many tourists drive for hours through near gale-force winds only to arrive here in virtually white-out conditions. Our day's weather was balmy by comparison.

This coastline is called the Shipwreck Coast, the appropriately named scene of hundreds of maritime disasters over the centuries. The most famous of all was the wreck of the Loch Ard in 1878, on the final night of its three-month voyage from England. Of fifty-five passengers and crew, only two eighteen-year-olds, a boy and a girl, survived, both miraculously swept into the same protection of Loch Ard Gorge. Legend says he rescued her, after hearing her cries for help above the storm; brought her into a picturesque cave; built a fire; and both survived the stormy night. The romantic tale made headlines worldwide, but no real romance ever ensued. She soon returned to Ireland, and the fortunate pair never saw each other again. But the scenic depths of Loch Ard Gorge provide the perfect setting for such a shipwreck fantasy. Here, tucked into a deep limestone fold, several hundred feet below the flat, windswept heath moor that stretches endlessly along this seacoast, one finds pockets of ferns and intricate moss gardens, nourished by the freshwater springs seeping out of the cliff faces. Deep, sandy-floored caves for shelter. Piles of ancient driftwood to provide ample firewood. Fish and seafood plucked fresh from the sea. A magical fairy-garden, where such dreams and fantasies might actually come to life.

Another surprise here is that this coastline contains much more of interest than just the well-known landmarks of the Twelve Apostles and London Bridge, an enormous, free-standing sea arch still further west down the coast. In fact, the entire limestone coastline is capped by a windswept, rolling heath plain that ends abruptly at the storming sea's ragged edge, several hundred feet below. This has created, over millennia, a complex, variegated system of gorges, caves and headlands, stretching for over fifty miles, that is constantly evolving with time and tide. In fact, the marquee Twelve Apostles are said to be down now to only Eight; but new novices are in the process of being formed, even as I write. And London Bridge has reportedly since collapsed into the devouring seas. It's a bracing, dynamic coastal experience. A long day trip really isn't time sufficient to see even the highlights of this fascinating, ends-of-the-earth environment. There are many trails to hike and nooks and crannies to explore. To my mind, it would be very satisfying to linger and absorb the fantastically remote ambiance of this sea-ravaged place on the planet for several days at least. One might be better served to stay a night or two in the quaint fishing hamlet of Port Campbell, a tiny speck (pop. 478 in 2016), set down seaside on a tight cove, below the protective limestone cliffs, just west of the Twelve Apostles. Or perhaps to continue along the coast farther west to Warrnambool, Port Fairy or points still further beyond. It takes so long to get out here, my advice would be to savor it, whatever the weather.

Unfortunately, having made prior plans, we turned reluctantly east to begin the three-hour, stomach-churning, but scenic, ride back to Lorne. At least the roads were empty, and we could ramble and stop at whim. We heard many stories of the mid-summer GOR becoming a bumper-to-bumper caravan and tour-bus traffic jam, with even the stunning, well-sited overlooks overfilled beyond capacity. So, a word to the wise; the GOR really is one of the great oceanside drives on the planet. I suppose the word's out. Consider that when planning. The off and shoulder seasons might give you the more pristine experience that we had, and the weather might even miraculously cooperate for you too!

DDU Blog entry: At Claire and Cate's insistence, we took a quick diversion out to scenic Cape Otway on the ride back to Lorne, for the express purpose of viewing the southern subspecies of Koala, larger, darker and much furrier than their tropical cousins, in order to survive in their harsher environment. Cape Otway is one of the best places to see them in the wild. We weren't disappointed, seeing several dozen large and very furry specimens, up quite close. The girls were so enthralled, they wanted to Koala-nap one back to Brisbane but were eventually dissuaded by reality. Unfortunately, there was simply no time to explore the famous and very picturesque Cape Otway lighthouse standing sentinel here. There are guided tours and extensive hiking trails across this wild, southernmost peninsula for those with more leisurely schedules.

Australian birdlife is famously prolific and exotic. It's called the Land of Parrots for good reason. On our return to Lorne, right on our condo balcony, several beautiful white Sulfur-Crested Cockatoos were hanging around awaiting a snack. Claire and Cate couldn't resist feeding them a treat. The birds are so intelligent and exotic, the girls just couldn't help themselves.

"Dad, look at these tame parrots!" they cooed, and headed out onto the open patio, offering food morsels, despite parental warnings and clear facility signage advising against such avian handouts.

"I'm not sure that's a good idea, girls. Those are wild birds, not pets," I called, unheeded. The girls were simply mesmerized by their wild beauty, so close at hand. Their generosity only encouraged more of the neighbors to flock over.

"Close the slider, Claire!", Stephanie called out, while we busily prepared dinner.

Before we realized, we had a full-fledged Cockatoo riot on our hands, involving several dozen large, vigorous birds, complete with avian fisticuffs, and aggressive jostling for premium railing space! When agitated, they spread their butter yellow crests dramatically, splay open their wings in a threat display, and squawk loudly while bobbing repeatedly. The birds literally swarmed the balcony for handouts; their rapidly growing numbers likely being artificially concentrated by the scarcity of other guests in this off-season.

Claire cried out in a panic. "Dad, help...!!" Cate simply shrieked repetitively at high pitch, as only a six-year-old girl can...

The noise of some twenty-odd, highly stimulated Cockatoos up close was absolutely deafening! They began to leap and land on the girls, with wings flailing like feathered fans. Claire and Cate, now trapped outside on the balcony, were essentially being accosted by this mob of agitated wild parrots, which can also deliver a nasty bite with their oversized beaks. And the girls only added to the din by screaming out in genuine terror...

"Oh my God, Stephanie, look at this!" I looked up, startled at the growing frenzy just outside the kitchen window...

Dropping the dinner prep, we ran out to save the girls from their well-deserved fates, with me yelling and waving my arms frantically, "Hya... get away...! Hya...!" as Stephanie pulled the panicked girls inside to safety.

The birds flew off in a raucous, complaining gaggle, leaving us both heaving with laughter, and gasping for air... A hilarious, if somewhat alarming, Aussie experience never to be forgotten! And a lesson I'm sure the girls will always remember vividly.

So, in future, please observe the facility signage and "Do Not Feed the Cockatoos." You've been forewarned.

On any trip you have only two real choices: stay local and explore a small area intimately or hit the road and try to see as much of a region as possible, within reason. We normally prefer the former, but the state of Victoria, by far the smallest and most populous of Australian states, is famous for the stunning diversity of its landscapes. Everything from hiking and skiing in the Snowy Mountains and Victorian Alps, to the Great Ocean Road and remote coastal ranges to the desert landscapes of the western Goldfields with the sprawling Outback beyond - all within a four-hour driving radius of Melbourne. Given that we might never get to this part of Australia again, we decided, unanimously as a team, to see as much as possible.

DDU Blog entry: Driving back east off the Great Ocean Road (GOR) we hugged the coast south of Melbourne, crossing the narrow entrance neck of Port Phillip Bay by ferry to the Mornington Peninsula and the resort town of Sorrento. The public ferry ride across the surprisingly tight inlet to Port Phillip Bay was made under flawless, sunny skies and glass flat seas. We could clearly see the towers of the Melbourne CBD far away to the north on the glimmering horizon of this massive bay; this water route provided vicarious glimpses of the opulent lifestyles enjoyed on the sheltered, and rapidly approaching, eastern peninsula. This area has been the playground of well-heeled Melbournians since the Victorian 1860's; think Boston-Cape Cod, or NYC-Hamptons. The local architecture is a fetching blend of graceful British-colonial Victorian and cutting-edge Mediterranean, with a mellow seaside, yachty ambience. Smell the money... The area is riddled with boutique wineries, hip restaurants and excellent B&B's. We were only passing through, but did stop for an excellent bakery snack, and a quick trip to the outer "back beaches" at classy Sorrento, and lunch in the town of Mornington.

Even though the Mornington Peninsula was perfectly magical, and could easily occupy a week, or an entire summer of your time, we had a few miles to go yet. On an Aussie friend's advice, we decided to head two additional hours northeast, to spend our final night in the Yarra Valley, a fine wine region famed for its cooler weather wines, and classic Pinot Noirs in particular. Healesville is the small agricultural town at its heart, like Healdsburg, in Sonoma, CA, well-regarded for fine, local-sourced ingredients and seasonal menus. The Healesville Hotel is a rustic foodie haven, so we decided to end the trip with a big splurge on a winter tasting dinner there, complete with roaring fireplace. What followed was one of the best meals we'd experienced while in Australia, and that's high praise indeed. Relaxed, attentive but not fussy service, and thoughtful pairing of courses with locally sourced wines. More than merely dinner, it was a shared learning and life experience with our beloved daughters, Claire and Cate, and hopefully a subtle education in the more refined pleasures of life. Good food, conversation, companionship; the very stuff of civilization. Fine indeed...

Next morning, we were up early as usual, and off to explore the Yarra Valley before catching an afternoon flight back to Brissie. There was method to my madness, as the agriculturally zoned Yarra Valley lies a mere ninety minutes northeast of Melbourne, almost hard up against its rapidly expanding outer suburbs. So, we were already well positioned to reach the airport, which is due north of the CBD. The Yarra Valley is surprisingly large and adamantly agricultural, surrounded by low, timbered hills, it feels similar to Napa or Sonoma. Being mid-winter, the vines were dormant, and all was quiet, rural bliss. It's a nice season to visit this very popular destination. In reality, one could spend many wonderful days getting to know the region, and its wines, on a more intimate level. And it was a special treat indeed, to have our lovely young daughters, Claire and Cate, along for another cultured, exciting and adventurous girls' road trip to graceful Melbourne and its scenic surrounds. We trust these memories made together will last them a lifetime and encourage their love of travel and exploration out on the open road.

CHAPTER 24: Balancing on the Fulcrum

November 2013

DDU Blog entry: As we approach the second anniversary of our living in Australia, and having never been expats before, lots of conflicting emotions arise. It's all going very well: the job secure, with lots of positive reviews and professional reinforcement, the money good, kids all busily engaged with school and friends; home life and Stephanie settled into a more predictable, comfortable rhythm. But it seems we are now balancing on the fulcrum. The issue confronts us almost daily, if indirectly. When/ how/ if this dream ends, what then? As we weigh the options and consider extrication now, versus possibly staying on for somewhat longer, diving in even deeper; what then? It seems as if our midlife sabbatical has somehow taken on a life of its own and is evolving into something far more complex and potentially permanent. Life never seems to stay static - so many complex considerations. And if it's not to be this life, then what life comes next? Bear with us, dear friends and family, this ain't easy. We are simply making it up as we go...

The kids continue to work hard at becoming seasoned Surf Lifesavers. It's a challenge for them to overcome ocean fears and learn the ways of the sea. If not a lifelong career move, at least an important education in understanding the vagaries of the ocean environment. As Stephanie and I tell them, "The life you save may be your own." Luke (14) continues trying to master the deceptively difficult art of surfing and is also learning the craft of crewing ocean-racing Catamarans with our sailing enthusiast landlord and friends. Now more established here in Cleveland, we are no longer visitors, and are living a rich community life completely unknown to the casual tourist. What once seemed so exotic is now becoming the stuff of weekend routines. We have a network of friends met via school and work, sharing common concerns and daily experiences. We even get the occasional invitation to go "Sailing On the Coral Sea" out on beautiful Moreton Bay.

Stephanie and I had a belated 20th anniversary celebration, four months late (!) Do you have any idea how hard it is to find a sane, live-in sitter for five young kids? Try it sometime. Anyway, we had a restful weekend away, up in the mountains ten km inland from the Sunshine Coast, aka the "Sunshine Coast hinterlands." Drive ninety minutes north of Brisbane, inland off the coast, and you enter into another world of hill farms, tropical fruit orchards, remote waterfalls, rainforest pockets and amazing B&Bs.

"Secrets On the Lake" is a remarkable enclave of fifteen beautiful, unique tree houses tucked away on a small lake near the mountain resort town of Montville. It feels, oddly enough, like being in a tropical Adirondack Great Camp, all woodsy and rustic elegance. The tree houses are famous for their extensive, one-of-a-kind carvings of local wildlife, every one unique. The whole complex is connected by extensive boardwalks set high off the ground and winding amongst the rainforest trees. It's a really exceptional place, Google it some time. We splurged and had a memorable dinner at the Spicers Clovelly Estate in nearby Montville. Considered one of the very finest restaurants in Queensland, and set in an elegant old Queenslander on acreage, there are only eleven tables, and all the food is locally sourced. It's a leisurely, full, romantic evening. Highly recommended for a special occasion.

The following day, we completed a ten km bushwalk on a portion of the newly- constructed Sunshine Coast Hinterland Great Walk, from impressive Kondalilla Falls to Baroon Pocket Lake, hiking up the river gorge and returning on foot directly to "Secrets On the Lake" in four hours flat, easily working off dinner from the night before. The Secrets owner was kind enough to drive us up to the starting point and we hiked right back to our cabin door. It was hot and pretty remote, with large Goanna lizards scampering through the undergrowth everywhere. Their noisy rustlings through the dried leaf litter kept us both on high snake alert, but none were spotted, though I'm sure they were all around, given the remoteness of the trail and the hot, dry weather. It was a fantastic, varied hike with waterfalls, gorges, rainforest pockets, dry eucalypt ridges, almost everything one could want, really.

Later that night, after a relaxing and romantic candle-lit, hot tub session in our treetop cabin, we were once again invaded by a wandering opossum, who entered our love shack through a window I'd carelessly left open. Awakened to action by his foraging, we found him pretty stubborn in his insistence on having a midnight snack with us, and at our expense. Hissing and posturing threateningly in the semi-dark, he made his stand. Finally, we encouraged him to depart without mutual bodily harm by means of some vigorous towel rat-tailing in the moonlight. He eventually realized he'd met his match and retreated back out the same window, disappearing silently into the surrounding treetops. Note to self: it pays to keep your windows screened or closed in this unpredictable country. And thus concluded another memorable, if mildly bizarre, anniversary in this always surprising land Down Under.

CHAPTER 25: Cheers!
South Australia: McLaren Vale, Barossa and Clare Valleys

December 2013

The following month, Stephanie and I, miraculously, had another opportunity to get away and experience yet another region of Australia: the vast and comparatively dry state of South Australia (SA). We'd located a new, younger nanny; actually a twenty-year-old, pre-medical student who needed the money, and seemed energetic and brave enough to take on the challenge of five nights alone with the Nolan kids. I had a five-day national ACEM conference to attend in Adelaide, and Stephanie came along for five nights leading up to the event. We spent four wonderful nights B&B exploring the world-renowned wine districts of McLaren Vale, Adelaide Hills, Barossa and Clare Valleys. A fertile arc running to the north, east and south, all are within a two-hour drive from central Adelaide, making them popular weekend destinations for Adelaideans. These regions contain some of the oldest and best vineyards in Australia, dating back to the arrival of German missionaries and settlers in the 1830's.

The date arrived, and we were on our way. Behave, you little monsters... Best of luck, sweet nanny! Adelaide is a green, graceful city of around one million, laid out by British military engineers in the 1830's. It was the first major, free-settler colony in Australia, and has no brutal penal colony history, unlike the cities on the East Coast and Tasmania. In fact, it's considered to be a rather posh repository of old-line families and money in Australia. Originating as a planned town, the CBD is completely encircled by a generous swath of verdant parklands and bisected by the Torrens River. The Gulf of Saint Vincent presses along the coastal, western edge of the city, providing residents with a long stretch of pristine beaches only twenty minutes west from downtown and running southward towards distant Kangaroo Island. The overall sense one gets on landing is similar to the central coast of California, with fertile, irrigated valleys backed by sparsely wooded, low, golden hills rising to the east. It gets pretty rural thirty minutes out of the CBD; and much beyond that, you suddenly feel as if you're heading somewhere out towards the very edge of the planet...Which, in fact, you are.

DDU Blog entry: We started the trip by getting right out on the road from the airport, heading south into the famed vinicultural region of McLaren Vale, which begins on the coast only forty-five minutes south of the CBD. Surprisingly, you wind through the rather featureless southern suburbs, then crest a rise to arrive almost instantaneously at an antipodean Eden of sorts. The landscape is quite hilly and becomes immediately rural. McLaren Vale has a cooler, maritime climate with refreshing ocean breezes sweeping in from the southwest coastlines, rising over the low hills that obscure the Adelaide CBD to the north and west. Within these undulating elevation changes there exist multiple micro-climates, and Mclaren Vale is home to some legendary Aussie wineries. The diverse moisture and climate conditions allow a wide variety of grapes to prosper to world-class status here: Shiraz, Grenache, Riesling, Chardonnay, even the finicky Pinot Noir. It's claimed that any grape grown in Australia can reach peak excellence somewhere in McLaren Vale, and my taste buds must happily concur!

On our first night out, we got a feel for the howling energy of the southwest winds coming in off the Gulf of Saint Vincent from the vast, sub-Antarctic, Great Southern Ocean beyond. We attempted a romantic sunset beach stroll but were soon defeated by the raw winds throwing fine sand up off the beach directly at us, stinging hands and faces. We retreated for cover, and hastily ducked into the cozy, well-regarded, and picturesquely sited, Victory Hotel, overlooking the entire darkening expanse of these sea-stormed coastlines, for the first of many great meals in SA. The sea and landscapes here are wild and ruggedly beautiful, and remain a vivid memory, as do the sublime local Coffin Bay oysters on a half-shell, with soy and seaweed garnish, burnished by several glasses of exquisite local wines.

Coastal South Australia boasts a Mediterranean climate and is often referred to as the Sonoma of Australia. The food and wines are local, diverse and world class: seafood, lamb and beef, charcuterie, cheeses, olives, fruits and veg of every variety. Wine tasting is the big activity in all these sub-regions. Tastings start around 1000 and end by 1700. At no charge, the wineries pour small samples, but you'll try six or eight different wines per stop, so a full glass. Most will pour some pretty high-end drops, $75-90 a bottle, if you're lucky. So, it's a fascinating, hands and lips-on, education on the various styles grown in each region. The stylistic variations, on the same grape varietal, can be startling. After four or five stops, you might begin to feel a bit tipsy, so a designated driver, or local tour company is recommended if you plan on diving-in fully. Many wineries have adjacent high-end restaurants which are also truly world-class. Funnily enough, many only serve lunch. After a few days, I began to realize that most everyone was probably back home napping by 1800, after a long, hard day sampling the local hooch. So, if you are going, plan on lunch, probably not dinner.

D'Arenberg is the largest family-owned winery in the Vale, where small family-owned and managed wineries are the norm. Fourth generation, and still very innovative, its wines are sublime and well-priced. We had one of our best meals in SA at their well-regarded d'Arry's Verandah restaurant. The staff was informative and laid back, as we arrived almost two hours late for lunch, waylaid by a hike and various tastings, but no worries! They are highly recommended for lunch to any visitors to McLaren Vale. Other highlights were tiny Coriole and Chapel Hill vineyards; the latter's tasting room stunningly set within the rebuilt ruin of an 1840's stone chapel, that sits atop a high hilltop overlooking this paradise. "The Prophet" Shiraz made here is an outstanding value for the quality found lurking, in deep violet, within.

After two nights at a B&B in McLaren Vale, we headed north through the twisting backroads of the Adelaide Hills, rising gently east of the city, and home to over fifty smaller boutique wineries that specialize in cooler climate, lighter-bodied wines. We had lunch in the old German settlement of Hahndorf. Dating back to the 1830-40's, it's an unexpected delight, full of stone heritage buildings and interesting shops. Well worth a day or two's exploration. As charming and varied as the Adelaide Hills were, we had miles to go before we slept, and drove still further north towards the "Big

Kahuna" of South Australia wine regions, the Barossa Valley, where we had dinner and B&B reservations waiting.

There are elaborate WW1 monuments all over Australia, even in the smallest rural towns, and the Adelaide region is no exception. Aussies mourn and remember that war in some ways more so than WW2. The young, colonially idealistic nation, population less than five million in 1914, suffered 220,000 casualties in WW1, approximately 60,000 killed and 160,000 wounded; almost 5% of the entire population and that occurring not on the home front, but far away overseas! Over 30% of Australian troops sent in support of the English monarchy were either killed or wounded - an astonishing figure by any historic measure. It was during these traumatic events of WW1 that Australia first developed a truly national identity, and the bi-national holiday of ANZAC Day, observed every April 25, celebrates the Australian/ New Zealand ideals of "Mateship, Sacrifice and Service" in a manner very similar to Memorial Day in the USA. These monuments are well-preserved, poignant reminders of the high costs borne by Australia in support of the British Empire. Australian losses in WW2 were comparatively mild, approximately 27,000 killed, 23,000 wounded and 30,000 taken prisoners of war. Australia's geographic isolation was then a blessing, although Darwin was bombed repeatedly, and there was some actual danger of invasion by the Japanese Imperial Forces into northern Queensland at one point.

DDU Blog entry: Heading north down out of the Adelaide Hills, the windy, forest-lined roads gradually straighten and flatten out and you arrive in an entirely different landscape: the broad, open, sunny and fertile Barossa Valley. This is the epicenter of the SA wine industry, which was begun by Prussian and German immigrants in the 1840s. Many of the wineries are still owned and worked by the 6th generations of the original settler families. Although the Barossa is home base to many of the giants of the Australian wine industry: Jacob's Creek, Wolf Blass, Peter Lehmann, Penfolds and Kalleske - it never feels crowded or overly commercialized. It's a very large landscape, full of wonderful food and wine-tasting opportunities, but remains adamantly rural, similar to Sonoma in California. Arriving in early summer, mid-week, we had the place almost to ourselves. One feature that gives the Barossa such a distinctive ambiance is the many stone heritage buildings constructed over one hundred and fifty years of settlement from the local bluestone. Beautiful stone churches stand sentinel in every hamlet.

The Seppelt Winery, established in 1851, is an Australian icon. The approach road takes you under a long arching parade of matching palm trees, a unique Australian landmark. The family made its vast fortune shipping fortified wines, Ports and Sherries, throughout the British empire when at its zenith. They still produce fortified wines here today, and possess the world's largest collection of ancient wines, with an unbroken lineage back almost to the founding of the winery. They are famous for their DP90 Tawny Port, which is only released when it reaches one hundred years of age! Generations of Seppelts are buried in the family crypt, a Grecian-style stone mausoleum that sits on a beautiful knoll above Seppeltsfield, the compact, family-owned company town. We then had dinner in Tanunda at a fabulous Asian fusion restaurant, Ferment Asia, set incongruously in an 1840's Germanic farmhouse. A phenomenal restaurant, especially the wine list! The Barossa Valley, an iconic Australian landscape and experience. It's an unexpected, intriguing place, a savory blend of solid Germanic tradition and cutting-edge gastronomic fusion.

Driving home, later that evening, we watched the rolling, golden-grassed hills deepen dramatically to bruised tangerine, then crimson, as the sun retreated farther away in the west, across the verdant valley floor, geometrically crisscrossed with myriad richly budding vines as far into the twilit afterglow as the eye could wander. Simply magical...

DDU Blog entry: In the brilliant, bright morning light, we were up with the sunrise to hike the gravel road that snakes up onto the hills backing up behind the Blickinstal B&B, our rural base in the Barossa. The sense of unfolding mystery just pulled us along, higher and higher, and we soon found ourselves in a different world once again. Wilder, a tumbled and rumpled straw-grass savannah, interspersed with ancient, gnarled gumtrees. Nothing like the manicured vineyards sprawling across the flat lands below. We started out in a refreshing, misty rain, but in these parts rain never lingers. The sky cleared as we moved higher, and the heat began to rise.

As we moved further into the bush, the birdlife, hidden away up on these forgotten and infertile heights, became simply unparalleled in numbers and diversity. Sudden bursts of rocket-fast Lorikeets, flashing by in a multi-colored blur; the hoarse challenges of Cockatoos and Galahs breaking the hot stillness; hawks riding thermals overhead. On this single ten-kilometer walk, we experienced some of the best birdwatching we've witnessed in Australia, which is really saying a lot! The hike back down was long and satisfying, an experience to be slowly savored...It was hard to leave these breezy, neglected back hills for the comparatively busy and hot valley floor.

Soon enough it was time to hit the road again, heading still further north, inland for another ninety minutes into the Clare Valley. Higher, cooler and famous for its white wines, especially Rieslings. But of course, always taking time to stop at a few wineries along the way. Wirra Wirra and Turkey Flats were two standouts among many fine contenders. You simply have to choose a few that have a personal connection to you and indulge, such is the bounty of the Barossa. There are dozens of equally worthy destinations that will have to await future trips.

Australia, being so geographically isolated, has some of the oldest commercial wine grape vines on the planet; most begun with transplants carried to the continent on sailing ships from Europe. In fact, after Phylloxera and other diseases decimated vineyards in Europe, grafts of some varietals were sent back from Australia to their countries of origin to help re-establish the vines there. We took a rural side road north though extensive wheat and barley fields, just now being harvested, bleached almost to white under the intense sun. I actually had to put on sunglasses; their intensity burned my eyes. A strange landscape of brilliant, bleached beige, pierced only by the deep, singular gray ribbon of macadam roadway; something I'd never experienced before. Driving thus, on undulating, two-lane blacktop for miles and miles, the effect is hard to describe, but somewhat like being immersed within some vast, pale-golden tapestry, that you maneuver over, around and through for hours on end. It was a singularly beautiful experience.

The name Clare Valley seems somewhat of a misnomer to me, as a first-time visitor. Where exactly is the valley again? It's actually a large region of almost imperceptible low, timbered ridges, running north to south, interspersed with rich, vinicultural flats. It's a bit hard to describe or get your head around at first. But it's certainly scenic, trust me on that. One Clare Valley must-see is the Australian landmark of Sevenhill Cellars. The oldest winery in the Clare Valley, and one of the oldest in Australia, it was founded by the Jesuits in 1851 and is still run by the Order as an active parish and retreat center. We learned that Sevenhill makes 80% of the sacramental wines used in Australia; as well as a wide range of highly regarded world-class varietals. The spacious grounds and European-styled stone architecture feel very non-Australian, and it's hard to believe you are in rural South Australia here at all.

DDU Blog entry: Sevenhill is most famous for its arched stone-ceilinged wine cellars, which date from the 1800s and are unique in Australia. Very unexpected in this final, fertile outpost on the edge of the increasingly desiccated Outback. The history gets even more unusual, as adjacent to the iconic wine cellars, and built directly under the impressive stone church above, lie the stone crypts where the Order has buried its deceased brothers since arrival. Literally, Australian catacombs, and again, entirely unique on the continent.

After the monied, somewhat posh Barossa, Clare Valley comes as a bit of a surprise. Firstly, as you drive up the main route north, it's hard to tell you're in a valley at all; the landscape is rather low, obscured and rolling. Also, while you'll see some roadside vines, it feels much tighter and more forested than the wide-open expanses of the Barossa. And the main town of Clare feels simply like a down-to-earth working agricultural town, which it most certainly is. Nothing fancy here at all, just all the services and equipment vendors you need to run large scale farm and vineyard enterprises.

And after all the upscale food and wine consumed since our landing in SA, we enthusiastically embraced the local dining scene. We couldn't resist having dinner at the Clare Hotel right downtown, dining among the local farmers and their wives. Pork roast dinner special with roasted root veg, including the salad bar for $9.95, which is a screaming deal in Australia, believe me - less than McDonald's. It was beautifully prepared food, a real highlight of the trip. And funnily enough, this humble country hotel pub also had a world-class list of high-end South Australian wines: $7 a glass, filled generously, almost to the rim. I commented to the bartender, that *"we'd been eating and drinking half as well, for twice the price, all week." He seemed very pleased, in an understated way. When I noted the impressive wine list, he smiled and just said modestly, "Well mate, you are in the Clare Valley..."*

Our lodgings, the 1970's era Clare Valley Hotel, were similarly down home. Clean and tidy, not at all posh. Perfect! When told the room rate included a complete cooked breakfast, the matronly Aussie owner asked if we'd like it in the dining room or brought to our door. I asked what the charge was for room service, and she just laughed and said, "Oh, no worries, we'll just bring it over."

Which they did, at no additional... and right on time too. A full-on British-style "fry up" even. Eggs, potatoes, sausage, toast, beans and grilled tomatoes, with mushrooms. Don't tell my Cardiologist, but certainly, my kind of place. After our unexpectedly awesome brekkie, we headed out on a hike, where we hoped to get a better idea of the vastness of the Clare region. From the summits of low rocky hilltops, the pale-golden flats below stretched away north and west until they dissolved indistinctly into the warm haze of the desert outback, undulating endlessly beyond. As always in Australia, this landscape is vaster and more intriguing than we expected. Further into the rolling back roads, we explored some of the wineries for which Clare is world famous, especially the Polish Hill River and Watervale districts. Pike's and Jim Barry were standouts. We then took a lonely, winding back road out to the heritage-listed hamlet of Mintaro. Very much lost in time, it's becoming something of an offbeat destination on the wine-tourist path. Surprisingly, many of the buildings are not yet fully renovated; a few still stand as empty ruins, echoes of a harsher, earlier existence, lived here at the very edge of the inhabitable earth. It's a fascinating glimpse into the not-so-distant past of South Australia. The Magpie and Stump Hotel, c 1851, is a funky local landmark that's worth a tuck into - a time capsule redolent of age and memory.

Another major feature of interest near Mintaro is the stunning Martindale Hall, an intact English Pastoral estate from the 1800's. It's been featured in several movies and earns its upkeep today as a high-end B&B. We had a stroll around the unexpectedly formal grounds, but didn't have time for the house tour, unfortunately. A rural landmark of a bygone age, Martindale Hall appears as a fantastical, intricate jewel set within this complex and austere landscape, that somehow still survives through the slow passage of time and seasons in rural South Australia.

CHAPTER 26: More Cheers! South Australia: "Rad"elaide and the Adelaide Hills.

December 2013

Stephanie could only stay one night in Adelaide. After our SA wine country touring, she had to get right back to Brissie to pack up the kids for their Christmas break adventures back in New York and at Fairview Farm. We'd been in Australia since January 2012, and this was their first trip back home to the USA in almost two years. They had sure earned it! They'd be away for five weeks, while I worked and held down the fort solo in Raby Bay. Yet another complication of raising a family overseas and juggling lives in two places. I dropped her off at the Adelaide airport and spent the day further exploring the Adelaide Hills, just thirty minutes east of downtown. It was difficult to part after such a full, fascinating week together, and I'd miss having her energetic and fun-loving spirit here with me. Traveling solo is an entirely different experience; a now infrequent immersion inwards that can be spiritually, as well as creatively, rewarding. I certainly spent many hours traveling solo in my younger seasons. But, these days, I always prefer to have Stephanie and/ or the kids along to share the experience and build bonding memories. Life is richer, if less meditative, now.

DDU Blog entry: The Botanic Garden here is beautifully maintained by volunteers. Entry is free with a goodwill offering if so moved. I happened upon a very strange looking tree here, a Wollomi Pine, named after the remote valley it was discovered in. It's the botanic equivalent of finding a living T. Rex in 2013. Some botanists found a few of these specimens growing up in a remote slot canyon in the Blue Mountains of NSW, only a hundred kilometers from the Sydney CBD. The genus was thought to be extinct for some 100 million years. This very tree was germinated from those original seeds and grows today here in Adelaide, now truly a Jurassic Park!

I then took the steep, windy drive, in contented silence, to the summit of Mount Lofty, rising just east of the city. At 2329 feet, it's a local landmark, with panoramic views over the greater Adelaide region and the coastlines undulating further west and south into the heat haze. The weather began to clear as I drove down off the summit. Now having hours of unstructured time, near the base, I took a small side road up the dead-end canyon at Waterfall Gully. Surprisingly, there was a little antique wooden cottage, in the alpine style, hidden away in the forest grove there. It looked very popular with the weekend brunch crowd. Tea and scones were featured. Aussies love their English-style Devonshire Tea, which includes a fresh, soft, plain and unsweetened scone with strawberry jam and clotted cream on the side. Makes for a great Sunday brekkie, so I ordered up and dug in. The day being hot, I innovated with an iced tea, without raising any eyebrows. The scones were fresh and delicious.

Thus fortified, I started up the three-kilometer (~ two mile) trail back towards the summit of Mount Lofty, not sure how far I would get after all the recent food and wine over-consumption. As is typical in Australia, the cooling cloud cover soon lifted completely, and the heat began quickly rising. The steepening trail really started to kick my aging butt. I had to admit, after all the past week's overeating and fine wine-tasting, the last five hundred meters was pretty tough. But flushed (and overheated) with success, I at last re-attained the summit of Mount Lofty, this time on foot. It was first sighted and named by Matthew Flinders, the famous British navigator, from far away at sea to the southwest, while he was exploring Kangaroo Island in 1802, aboard HMS Investigator. The summit views west over the Adelaide CBD are stunning, and on a clear day such as I had, one can see down the coast to the southwest all the way to the remote, legendary Kangaroo Island offshore. Far larger than it appears on a map, it's a bucket-list destination; an island ark of Australian mammals now endangered on the mainland by dingoes, domestic cats and dogs and car traffic. Friends who've gone over on the ferry say the dramatic seascapes and tame, plentiful wildlife are simply incredible; but it's a completely separate trip, requiring three-days at a minimum.

After sufficient rest and rehydration, I started back down the three-kilometer return to the valley floor. On the down hike, I was intrigued to hear a soft digging sound in the bush and noted dirt falling trailside. As I stopped to listen, it continued on... Hiking off trail, into the steep bush (watch those snakes, mate!), I soon came right upon a Short-eared Echidna, busily searching for dinner. Pretty uncommon, it's a porcupine-sized, spine-covered hedgehog of sorts. And the only other egg-laying mammal on earth, along with the Platypus. I was able to stand right over it, as it seemed fully occupied face down in the earth, hungrily tunneling for insects. My attempts to gently pop the critter out with a stick, to get a glimpse of its unusually shaped snout and face, were met with more furious burrowing by means of burly forelegs. It held fast. So, I had to be content with looking at, and photographing, its spikey butt-end. This was yet another in a long series of memorable, up close and in-the-wild encounters with the fascinating wildlife of Australia.

Finally, it was down to business and the reason we'd traveled all the way to Adelaide and South Australia. The opening night party of the Australasian College for Emergency Medicine conference was a superb blend of Adelaide Festival weirdness and sublime foods showcasing the very best of South Australia. There was a lively mix-and-mingle on the back verandah of the convention center, on the Torrens River, right downtown. And the weather was flawless - not at all unusual in SA. The food and wines were superb and well-chosen to represent the marvelous local bounty of the region: oceanic, vineyard, diverse artisanal cheeses, as well as farm and ranch offerings. Roving entertainers from the Adelaide Festival - jugglers, clowns, gypsy snake handlers, even a guy on stilts - were complemented and enhanced by a groovy live band and unlimited quantities of wines from the now somewhat more familiar SA wineries. All in all, it was a fantastic, welcoming event, and an invigorating conference among my EM peers and colleagues. The only element missing was Stephanie.

Exploring the city further on my off hours, I spent some rare and contemplative time indoors. Adelaide has several highly regarded museums, including one of the world's finest collections of Aboriginal and Pacific Island artifacts. I almost missed the Pacific Island display, it's upstairs in a side gallery at the Adelaide Museum. Over a hundred years old and brought to Adelaide by various missionaries and adventurers over many decades, each island group has its own unique display: rare head-

dresses, spears, tools and weavings, all beautifully arranged and encased in antique hardwood framed cases. Many of these traditional arts on display are long-extinct on their home islands today. It's a fascinating glimpse into now vanished worlds - eerie, primordial, even a bit spooky. Do not miss this exhibit if at the Adelaide Museum, as it's unique and comprehensive, a truly stunning collection of irreplaceable Pacific Island indigenous history.

In complementary contrast to its hipster-vibe reputation, Adelaide, to this visitor, is also a city of impressive colonial sandstone architecture and graceful English-style parks and gardens. A winning combination in my book. It really is a fascinating contrast of old colonial wealth and charm, cutting edge, Mod-Aussie innovation and playful weirdness. Adelaide, South Australia is a city and region that, while somewhat off the beaten track, is definitely worthy of being on any Australian visitor's itinerary.

CHAPTER 27: Nuh Zilla (New Zealand) #1: Solo Hiking the Milford Track

January 2014

DDU Blog entry: Stephanie and the kids were back in the USA for the long Christmas break. I worked over the holidays, payin' those pesky bills, and then took this rare opportunity to see a new part of the world solo, and accomplish a lifelong goal of hiking the Milford Track in the Fiordlands region of southwest New Zealand.

So, New Zealand... big subject. I'd never been, and after two years living in Australia, I assumed it would basically be like an alpine Aussie experience. So mistaken! It's only a three-hour direct flight from Brisbane to Christchurch, on the east coast of the South Island, but you're entering into another world entirely. Although it's widely understood that the two countries share a common English Commonwealth heritage and language, it's not so well-known that at Australian Federation in 1901, New Zealand was actually invited to enter the Federation as an Australian state, but declined, and later negotiated its eventual independence from Great Britain separately. And although there's heaps of camaraderie between the two nations, there also remains a vigorous, friendly rivalry between the neighbors "across the ditch" (aka, the Tasman Sea) about nearly everything imaginable, and especially Rugby Union: the NZ All Blacks vs Aussie Wallabies. In many respects, New Zealand (NZ) and Australia (AU) are very different worlds indeed.

As a brief primer, consider the following surprising contrasts:

- NZ is currently one of the most volcanically active places on the planet, while the last active AU volcanic period was around 20 million years ago.
- There are some 700 species of Eucalypt in AU, by far the most dominant plant genus. There are none in NZ.
- AU is world-famous for its curious mammals, many of which are entirely unique, endemic marsupials. NZ has no native mammal species except for two species of bat. There are also no snakes in NZ, while its sister country is literally chockers with many impressively lethal varieties. Oh, nor poisonous spiders or jellyfish either. In all, NZ is a peaceful oasis, biologically speaking.
- NZ was the last major, fertile landform on earth to be inhabited by humans. The native Maori (~15% of the population today) arrived only 800-1000 years ago, crossing the vast Pacific from Polynesia in small boats. Maori are closely related linguistically to Hawaiian Islanders, and still use some terms that are archaic in modern Hawaiian today. These common linguistic roots were one of the primary ways researchers pieced the Maori origin puzzle together.
- There once existed an enormous species of bird in NZ, the Moa, which stood up to 12 feet tall and weighed in at almost 500 pounds. Recognizing an easy and excellent meal, the Maori eventually hunted these impressively large, but unfortunately flightless, prehistoric birds into extinction, well before European arrival. There is no evidence of Moa ever existing in neighboring AU.
- The Aboriginals of AU are considered to be the oldest continually active human culture on earth. Origins somewhat obscure, they have been in AU for at least 65,000, and perhaps as long as 100,000 years. For time-scale reference, Neanderthals were still in existence in central Europe as recently as 40,000 years ago. The Australian Aboriginals have no genetic or cultural connections to the Maori or greater Polynesia in general.
- And even today, the Anglo NZ folks, so-called "Kiwis", seem a different breed to their Aussie cousins. Perhaps it's the harsher, more demanding climate, but I find Kiwis in general to be more direct, focused and no-nonsense (i.e., blunt) than the laid-back, good-timing Aussies. If Kiwis are perhaps similar to taciturn northern New Englanders in the USA, coastal Aussies generally display the more laid-back cultural attitudes of southern

Californians, or if rural and ranchy, perhaps Texans. Again, just my own observations here.

DDU Blog entry: I took the quick flight "across the ditch" from Brisbane and landed in Christchurch, on the South Island. Traveling solo, I had all my hiking kit field-tested and ready for adventure... Christchurch was historically considered the most English of New Zealand cities. A small (~500K) compact, college and literary center, founded in the 1840s, it's the capital of the Canterbury region, and sits on a vast alluvial basin right on the South Island 's mid-east coast. Famous for its extensive and beautiful heritage stone buildings and graceful parks, a genteel pastime is punting (yes, in quaint wooden skiffs, each propelled by a pole...) on the Avon River that flows through downtown.

Life changed abruptly for Canterburians on 04 September 2010 when the city was struck by a 7.1 magnitude earthquake. A second 6.3 magnitude tremblor struck on 22 February 2011; very shallow and centered less than ten km from the CBD, this second quake essentially destroyed central Christchurch in under thirty seconds. A heroic rescue and rebuilding effort has been underway in the ensuing three years, and I was very interested to see how the city was recovering. Eighty-five percent of the buildings in the Central Business District (CBD) were damaged beyond repair, and most of the ones still standing are condemned and will be torn down. Extensive, and ingenious, re-engineering is ongoing to salvage the remaining fragile heritage buildings and make them more earthquake resilient. In some cases, experts are literally recording the original dimensions, removing heritage stonework, pouring rebar-reinforced concrete under-walls, then meticulously replacing the heritage stonework, true to the original dimensions. Such precision work moves ahead slowly, impeded by over two thousand aftershocks. In spite of the destruction, life continues, as close to normal as is possible. The Botanic Gardens and adjacent Canterbury Museum were miraculously spared destruction, and are wonderful, orderly spaces of normalcy that are highly recommended refuges while in the Christchurch city center.

Downtown, the scrappy local community soon got a temporary shopping district up and running, opening on 29 October 2011 as the Re:START Mall. Using shipping containers, painted in uplifting, bright colors as temporary retail spaces, it's become an iconic testimony to human ingenuity and resilience in the face of overwhelming loss. Unfortunately, much of the CBD today remains a vast network of barren, vacant lots with the debris now leveled, cleared and awaiting the next, uncertain phase. Frankly, I was overwhelmed by the scale of loss and how much recovery remains to be accomplished. The main spire of the iconic stone Canterbury Cathedral still lies in partial ruin where it fell into the square below. There was an attempt by the government to raze the entire cathedral as unsalvageable, but determined citizens mobilized and are attempting to raise funds for its restoration. Its fate remains in the balance at the time of this visit. And it's daunting to consider all the subsurface "stuff" that was also destroyed. Sewer, electric, water lines all needing to be meticulously reconstructed while life continues apace above ground. So, my hopeful thoughts and prayers go out to the resilient residents of Christchurch, as they continue to rebuild their shattered city.

After two nights exploring Christchurch, it was time to hit the road west, through Arthur's Pass to the South Island's west coast region, called the Westlands. It's a wild and stormy coastline, home only to around thirty thousand permanent residents - hardy souls all. The beaches here are cold, gray, windswept and stony; simply worlds away from the aquamarine swells and sugar-sandy crescents of the eastern Oz seaboard. The drive down this remote coastline is stunningly scenic and full of fascinating diversions: caves, rock formations and unusual coastal glaciers. But it's definitely not Club Med.

Another striking realization about New Zealand is that it's a very rural place. It may seem obvious, but actually is still more so than you'd probably imagine. It's about equal in size to Great Britain, with less than one fourteenth the population (~ 64 vs 4.5 million). Consider that NZ is approximately four times the size of Ireland with half a million fewer people. Fully half the entire population lives in the greater Auckland region, on the northern end of the North Island. Only around 1 million people inhabit the larger South Island. So, you are well and truly into farm country, complete with innumerable and picturesquely grazing sheep, within thirty minutes of leaving the Christchurch CBD. The extensive use of tall, tightly spaced tree plantings as field hedgerows and windbreaks is a distinct feature of the breezy Canterbury plains surrounding Christchurch. They whir past like a giant, leafy kaleidoscope as you drive west, out of the city and into the mountains ahead.

With the towering, jagged and snow-capped peaks of the Southern Alps forming the backdrop to the entire western horizon, it's a landscape that's guaranteed to get your explorer's blood running hot. The serpentine road beckons you to follow further into the west, as the mellowing afternoon sunset fades gradually to a rose-orange alpenglow, highlighting the stark, treeless ridgelines and summits as the cooling evening settles.

DDU Blog entry: I was fortunate to have unusually fine weather for several days while traveling down the west coast, camping and exploring the iconic Franz Josef and Fox glaciers under rare, clearing skies, that exposed even the highest, snow-clad summits to brilliant sunshine; this was high adventure indeed! Hiking several kilometers up the rubble-strewn moraine valleys left behind by these retreating glaciers put one in mind of the setting of Helm's Deep in the Lord of the Rings. "Let's go hunt some Orc." felt like an entirely possible suggestion in these wild lands. Still further south, the remote coastlines become impassable, and the road turns inland, heading southeast through the sublime, alpine Haast Pass, and up onto the high, dry Central Otago plateau. Blocked off from the prevailing maritime weather patterns and moisture, this is a landscape of vast, drier alpine valleys, cradling crystalline mountain lakes, all ringed by jagged, snow-brushed mountain ranges. Similar in feel to western Montana, it's the genuine Lord of the Rings landscape, fantastic in scale and grandeur, which I meditatively explored for days on-end while a Lord of The Rings orchestral soundtrack CD played dramatically, on endless repeat, over the rental car stereo. A truly transcendent experience, with Howard Shore's melodies creating an indelible backdrop to this entirely magical country.

Next stop, tiny, funky Wanaka, probably my favorite NZ town yet, for some camping just down the road, alongside the very photogenic, mountain-hemmed Lake Wanaka, before eventually heading onwards to Queenstown, the adrenaline-adventure capital of NZ. Sitting meditatively by Lake Wanaka, it lies limpid in the final lingering southern twilight, and is one of the truly awe-inspiring natural settings I've experienced. Simply pristine and magnificent. But next morning, it was up early, the weather now turning hot and very dry. My immediate goal was a challenging training hike up Mt. Roy, starting out right from the Wanaka lakeshore. It's a popular local workout, around sixteen km (ten miles) round-trip and with ~ 3000 feet elevation gain. I planned it as my final buildup for the impending Milford Track. It turned out to be a very challenging hike, indeed; the trail relentlessly switching-back ever uphill. And the weather was surprisingly hot for late summer here. Up, upwards higher still, leg muscles burning, past the gorse and wild rose thickets, striding close by the ubiquitous, placidly grazing sheep. And finally, the celebrated views over Lake Wanaka, shimmering far below, in the bright, penetrating, high-altitude sunshine, like a distant, sapphire-blue jewel. And sweeping away still further southward loomed the glaciated spires of Mount Aspiring and the remote Mount Aspiring National Park. A vast and wild country indeed...

In retrospect, this warm-up hike turned out to be as strenuous as anything encountered on the Milford Track just days later. But I wanted to pace myself and save reserve strength for the challenges soon to come. I took it easy on the down hike but was actually pretty whipped on finally making it back to the trailhead, some six tough hours later.

DDU Blog entry: The following day, I took the scenic drive over Cardrona Pass down into Queenstown, which lies in a deep valley alongside the vast, austere Lake Wakatipu. Queenstown is the outdoor adventure capital of NZ, and the birthplace of bungee- jumping. There are a million ways to break a sweat, strain your liver and spend a buck in this town. At mid-summer, mid-winter in the Northern Hemisphere, the place is literally chockers with adventure seekers from seemingly everywhere on the planet. It's perfectly pleasant to visit in its own right, but I was here for a very specific purpose: as the link-up for a five-day, 56-kilometer (~35 mile) hike on the Milford Track with Ultimate Hikes NZ. After spending the afternoon exploring the compact, busy, lakeside downtown, there was a pre-trip orientation at the Ultimate Hikes headquarters. That meeting really built-up the sense of impending epic adventure. Meeting and greeting fellow hikers from around the world, as well as the young, highly enthusiastic guide crew was energizing. Show time! Then it was off to bed for a fitful night's sleep and an early morning departure for Lake Te Anau and further wild places beyond. Stay tuned for the next, riveting installment. Will they make it out alive? With how many life-threatening blisters sustained? Or perhaps resort to cannibalism in the trackless wilds of South Island New Zealand? We'll have to see how it all plays out, gentle reader...

Solo Hiking the Milford Track:

The Milford is considered one of the finest multi-day hikes in the world. It's not the hardest by any means. Rather, the way it's laid-out builds the excitement gradually, across diverse New Zealand environments of sublime beauty, all culminating in a challenging thousand-foot, over-ridge hike and finally a long rainforest slog out. It covers around 56 km (35 miles), with most of the hiking occurring over three 16- 21 km (10-13 mile) days. Thus, considered only a moderately difficult long hike, it's more of an orthopedic endurance test than a technical challenge. But it is a pretty fair cardio-vascular workout, without question.

The Fiordland region of southwestern New Zealand is a vast temperate rainforest, and World Heritage area. Parts are still so remote that the Takahe, a large, blue and unfortunately flightless bird, was recently rediscovered here in the wild, densely forested mountains. Takahe had been considered extinct for over fifty years but had somehow found hidden refuge in these remote forests! There's now a reserve, near the tiny town of Te Anau we passed through, that's dedicated to propagating Takahe chicks and releasing them back into the Fiordland wilderness.

DDU Blog entry: The Milford Track is really popular, but still quite remote. You have to drive three and a half hours south from Queenstown, and then take a local ferry up Lake Te Anau for another hour and a half just to get to the trailhead. There are public shelters on the trail but permits need to be booked a year in advance. The hiking season only runs for around six months, from October to April, as frigid weather, flash flooding and avalanche danger close the track seasonally for fully half the year. You must carry shelter, even if you have cabin permits; hiking is one-way, and you must move onward daily. If you miss a bus or ferry connection, well you're stuffed, mate...

Ultimate Hikes NZ is the only private company licensed to operate on the Track and removes all the pesky logistical details for the busy visitor. For a very fair price they arrange all permits and transportation, provide private bunk rooms with hot showers and real beds, and prepare all food and snacks for four nights and five days. For me, as a first timer to NZ, it was definitely the way to go. NB: you still have to put in the hard yakka and hike those miles, though with a lighter daypack of less than fifteen kg. Another really great aspect of the guided hike is the friendly, knowledgeable guides. Every evening, they hold an informative talk on the day's events, local history, flora/fauna and a preview of the next day's challenges.

After the long, scenic bus ride around the shores of Lake Wakatipu, down to the tiny lakeside village of Te Anau, we linked up with the ferry to the head of Lake Te Anau and the trailhead. It was a pretty wild and windy affair, with whitecaps and angry gray cloud-cover brooding overhead, as we motored some twenty miles north, up to the very head of the lake and into the impressively steep and threatening alpine mountains dead ahead. Very reminiscent of the Alaskan panhandle around Sitka, taking me back to my times living there (1977-80) in my introspective, rail-side reminisces. Like every other hiker on this adventure, I was lost in thought, quietly calculating my current level of fitness versus the challenges awaiting just before me. I was no longer a strapping twenty-four-year-old lad, that much was certain! Towards evening, the ceiling lifted partially, and we had high hopes for better weather and visibility by morning. An interesting aspect of this, my first-ever group hike, was to meet people from all over the world and hear their stories. On our first overnight at the rustic Glade House, after dinner, we each got up and gave a five-minute introduction and statement of purpose to the entire group. Many of the stories were quite touching. Newly minted widows, cancer survivors, honeymooners, family reunions... Fifty strangers all working towards the same goal, for many disparate reasons. The esprit de corps was high and over the next three challenging days, bonds and memories were forged.

As a marquee hiking destination, the trails, bridges and shelters along the Milford are maintained to a world-class standard. The public overnight shelters are placed a mile or so beyond the Ultimate Hikes private camps, so you rarely encounter the groups ahead of you, as they have a healthy head start every morning. No fires or bush camping are allowed on the track, and hikers must keep moving every day. Another nice feature of the Milford is that it's a one-way trail. Once you get into your groove, you hardly see anyone else all day long except at rest stops. No "trail etiquette" required working past oncoming groups. The entire experience is well-managed and feels authentic, uncrowded and still somehow pristine. Very fine indeed.

After the first night's excellent dinner and orientation at cozy, historic Glade House, right alongside Lake Te Anau, we settled in for a furtive night's rest on unfamiliar bunks, each silently hoping we were truly prepared for the strenuous days ahead. Morning dawned crystal-clear and chilly. We were soon out on the trail, each lost in our own thoughts, wending our way gradually higher through the pristine, virgin New Zealand Silver and Red Beech forests, up into the higher reaches of the Clinton River Valley. It's a long sixteen km day, but the intriguing excitement of the unfolding trail keeps you alert and engaged. High in the Clinton Canyon, after breaking out above timberline, except for scattered and sparse stands of stunted alpine beech, the sheer granite walls rise dramatically for thousands of feet, on both sides above the rocky, thread-like trail. Later that evening, at remote but well-appointed Pompolona Lodge, we spent a memorable alpenglow sharing our trail experiences of the first day's hike while sipping a glass of well-earned Kiwi wine and watching the dusk deepen over the snow-sharpened summits towering overhead. A tiring but successful day, building confidence for the next day's challenge, and hardest bit: getting intact over MacKinnon Pass, 1069m (3507 ft), which sits as a steep ridge blocking the dead-end canyon at the terminus of the glacial valley; and lying unseen, massive and immovable, just ahead.

On day three (full hiking day two) the weather dawned perfectly bright and clear, and we were packed up and moving again, on the trail while the valley floor still lay in deep, finger-numbing shadow. The ridge gradually revealed itself as a large bread loaf saddle looming straight ahead, directly across our path. Deep, confident breaths...steady... No turning back now; we were all fully committed and moving forward determinedly, not wanting to appear to straggle or need guide assistance. The tight switchbacks provided brief, welcome relief for burning calves and thighs, as the terrain steepened dramatically. The vistas looking back down the ground fog-enshrouded Clinton Valley were utterly sublime: the sheer, exposed cliffs plunging thousands of feet, straight down into the cloud-covered valley floor now far below. The actual dreamscape of a mythical New Zealand, that you are now fully immersed within...and the unforgettable reward for undertaking such a journey.

But the stronger urge to get this tough bit behind you kept one moving forward, even through the fatigue. After an hour or so of hard going, I could sense success near at hand. We were now breaking out of the stunted timberline, sheltered in a lee just under the treeless ridgetop. A raw wind was rising sharply, and ragged clouds were moving in fast flight, just overhead. The guides paused and were rugging-up for the final move over the exposed summit ridge and I did the same. It was all very thrilling, as less than fifteen adrenalized minutes later, we crossed over the windswept Pass summit and came upon the austere, iconic MacKinnon Memorial. Ultimate Hikes sure lived up to its moniker then, as a cheery guide walked over and offered, "Care for a spot of hot tea?" as he extended the proffered beverage, along with a few sweet bikkies (biscuits, or cookies) to boot. Well, never... in my entire hiking life...! It was, truly, an awesome, even ultimate, on-trail moment. And marked a minor celebration of this very personal achievement. Here at the Pass, we also saw Keas up close; the cheeky, large, forest-green, native mountain parrots of NZ. Beautiful, stocky birds with a deep red underwing, they are the only true alpine parrots in the world. Just watch your gear, as they are real rascals and will make off with whatever they can, edible or not, and quicker than you might expect!

After reaching MacKinnon Pass, the work's certainly not over. For many hikers, the final 5.5 km (3.5 mile), steep down-hike to Quintin Lodge on day three is the real crux and knee-strainer of the trip. We took a short break out of the rising weather at the functional, but basic shelter lying just below the Pass; and tried out the iconic and well-named "Loo with a View" perched and bolted precariously onto the ridge, and looked out high over the Clinton Valley, right from the toilet seat. Still higher above, mountain summits and snowfields danced fleetingly with the shifting sunlight and breeze-racing cloud shadows in 360 degrees. Not a place to linger, it was time to move on... I gathered my energy reserves and prepared mentally for the long slog down to Quintin Lodge, sited thousands of feet below, on the Arthur River Valley floor. The Arthur River was intermittently visible as a silver thread, shimmering under the shattered sunlight and swirling cloud cover, from atop the aptly named "Twelve-second Drop" off the back side of the Pass. And it looked a very long drop, indeed. It was a strenuous down-hike, which grew somewhat painful towards the end of the steep and long fifteen km (ten mile) day; but one that was passed dreamily weaving through beautiful re-emerging beech forest pockets and along musically tumbling alpine streams. The down-climb was assisted greatly by the most extensive use of metal ladders and temporary stair sections I've ever experienced in the wilds. Beautifully engineered, and protective of the delicate alpine environment, the trail traveled right along the pristine, tumbling headwaters of the Arthur River, and allowed safe access to intimate views of numerous small cataracts and hidden waterholes. Passing rhythmically through this unique and mystical forest landscape kept the curiosity and energy levels high; but it was so easy to zone out mentally. You need to watch your footing at all times, as it's rough and slippery underfoot. Having arrived at Quintin Lodge, now under a light, misty rain, I really just wanted a hot shower, a cold beer and a well-earned rest. However, the rest must be brief, and the beer delayed, if you intend to make the optional five km (three mile), ninety-minute, additional side trip out to Sutherland Falls and back before dark.

At 580m, nearly 2000 feet, it's the world's fifth highest waterfall and New Zealand's highest. A thunderous triple cascade that overwhelms with its raw power, it's definitely worth the extra effort. You can hear the roar increasing as you approach from a mile away. Thrilling! Once finally at its base, yet another awesome NZ experience is to brave the gale-force blast off the falls and hike laterally up towards the cliff face, over slippery, moss-strewn boulders, while staying just clear of the main stream of the falls. As you get closer, the water is blown horizontally off the rocks with remarkable energy. An icy, stinging spray, it's reminiscent of being hit in the face by a massive hose of blinding, frigid water...What fun! Up this close, the noise is simply deafening, thrusting fiercely like a jet engine. You must keep moving, quickly. Once safely tucked in the lee alongside the perpetually soaked wall face, you can then inch along behind the falls, and are suddenly standing within a relatively quiet pocket directly behind the thunderous cataract, which is striking the rocky base thirty feet out in front of you with tremendous force. You return along the same hazardous path, but with the wind and spray now thankfully at your back. Soaked to the bone, right through your rain gear, but feeling more alive than you have in a very long while, it's time to high-five your mates, and head back to the Quintin Lodge for that hot shower before full nightfall. Sutherland Falls was an utterly exhilarating side trip, one that was certainly worth the extra exertion at the end of an already tiring day.

We'd been fortunate and had relatively excellent weather crossing over MacKinnon Pass, but that was now changing rapidly and threatening to close in fully at any time. This actually added to the sense of high adventure, if not perhaps actual danger. It had finally begun raining in earnest late on the third day as we approached Quintin Lodge. But we'd been lucky indeed. The guides remarked that on the past two, five-day hikes, they saw not one ray of sunlight over ten days! And apparently, only one third of days on the Pass has any visibility at all. So, we were quite fortunate to enjoy the dramatic, broad vistas of the Southern Alps under widely broken cloud cover. In an unexpected sense, having the rain falling now that we were all safely, and scenically, over MacKinnon Pass, became somehow a positive feature - giving the track an entirely different feel. Numerous waterfalls magically appeared, flowing lace-like from over the cliff faces on both sides of the valley, a thousand feet overhead. The rivulets and creeks were all running hard, filling the air with water music from every direction. And the verdant, variegated greens of the dense foliage glistened with a magical iridescence. It completed the rainforest effect, you might say... I slept soundly in the dry, heated cabin, on a basic but supportive mattress. Certainly, a luxurious giant step above my usual and customary back-country digs!

Day four is a long one, ~22 km (13.5 miles), but you are relieved to be over the Pass and on the long downhill lope out to Sandfly Point and the ferry to Milford Sound village. The miles and hours pass pleasantly, as you get into the rhythm of the trail; your boots working the gradually flattening ground, and you drift away into your deepest, meditative thoughts. It's one of the aspects I most love about long hikes. When else do you get to experience that degree of private, undisturbed mindfulness for rhythmic hours on end?

There was a real sense of accomplishment and camaraderie on our finally reaching the trail terminus at Sandfly Point. After group photos and a short wait, we were soon aboard the antique local ferry for the brief transfer downriver to the Mitre Peak Lodge on Milford Sound, our final night's lodging. And then, almost miraculously, the low cloud ceiling began to lift again towards evening, and we were treated to the sublime Grand Finale of the stunning Mitre Peak looming over placid Milford Sound in the clearing evening twilight. This is a view that many travel great distances to see, and are often denied, due to the persistent, low-hanging cloud cover. Fortunate folks indeed... The evening finished off with a bountiful dinner and a really funny awards ceremony and talent show, liberally lubricated with adult beverages, now that we were all safely off the track. Only then did we discover that a quiet, unassuming Japanese gentleman had been the oldest person in our group. He had completed the Milford Track, without assistance, at seventy-nine years old. How inspiring!

The final morning dawned, offering a robin's-egg blue, cloudless sky. The fine adventure, and great weather, continued as the hike culminated with a two-hour cruise of the entire, fabled Milford Sound, even out onto the open Tasman Sea, all arranged by Ultimate Hikes and part of the package. None of us could believe our good fortune with the sudden weather change. The boat pilot said it was the best day on the Sound in over three months! We glided over puddle-smooth waters out through the fiord mouth, and onto the now limpid, but rarely placid, Tasman Sea, enjoying the majestic spectacle of the peak-hemmed fiord completely unimpeded by cloud cover. A lifetime memory certainly; and a wonderful way to cap off our successful hike.

Finally, the Ultimate Hikes custom coach was waiting to take us back around Lakes Te Anau and Wakatipu, and into Queenstown and civilization. Spirits were high, legs sore, and a real sense of shared success pervaded the group. You sit back, stretch out and relax. Enjoying the passing scenery, you've sure earned it. And then suddenly, too soon in fact, the bus halts, you step off and are thrust back into reality in busy downtown Queenstown. The past five days of camaraderie, shared effort and accomplishment - a sweet memory, but already passing. Fifty people working towards a common goal, each for very different reasons, now scattering around the globe, most never to be seen again.

In sum, hiking the Milford Track accomplished a life-long personal goal, which, while certainly not the extreme technical climbing adventures of my younger, wilder days, provided a challenge to work up to and complete with reasonable odds of success. The trip was even better than anticipated, and I expected it would be great! Ultimate Hikes took care of all the tricky logistical considerations, and allowed for peace of mind, as well as a lighter pack, which made the entire experience more enjoyable. They come very highly recommended for those with a little extra coin in pocket, and the desire to experience such an epic adventure while touring

New Zealand. In fact, I'm now planning to attempt the Routeburn Track, a three-day, high-alpine hike, with them next year, if all the logistics can be worked out.

Queenstown North to Christchurch:

DDU Blog entry: An easy attraction to miss is the beautiful botanic garden in Queenstown; on a point in the lake, right downtown, it's definitely worth a few hours of your time. There are moving memorials to New Zealand climbers who died exploring and climbing in these beautiful, but treacherous mountains. But, after a relaxing garden stroll, the open road once again beckoned...

Heading north into the Gibbston Valley and beyond is a very different experience than the road south. First stop: the actual birthplace of bungee-jumping in 1988, at Kawarau Bridge, over Kawarau Gorge, only a few miles out of Queenstown. It's all been upgraded into a high-tech, adrenaline-pumping machine, but the heritage wooden railroad bridge, c 1880, remains intact. Surprisingly, they let you walk right up close to the action. Close enough, indeed, to "smell the fear..." as people get their courage up and submit to the adrenaline rush of willingly free-falling for a hundred feet or so down into the surging river below. You can even choose the degree of ice-water dunking you prefer, from "None, thanks" up to and including whole-hog immersion. With five young kids to raise, Stephanie had made me promise not to try anything foolish, like this... So, I had an airtight excuse for not participating. Movie scenes from the Lord of The Rings were filmed here; it's a very dramatic river canyon landscape. For any travelers, this is a very entertaining, and free stop, even if you don't plan on hurling yourself off the bridge into the canyon below.

Soon after leaving the irrigated Gibbston Valley vineyards and orchards of the Central Otago plateau, the landscape changes dramatically, becoming higher and much drier. Beyond the fruit-growing areas around Bannockburn and Cromwell, where I bought a bagful of gorgeous, juicy, local cherries for the ride, the landscape feels reminiscent of the arid American west - Wyoming or even Nevada. Vast plains of dry button-grass stretch to the rolling, treeless horizons out here. The only thing missing is the evensong of lonesome coyotes...

The long, rural drive north takes you through the old company town of Twizel, built to house workers on the surrounding hydro-electric projects, and finally along man-made Lake Pukaki towards the towering heights of the very ruggedly alpine Southern Alps. The storm clouds were building ominously over the mountains to the west and the landscape became even more infertile. Open vistas with wide, braided-river flats backed by towering glaciated peaks... Suddenly, interior Alaska! It felt as if I were suddenly transported, and again driving alone on an approach road to Denali, Alaska circa 1979; now some decades and a million miles in my past from this breathtaking moment. Miraculously, once again on this trip, the clouds parted at the critical juncture and there loomed the very summit of ice bound Aoraki/ Mt Cook, luminescent in the evening light at 3724m (over 12,000 ft) above the valley floor and mirrored across the placid face of Lake Pukaki. Similar to Milford Sound, it's a vista many travel long miles to see, though oftentimes in vain, obscured, as it so often is, by dense, lingering cloud cover. That old Nolan luck was holding fast once again, it seemed.

Heading west into the National Park past Lake Pukaki, the terrain becomes resolutely alpine, essentially tundra. High up in the Hooker Valley, I spent a rather sleepless night in my trusty mountain tent, being rattled by clear, sharp winds gusting to over 100 km/hr (60 mph) off the mountains rising just above me. Curiously, the wind built up in force and then barreled down off the high glaciers into the valley and hit with a sudden, violent rush. I could hear them approaching. Things would then quiet down for a bit, only for the process to repeat again. I've been in lots of severe mountain weather in Alaska and the Northern Rockies, with it typically being more continuous over the hours. A few times, I actually thought my stout little tent would be shredded, it shook so violently; but no, we passed the sleepless hours without disaster. Perhaps I should've shelled out the dough for a calmer night tucked away within the steel-clad Hermitage Hotel, standing sentinel across the austere valley...

One thing not to miss at Mt Cook NP is the wonderful, free museum that details the history of NZ mountaineering, including the storied career of Sir Edmund Hillary, who trained here for his successful first ascent of Mt Everest. There's a larger, fee-based museum too, but the little one I visited seemed perfectly adequate. It contains a very moving display and memorial to all the lives lost while climbing among the NZ mountaineering fraternity over the years. And the tally is fairly sobering indeed, and ongoing...

Next morning, awakening under beautiful sunshine and light breezes for a four-hour solo hike up the Hooker Valley, I felt tired but rejuvenated. Under fair skies, the Hooker Valley appears like the perfect alpine valley of your dreams. There are tour operators who do guided day tours here-but save your money. This is an easy, exciting hike that you can plan on your own. Just pack a lunch, water and sunblock and head off. The clear trail follows a glacial stream, including crossing a very high, iconic NZ swing-bridge, for several miles up to a moraine lake, terminating right at the very foot of Mt Cook. Impressive, glaciated peaks tower all around if the weather is favorable. I hiked under flawless, azure skies, feeling like the luckiest guy alive. High up, the vegetation becomes sparse due to the many months of snow cover and poor soils. There are some remarkable high-altitude plants, some actually flowering, hanging on tenaciously in small depressions or hard against the sheltering rocks. Mt Cook NP was a definite highlight of the trip. Much more austerely alpine than I expected. The fine weather and impressive scenery helped; but if you come well-prepared, even in less-than-ideal conditions you won't regret the effort required to get here.

Heading still north a further few hours towards Christchurch, you'll arrive at Lake Tekapo, one of a series of large, turquoise, glacial lakes flowing out of the Southern Alps. This is the heart of the MacKenzie Country - a vast, sub-alpine plateau, settled by tough Scottish/Irish shepherds in the 1840's and still wild and sparsely populated to this day. Sheep herding remains the primary occupation in this austere, but intensely scenic, area. Hiking up Mt John, a small mountain on the southwestern corner of Lake Tekapo, is a must do. The views across this sprawling region are awe-inspiring, and there's even a highly regarded summit cafe, as well as a natural hot spring at the base, for an after-hike reward. The campground here is beautiful, being right on the lake, and sited next to the hot springs. Plan on two nights at least. Because of its isolation and clear, dark skies, Mt John is also the site of a major Observatory for the Canterbury University of Christchurch. Not something you see on many summits, and it adds an interesting dimension to an already sublime day hike. In terms of bang-for-the-buck, Mt. John is certainly one of the best short-day hikes I've *ever done, and I've done quite a few in my day. Give it a go, you'll be richly rewarded for your efforts.*

Just out of town is the ridiculously photogenic, rugged stone Church of the Good Shepherd, built in 1935, the scene of uncountable, lakeside weddings and calendar shoots. Much less known is the nearby Collie monument, a touching tribute to the sheep dogs that helped settle this wild country. Both are well worth your time; just make sure you have a camera along. Tekapo also has, surprisingly, one of the best Japanese restaurants in New Zealand at Kohan. Try the locally raised Salmon Teriyaki; it's wonderful. A surprising find in this tiny Kiwi community, and highly recommended.

Heading several hours still further north brings us back into Christchurch. I arrived a full day early for one final Kiwi adventure. A Belgian hitchhiker I'd picked up on my journey had raved about the unusual beauty of the Banks Peninsula, an unusually variegated coastline which is actually a massive, collapsed and flooded volcano caldera. And even better, it's only an hour's drive southeast of the Christchurch CBD. Surprisingly, the main town and harbor, Akaroa (literally meaning "Long Harbor" in Maori), was originally settled by French sailors in August 1840, prior to New Zealand being claimed by Great Britain. They stayed on, and now, over one hundred and fifty years later, there exists a tiny outpost of Gallic culture on the South Island of NZ. A most remarkable historical anomaly. The peninsula is a genteel weekend playground for Christchurchians, and retains a very charming, pastoral feel, like some long lost Caribbean isle.

But the activity I was specifically here for was a dolphin cruise on the Fox 2, a restored, antique wooden 1920's ketch, run by an American expat couple from New York City. Several people told me it was a "Top Three" New Zealand experience, so I just had to get aboard. The weather was, again, eerily perfect; the companionship lively and fun; and the American skipper very enthusiastic and informative. It was a perfect way to spend my final full day in NZ. Under fine skies and light, favorable winds we sailed down the long harbor of Akaroa, through the ancient, collapsed caldera wall and out onto the open sea, passing the impressive caldera sea cliffs and seeing lots of bird and wildlife.

As fantastic as the entire experience was, the star feature of the day was the gregarious pod of Hector's Dolphins that played in the rolling swells, right alongside the boat, once we were outside the harbor mouth. They are the world's smallest (~ three feet) and rarest dolphin; less than two thousand are estimated to remain in the wild. This is the only place on earth you are likely to encounter them, so we felt very blessed and fortunate to have had the experience. And I have to agree, a day sail on the Fox 2 out of Akaroa was a top Kiwi experience for me too. If you are in the area, and have the time, it's a must do...

From Akaroa town, you can drive the impossibly windy, caldera summit road back towards Christchurch. It's an outstanding drive, feeling very remote and somehow Mediterranean, but "keep your eyes on the road and your hands upon the wheel..." for sure. Rural side roads drop invitingly down into hidden coves and inlets along the deeply fissured coastline, inviting leisurely exploration. But I had to get back for the next day's flight out to Brisbane. If you had time sufficient, one could easily spend a very pleasant week or two out here exploring all the little harbors, hamlets, nooks and crannies along the rural byways. And there are said to be excellent long-distance hiking trails to some of the more remote outlooks on the Peninsula as well. Perhaps for another time...

Alas, even the best adventures have to end; and life, work, family, reality soon enough intrude. That said, these eighteen days spent solo, out on the backroads of SINZ felt like a real gift, and a vital rejuvenation of my busy life back in Brisbane. And that's how the perfect trip should end: not with regret, but anticipation. As great as it all was, I found myself feeling ready to get home, sleep in my own bed, pick up Stephanie and the kids returning from the USA the following day, and settle back into our familiar routine together. Hopefully, there will be many further adventures still to come; but the warm, vivid memories of this one can sustain me for a long while, indeed, until then. I headed back to Brisbane well-satisfied, fulfilled and fairly certain that I would be returning to Aotearoa, the Land of the Long White Cloud, for further Kiwi adventures in the not-too-distant future.

And I'm sure Stephanie and the kids felt that same anticipation to see Dad once again and settle back into our "home" in Raby Bay, Cleveland, Queensland... Australia, after their own exciting adventures back in the USA for Christmas 2013, New Years 2014 and beyond. The kids love to tease me endlessly about being a tightwad. But when you have five kids, spending decisions are always about priorities, believe me... You can always spend more on, well, everything! Our second car is a beat-up old Nissan sedan that the kids aptly nicknamed the "beach banger." Whatever, it gets me the two miles to work and back dependably. We don't have a big power boat, though I'd love to. Only an aluminum dinghy, powered with oars. I try to impart a life lesson here, by repeatedly saying "You'll know what I really value by what I spend my money on." For us that looks like kids, travel experiences, active adventures in the outdoors and perhaps the occasional guitar or fishing rod. That's, self-evidently, what I value. And I think we've made some very good choices. We had an energetic, cheerful reunion the next day at the Brisbane airport, followed by us eagerly sharing our many travelers' tales, recounted over a feast of excellent Aussie fish and chips. For each of us, home now really felt like the place we were all together, safe and sound, "Team Nolan".

CHAPTER 28: More Aussie Emergency Medical Adventures

July 2014

Going into our third year overseas, I was now settled into the work routine at our local Emergency Department (ED). I had attained my FACEM, or Fellowship in Australian Emergency Medicine, so was a fully credentialed senior Consultant, and was fully integrated into the culture of the ED and larger hospital system. And over this time, I was also becoming more aware of both the pros and cons of working in such a publicly-funded healthcare system.

As a Queensland state employee, I appreciated the job stability, and the pay and benefits. By US standards they were quite generous. Also, the Australian, team-based teaching model was very satisfying professionally. I was supervising teams of doctors, at every level from medical student up to very senior, fifth- and sixth-year EM trainees. This British-modeled training pathway can be very long, requiring up to twelve years to attain full specialty Fellowship. So, there was a robust educational training program on-site, happening daily, which I was actively participating in.

But, on the other hand, our patient census and acuity seemed to be ever increasing, and it was becoming obvious to me that our local long-term, public healthcare planning was not keeping up with the area's burgeoning population growth and healthcare needs. The number of new housing developments that had started up, even since our arrival, was astonishing. Springing up like mushrooms after a rain, and ever more increasing.

The need for ambulance "ramping", i.e., holding patients at the front door, literally "on the ramp", was now becoming our daily, near continuous reality. By 1000 am on most days, the place was chockers, with minimal forward movement, especially of already admitted patients, seen overnight and awaiting very tight in-patient beds. The ED staff were very professional and hard working - screening (or triaging) incoming patients and trying to prioritize who got moved ahead in the queue. The prior regional model of evaluating all patients at the less-resourced outlying community hospitals, such as ours, and then transferring those needing emergency specialist care efficiently into the larger tertiary hospitals in Brisbane was starting to break down, as these larger hospitals were straining under their own insatiable patient demands. That older patient-flow model was predicated on there being upstream in-patient capacity that no longer existed predictably. Very sick people were routinely sitting for hours, with nowhere to go. Acute mental health patients waited the longest for definitive care, as in the US. We would often discharge marginal patients home from the ED for outpatient management, many of whom would ideally have been admitted to hospital if more capacity existed. In fact, a large portion of my expertise was now consumed by rounding with the team and making the final determination as to who could safely go, and who had to stay, or be transferred into Brisbane. Final decisions were oftentimes driven by that day's bed situation frankly, because there were always more at the door, seeking emergency care. It became common to admit a patient, and then fully manage their care in the ED or adjacent short-stay area, and finally discharge them directly home from the ED after 24-72 hours. They might never actually make it to their assigned inpatient bed at all! But this discussion is in no way meant to disparage the Australian publicly-funded healthcare system, which I feel is probably as good a system as you'll find. My intent is to give the non-medical reader a sense of the daily realities faced by staff and patients on the Emergency Medicine front-lines. These same issues of lack of capacity and supply-demand- funding realities exist in the USA and probably worldwide. It's just a matter of degrees, and proactive systems planning, or not... "Older, sicker, poorer, fatter..." Drip, drip, drip...

At our local hospital, the short-term, politically and fiscally expedient fix had been to attach a much larger, fully modern ED, to the very basic, existent community hospital, with no after-hours specialty services or expanded inpatient capacity. But this model was now clearly failing. We currently had a sixty-thousand patient annual ED census, rapidly growing along with the community, managed in our fifty-four bed ED. The local hospital had no ICU, and only general Internists in house. Surgical capacity was nil, especially after hours and on weekends. We had no Orthopedic service locally at all, and thus were managing complex Ortho cases in the ED without local back-up. In fairness, permanently staffing all these services, while highly desirable for all involved, is a very expensive and lengthy process; but it was becoming clear that we were falling behind the predictable needs of the area.

There were some innovative, out-patient follow-up and home care initiatives being put into place, but they were only partial solutions. We essentially needed an entirely new hospital - a very expensive proposition indeed, and one with a multi-year lead time. Our patient metrics, "waiting to be seen" and "ED throughput times" were among the worst in the entire state. On the back end, "patient in-patient days" were among the shortest state-wide, by necessity, as patients were being discharged as quickly as possible to free up critically needed in-patient capacity. But this inevitably caused our "unexpected 48-hour returns", or "bounce-backs" to rise as well, both from the ED as well as in-patient services. In truth, many patients were being discharged, that might not have been, in a more fully resourced system.

But these systemic capacity issues are in no way unique to QLDH or Australia. They're a very real and growing problem virtually worldwide. The only meaningful discussion, to my mind, revolves around how honestly and efficiently a system can acknowledge and try to respond to them. And at what sustainable cost. These are ultimately broader societal issues and decisions being played out daily in the ED environment. Many healthcare systems appear to me to be dangerously stressed and fraying.

Again, none of this discussion is meant to disparage the incredibly hardworking and capable QLDH Medical, Nursing and ancillary personnel in any way. But, when you have good people working in a dysfunctional, or under-funded system, bad outcomes become inevitable. At least as a Queensland state employee, I didn't have that overwhelming sense of naked exposure to litigation that all American physicians face on a daily basis. If a lawsuit were to arise, the plaintiff essentially would have to sue the state government, as opposed to the individual physician, who is working as an agent of the state - absent gross misconduct or professional incompetence. This seemed a major benefit of the Australian system to me.

I reveal these issues as a warning of sorts to those in the USA who imagine that a single-payer, state-run healthcare system would somehow be a panacea and solve all healthcare issues, neatly and cleanly, and at low-cost. Not so - and in some ways, considering my professional experiences, some aspects may actually be a worse construct from the patient's perspective. Some American politicians actually propose a direct government take-over of the extant private system and implementation of a mandatory public system. Soundbites are cheap; most politicians appear utterly clueless to me, and the public, in general, seems to want easy solutions. But that won't get you to a more functional, sustainable healthcare system. Trust me...I'm a doctor.

Doctor Dennis March, my direct medical supervisor, increasingly began to seek my opinions and observations, coming as I was, from a very different healthcare background. We had many deep and incisive conversations on improving our current situation by "working with what we had at hand." Through him, I also began gradually to understand the political and funding realities that existed within the Australian system.

Every system will have, by definition, its limitations and fiscal realities. The pie really is only so large. And the voters ultimately decide how large a pie they're willing to fund. Absent gross deficit spending, which seems a painless, short-term solution, but isn't ethical or sustainable in the long-term, budget constraints inevitably become clinical realities. Once any system begins to strain against the essentially limitless demands placed on it, all sorts of unanticipated deformities and perversions begin to appear. With my background, I consider this as a given. The primary questions I then raise are along the lines of: How transparent and honest is the system in identifying and promptly addressing its high-risk areas? How transparent and accurate is the data collection being used to drive clinical and policy initiatives? Are resource allocation decisions being made in the interest of legitimate patient care demands, or political expediency? How accepting and protective of whistle-blowers and challengers to the in-grained status-quo is the organization? While not probably on the top of everyone's mind, understanding how these systemic questions reinforce or ameliorate system inefficiencies and misaligned incentives ultimately affects outcomes across broad populations, i.e., allows for better or worse healthcare outcomes. These questions ultimately get to the heart of a healthcare organization's culture and its willingness and capacity to healthily evolve.

I began to understand that the most significant flaw in a publicly-funded system such as Australia's is that ultimately, control of the funding, and thus resource allocation, is moved almost entirely out of the healthcare and medical systems administration realms, and into the political. Lacking any significant, countervailing, private revenue stream, most financial resources available to the public healthcare facilities ultimately come from government policy makers. This may result in healthcare policy decisions that, from my observations, may not be made on a strictly medical-need basis.

So, for instance, an electoral swing seat may get a huge infusion of healthcare funding leading up to a tight election, while an area of greater need, that's less contested politically, goes without. This can have real-world, patient care implications. My Aussie mates observe these sorts of schemes with an attitude of somewhat resigned cynicism. Of course, these kinds of political deals happen in American politics too, but because, in the USA, the bulk of political healthcare influence lies within the private healthcare industry, they have more leeway to make independent resourcing decisions. For example, the Mayo Clinic doesn't depend directly on the State of Minnesota to plan or fund its ongoing operations. The primarily publicly-funded Australian healthcare system appears much more dependent on the whims of the political class for its funding, to this observer. And in truth, the last group of people I'd want setting our healthcare resourcing priorities and agendas would be the politicians.

Even more concerning, because Australia functions under a Parliamentary system, an election can be called, and a government changed, whenever it's deemed politically expedient. This occurred with surprising frequency during our six years in-country. But unfortunately, as Aussie public healthcare funding is tied much more tightly to the political system, the various funding priorities seemed to change regularly with the changing of the political guard. While I'm not an expert in these matters, longer-term healthcare funding decisions and priorities seemed intimately caught up in the ongoing political scrum. In any ideal healthcare model, the long-term funding stream and planning priorities should be as sequestered as possible from the political arena and administered by a more stable cadre of professional healthcare systems administrative and financial specialists, working closely with clinicians. This, by the way, is more typical of the larger not-for-profit private healthcare networks currently operating in the USA, such as the Mayo, Geisinger and Cleveland Clinics etc.

On the other hand, back in the USA, in our understandable attempts to avoid an overarching government-run healthcare bureaucracy, we have in large measure succumbed to a corporate-model bureaucracy that, while generally delivering high-quality clinical healthcare in a cost-efficient manner, comes with much higher charges to the patient. Due to the ever-growing need for profitability and sky-high managerial margins, we have perhaps traded one set of problems for another. Excessive clinical patient care charges and billing thus subsidize extensive non-clinical activities and administrative expenses. Sure, the healthcare in the USA is generally good, but how many citizens can't afford it, and are thus going without? On balance, I believe that the Australian model of universal access to basic, high-quality care for all citizens is the superior model, although one with its own set of complex issues and limitations.

One real-world example of what can go wrong with a distant, centrally-planned, healthcare bureaucracy was the new six-bed pediatric emergency area built adjacent to our current ED. Again, not to disparage, but perhaps enlighten. Dr. March explained to me that he'd had zero input into its design or implementation, even though he'd been the long-term, highly experienced medical director of the ED. A team of "experts" was brought in from Brisbane, who over-designed the unit for daily community ED needs. Each bay was fully outfitted, at great additional cost, with full cardiac monitors, critical-care style trolleys, wall oxygen and suction, the whole kit bag. Equipment that you might need to treat perhaps one or two percent of a community ED pediatric population. But curiously, there were no fast-track bays, asthma chairs, or rapid assessment and throughput areas. Even stranger, although the unit was built hard up against the current ED waiting room, someone in authority decided it was "unsafe" to have the door to the pediatric area open directly into the common ED waiting area, which also happened to contain all the patient intake and registration functions. Thus, they then built an alternate, sequestered pediatric ED entrance inside the hospital, again at additional cost. And unfortunately, because these designers didn't actually work clinically at our facility, or apparently understand basic ED patient flow patterns, this caused the pediatric patients and their families to have to routinely enter the common ED intake area anyway (to register), then enter through the standard ED entrance, only to then have to traverse the busiest corridor in the hospital, lying as it was between the main ED and the ED Radiology suite! Thus, they're dodging moving patient trolleys and portable X-Ray machines, just to be able to enter the brand-new entrance to the pediatric area; all in the name of patient safety. Incredible, but true.

But it gets even better! Our beautiful, if costly, pediatric area was finally opened to great fanfare. The regional politicians and administrators all came out for the opening ceremony. There were articles and photos in the local papers. Everyone took a bit of credit for their good works. But then, stasis... Nothing changed... We weren't allowed to bring patients back into the unit. It seems no one had budgeted for the additional personnel required to actually staff the unit. And given that it was purposely designed as a separate, enclosed space, it was deemed to be unsafe to utilize, unless it had dedicated staff on-site. Thus, this shining little unit of critically needed capacity sat unused, but fully stocked and ready for action, for over a year, until the staffing logistics could be worked out, budgeted for and implemented. Struth mate, fair dinkum? Bloody oath! Somehow, I have difficulty imagining a high-performing US healthcare organization, such as the Mayo Clinic, allowing planning inefficiencies of this sort. But conversely, another gradual realization for me was to consider that in a completely publicly-funded system, with no billing for even basic services, and therefore no recurring operational cash-flow, every additional service or patient encounter represents an additional expenditure or cost to the system. Thus, from an administrator's point of view, less services provided might be considered a positive, without robust additional funding from the state government. This financial reality might partially explain the apparent lack of incentive to get our new pediatric area up and running. I can only surmise, as I had no direct input or communication in these matters.

So, in brief summary, I think it's important for all to have a healthy skepticism of non-clinical healthcare "experts" offering simple solutions. If there were any, they'd already be implemented. Change must and will come to the delivery of healthcare in the USA, by necessity, and driven by fiscal reality. But it should be openly and honestly discussed and be incremental. It will ideally be centered on transparency in actual delivery costs of services versus pricing, aggressive reduction of non-clinical expenditures and improved access to lower-priced insurance policies, not by a wholesale take-over of the healthcare system by the political classes and their various, vocal constituencies. I personally would not look for healthcare system salvation or stability from that demonstrably inept quarter. You might be sorely disappointed at the results; and things can indeed get a lot more dysfunctional than they currently are, if the initiatives implemented, however well-intentioned, are off the mark. Further discussions of these policy issues can be found at my blog site, www.docdownunder.com under "Medicine" for those with a deeper interest in such arcana. I look forward to reading your comments and exploring ideas.

But a major factor of my wanting to practice overseas in another healthcare system was to learn, and I was learning a lot. The good, which was predominant in Australia; and the not so good, which was perhaps more subtle and understood only more gradually by observation and hard practical experience.

CHAPTER 29: Coastal Queensland: The Whitsunday Islands

July 2014

DDU Blog entry: It's now mid-winter in Australia. The kids have a two-week winter break in July, so we headed north along the vast coastline of Queensland, to see some new sights and find some warmer weather, believe it or not. I guess we're getting soft; mid-60's just doesn't cut it anymore! When you're Down Under, heading north means heading towards the tropical equator and our balmy destination, the fabled Whitsunday Islands. It turned out to be an epic 2500 km (1600 mile), twelve-day Team Nolan adventure.

Given that we were traveling with seven, plus gear, in a single Toyota van, now growing increasingly snug as the kids rapidly enlarged, we broke the trip up into manageable bites. Twenty hours of driving over three days, and you're still only halfway up the Queensland coast! First stop, the whale-watching center of Hervey Bay. The Bay is a massive natural shelter that thousands of whales, Humpbacks especially, use to calve and feed, resting for weeks at a time during their seasonal migrations, both north and south from the Antarctic to northern hemisphere waters. It's one of the best places in the world to see these incredible sea mammals up close, under calm conditions. In season, it's not unusual to see thirty or forty whales, often with their young, on a single whale-watching trip, many coming right alongside the boat. Unfortunately, by this season, they were already far into the northern Pacific for summer season in the northern hemisphere; so, the bay and town were quiet.

The Urangan Pier, circa 1913-17, is a coastal landmark here. Constructed of local tropical hardwood, it was originally over 1100 meters (3/4 mile) long at completion; the extreme length being necessary to allow ships to dock in the shallow, sandy bay. It actually had a railroad line running its entire length to carry out coal and off-load supplies. Consolidated now to "only" 900 meters, over half a mile, it's been fully restored and is an impressive maritime structure. Popular with fishermen, it takes a full twenty-minute walk to reach the end, and incredibly, it was all built by hand! We enjoyed chatting with the local fishermen, getting the local fishing report, as a brilliant sunset colored the limpid expanse of water, before fading into an enveloping indigo evening.

Next morning, we planned a nine-hour drive north through the vast cattle country of central coast Queensland around Rockhampton. Winter is the dry season in Oz, so we passed through hours of dusty-brown, cattle-flecked savannah under flawless blue skies. Our second night was spent out on the beautiful coastal peninsula near Yeppoon at Kinka Beach; the crescent beaches and rocky headlands again almost deserted at mid-winter.

It amazes me that much of the M1 coastal highway, the major north-south artery along the populous east coast from Sydney to Cairns, is still an undivided two-lane road. This is such a newly developing country in some ways. Especially north of Brisbane, you really have to stay alert for cattle, kangaroos and oncoming tractor trailers! The wrecks in these parts can be truly epic, and fatalities occur pretty regularly. The Federal government's stated plan is to complete a modern, four-lane, limited access highway all the way along the eastern seaboard to Cairns within the next thirty years. That's not until around 2045! There is an enormous amount of construction going on, which can really snarl things up along this heavily trafficked, vital lifeline. But it's a vivid reminder of just how young and vast this country really is, once you leave the very few major metro areas behind.

North of Rockhampton, now entering into the tropics with its increasing natural rainfall, the cattle ranges gradually give way to widespread sugar cane plantations. They grow, cut and harvest cane year-round up north, so you'll pass vast fields at varying stages of growth simultaneously. Small country town-centers can be located off in the distance by their distinctive sugar mill smokestacks, which send skyward feather-like plumes of the ashen remains of the burnt cane stalks. The cane grows here to prodigious heights, twelve feet or so, and when fully mature develops a large, creamy-white seed frond. It's quite beautiful to witness the vast fields of deeply verdant cane, topped by a foaming sea of windswept, waving fronds, scattering like so much confetti. And with the whole scene backed up and framed by the deeply fissured, tropical peaks of the Great Dividing Range, which form the entire western horizon. It's a vastly different world up here than down south in sprawling, busy Brisbane.

Finally, we passed through the sugar capital of Australia, Mackay, (pronounced "Muck-I") and arrived at hip little Airlie Beach, the jumping-off point for the Whitsunday Islands. Although we were now about 1200 km north of Brisbane, that's still less than halfway up the coast to the northern tip at Cape York. The seventy-four Whitsunday Islands are a major winter playground for Australians, and the international yachting fraternity. Only six islands have any development; the remainder are protected as a National Park and look very much unchanged since Lt. (later Captain) James Cook named the passage he sailed through on Whitsunday (Pentecost Sunday) in 1770. The islands are actually the flooded tops of an ancient mountain range, now cut off from the mainland for thousands of years by rising sea levels. The entire chain is protected from the open ocean swells by the Great Barrier Reef, still some miles further offshore; and the brisk southeasterly breezes here make for world class sailing throughout the complex, variegated archipelago. Think Caribbean islands, but circa 1940s. It feels wild and sparsely populated...

Hamilton Island is the most well-known resort island, but even when fully booked out, only holds ~ ten thousand people. Though you can fly direct in high season, most people arrive on the rollicking three-hour ferry ride that leaves daily from Airlie Beach marina. It's not cheap, but when you witness the vast scale of the environment here you understand why. The ferry also stops at several other resorts along the way and makes for a nice way to sightsee among the passing islands. Surprisingly, some very famous people have had private homes hidden away out here, including the late George Harrison and the actress Angelina Jolie. We decided to rent a three-bedroom hilltop condo for five nights, which came with its own golf cart and incredible views of the Whitsunday Passage below. The older kids loved being able to drive around without even a learner's permit. No private cars are allowed on the island, which maintains the pretty relaxed *vibe. The other great thing about getting a condo is that you have a full kitchen, so you can self-cater and not have to go out for every meal; as "Hammo" is a closed shop, the entire island, including the restaurants, being run by one corporation. The supermarket at Airlie Beach actually took our shopping order online before we left Brisbane, and there was a pile of styrofoam boxes, holding everything in perfect condition, stacked up at the door on our arrival. Door to door delivery via ferry only cost around $30, which was a fantastic bargain.*

The boys and I fished nightly from a local pier, catching a variety of colorful reef fish. All released unharmed, it felt like gathering very beautiful gems under the warm tropical stars, while we watched sailboats drifting noiselessly by, dreamlike across the calm, warm waters. Only one area of Hamilton Island contains the hotels; and, as a single company manages the entire island, you have access to all the hotel pools and facilities if you rent a condo in the much more private hilltop neighborhood area away from the resorts. We would highly recommend the condo and self-catering option to any potential visitors to this magical, somewhat remote, island group.

A nightly ritual is the golf cart congregation atop One Tree Hill, one of the highest vantage points on the island, looking dead west, to watch the sublime sunset over the Whitsunday Passage below. They even set up a temporary bar nightly. Passing sailboats look like tiny toys threading a river of silver, against the immensity of the darkening landscape of the Australian mainland beyond. Barely a light can be seen coming from any of the vast surrounding landforms, as the darkness stealthily advances, enfolds and becomes complete. Being so isolated, the stars here revealed themselves more radiantly than we could imagine.

Hamilton Island is seventy percent undeveloped National Park, and quite mountainous, so there are some really great hikes right out the door, for those so motivated. We took all five kids on the six km hike up to Passage Peak, high above Catseye Bay, and the main resort's beach. They handled the challenge eagerly and raced excitedly ahead, even little Owen. The views across the archipelago stretched out below were stunning.

With its rocky ledges, deep-blue water passages, pine-like trees, and pervasive boating culture, it felt strangely enough, as if we were hiking in coastal Maine or at Blue Mountain Lake in the Adirondacks of upstate New York. But then a cluster of parrots would fly raucously overhead, shattering the reverie, so.... not really.

We took Claire and Cate over to the Dent Island Golf Club for a tour and classy girls' lunch. Built by the Oatley family, famous Australian wine makers and world-class sailors, for forty-five million dollars, it might someday break even. You take an elegant motor launch just across the straight from the main marina on Hamilton Island. I'm sure large-scale planned developments are in the works, but for now, it's a well-designed, full 18-hole course on an otherwise uninhabited island. The views from the fairways are spectacular. The golf cart tour and lunch of fresh, locally caught Spanish Mackerel, in the modern clubhouse, were superb. It's a well-priced, highly recommended excursion if you are ever out on Hammo.

The next morning, it was the boys' turn. We'd signed onto a fishing charter out around the outer islands. The Spanish Mackerel were running strong, and our hopes were high. Unfortunately, though there were fish on the depth finder, they had plenty of natural baitfish for food and weren't hitting, so we switched over to bottom gear for some reef fishing. We caught some very nice, deeply crimson Nannygai, a variety of snapper, each weighing seven to ten pounds, which made for an excellent dinner later that evening. The austere scenery of the remote, outer islands was also a thrilling experience in its own right. The next day, we heard reports that the same boat landed some fifteen, highly prized Spanish Mackerel! But that's fishing... you've just gotta get out there to have any chance at all.

On our final day's departure, we headed via the northern route on the ferry to visit Whitehaven Beach on the eastern side of enormous and uninhabited Whitsunday Island, deep within the National Park. World famous for its pure silica sand, it's considered one of the most pristine and beautiful beaches on the entire planet. In a country that's literally surrounded by world-class beaches, this one's a standout. Part of that classification extends beyond the actual beach, to the stunningly remote and mountainous setting behind it. The only development at all, on the entire island, is a few primitive campsites and a pit toilet. You can reserve these campsites as part of a well-developed sea kayak route or take the daily ferry right to your destination. It's an excellent place to play Robinson Crusoe for a few days; just be sure to bring all your own food and water.

Once the ferry departs, you are well and truly on your own, until the next day at least. The beach here is really impressive, the sand is the color and consistency of flour, and the waters shimmer a crystalline aqua blue. You can polish your jewelry, so fine is the sand, to glitter in the tropical sunlight. Even though I was expecting just another amazing Aussie beach (yawn...), I must admit, it's a really fine one, indeed - and an experience not to be missed while in the Whitsundays.

A thrifty traveler's tip: rather than take a pricey day tour out to Whitehaven Beach from Hammo, and then have to pay for the ferry ride again back to Airlie Beach, you can instead take the return ferry first north, to Whitehaven Beach. On your last day on Hammo, take the early ferry directly to Whitehaven. You can disembark there, frolic in paradise for several hours, and be picked up by the later afternoon ferry, returning directly to Airlie Beach by the northern route, at no additional charge. An added bonus is that you get to see another entire area of the northern Whitsundays, which is a lovely, leisurely experience. With seven, we saved hundreds of dollars by this strategy, and had a wonderful adventure to boot.

DDU Blog entry: So, after five blissful nights and six days, it was time to bid the Whitsundays a fond adieu and head out on the long drive south, back to Brisbane. All the kids were unanimous in naming this the best Team Nolan road trip yet.

We spent our last night in the beautiful beach town of Noosa on the Sunshine Coast much further south and only three hours north of Brisbane. It's a high-end resort town surrounded by National Parks, wilderness coastline, surf breaks, rainforested mountains, and inland lakes, and the restaurants are great too. In short, it's got everything you could want except urban sprawl...Per-fect!

In shimmering Noosa, we had a final Thai feast to celebrate yet another safe and successful road trip together. The Thai food in Oz is generally excellent, and this meal did not disappoint. After dinner, we experienced yet another, completely unanticipated, peak Australian moment. Walking along Noosa's funky, commercial, Hastings Street alone with Stephanie, the kids scattered out window-shopping together; then we turned east, and headed right out onto the sandy main beach, now lying under a serene, luminescent moon. The tide was up, so the beach was considerably narrower than usual, and being right on slack tide, the waves were reduced to a gentle swell. Ripples really. As we walked quietly, arm in arm, recounting the trip's many highlights, suddenly a small pod of dolphins surfaced, breaking the calm face of the sea, not ten feet offshore. The soft whistling of their exhalations produced an unexpected exclamation point of sorts, as if to emphasize our very good fortune! Under the warm tropical night skies, the effect was startling and spellbindingly beautiful. Then, just as suddenly, they dove and disappeared like a mirage into the moon-brushed sea. The image, so perfectly framed, has stayed with me since. Blessed folks indeed!

In the following bright morning's clear light, it all seemed an evanescent, nocturnal dream, images from another world entirely. We had time for a final hike out onto the Noosa Point National Park headland. This is a very beautiful environment, with the wind-driven tide and swell piling roaring seawater into the gaping mouth of Hell's Gate, and surging hundreds of feet below the headland here at land's very end. The noise can be deafening, and it's a very thrilling experience. Just watch your step though - it's a long, deadly drop onto the rocks below.

CHAPTER 30: The Blue Mountains and a Return to Sydney, New South Wales

November 2014

DDU Blog entry: The Royal Flying Doctors Service (RFDS) is an Australian institution. Staffed by a highly motivated team of experts, it's a lifeline to specialist medical care for many remote bush communities to this day. The RFDS teaches a well-regarded Aeromedical Retrieval (STAR) Course regularly throughout Australia. It's a full three days, hands-on primer on all things related to pre-hospital emergency stabilization and aviation transport of critically ill and injured patients in remote environments, i.e., most of Australia. I'd scheduled to attend the STAR course in Sydney. As school was now in mid-session, we couldn't all get up and go. Thus, a father-son road trip with Luke, now fifteen, was hatched. He missed a week of school but gained a lifetime of new experiences and memories.

On day one, we left right out of Sydney airport and headed west into the Blue Mountains. Given that Sydney, population ~ 4.5 million is, along with Melbourne also ~ 4.5 million, one of the two largest population centers in Australia by far, it's remarkable how quickly you leave the "Big Smoke" behind. Within eighty km (fifty miles) we were heading up into the vast, Great Dividing Range, home to three major national parks, and covering over 2.5 million acres of mostly wilderness.

DDU Blog entry: The World Heritage-listed Blue Mountains have been a summer playground for wealthy Sydney-siders for one hundred and fifty years. The infrastructure, trails and overlooks are all well laid-out and safely constructed. In the small mountain hamlets of Leura, Katoomba, Blackheath and Mount Victoria you find impressively preserved Victorian-era hotels and country estates with formal English-style gardens. A bit of an Australian-imagined version of the distant motherland. But if you veer off the established walkways and paths only a few hundred meters you are suddenly thrust into the wild Australian bush, with treacherous five-hundred-foot drop- offs everywhere. Watch your footing!

As always in Australia, whatever your expectations, expect grander, vaster, more awe-inspiring. These mountains really are the most curious, variegated shades of blue, said to be due to suspended eucalypt oils evaporating off the forests and refracting in the sunlight. Whatever the reason, they are indeed, impressively and deeply blue.

We had a good connection to renting a simple, restored coal miner's cottage in Leura - Strathearn Cottage, circa 1930. Owned by our Cleveland landlady's sister, it made a handy and quaint base for exploring the region. The weather was favorable, and on the first night we had fantastic views of the iconic Three Sisters in the evening light. Storms were rolling in; it was a mid-week evening, and the place was deserted. Just how we like it. Unfortunately, for many visitors the famously fickle Blue Mountain weather settles in and leaves this view limited to your basic, monochrome cloudbank. That old Nolan luck was holding once again. The Sisters are not only much larger than anticipated, but the drop to the valley floor, some eight hundred feet below, is dramatically more vertical than any pictures I've ever seen capture.

It's a very ancient, complex landscape, and though truly mountainous, the real geologic wonder is that the entire area is actually a massively fissured erosion plateau. The only landscape I've seen similar is the Ozark Mountains plateau in NW Arkansas, and spreading into adjacent Oklahoma, Missouri and Kansas. There, the locals have a very apt saying that sums up the geology succinctly, "The hills ain't high, but the hollers sure are deep..." Exactly that, now try saying it with an ocker Aussie accent mate!

DDU Blog entry: The following morning, we returned to the Three Sisters to explore a bit more. There's a famous bridge out to the first Sister that you might just barely see in most photos, if you know where to look. Look lower left, as it provides a much-needed sense of scale to the whole scene. But I didn't realize that you first have to clamber down ladders to get onto it - a truly vertigo-inducing experience! It's an unexpected surprise then, to witness just how high off the valley floor the eroded rock formations actually are. The spires you see in all the calendars are just the tops of a ridgeline that falls away some eight hundred feet to the forest floor below. This holler sure is deep... And if you're feeling exceptionally fit, you can also hike all the way down into, and/or back up from, the valley floor from here. We deferred, for once.

Another wonderful feature of the Blue Mountains is the number of cascades flowing off these escarpments. Virtually every eroded canyon contains a creek at its base, patiently eroding things away over eons; so, water music fills the air everywhere. And, as water is essential for life, each riparian stream verge is a veritable cool fern grotto, tucked beneath the jagged sandstone cliffs overhead. It's a truly singular, and magical hiking experience.

In keeping with the well-heeled, resort-y feel of the area, the restaurants were really good too. Even the basic Asian/ Malaysian places were top notch. We got a tip on Tripadvisor about a highly rated family pizza place in Katoomba. I walked in and saw a USA-style, authentic pizza oven - something so rare in Australia that I wanted to cry out. I exclaimed to the waiter, "You have a real pizza oven...!" Surprised at my passion, he apologized, "It's not wood-fired, only gas, mate..." Suddenly overwhelmed, I then cried, just slightly... tears of joy, mixed with a sudden rush of homesickness for the land of real pizzas, and calzones too.

What ensued was "the best Aussie pizza ever," an easy 8.5 on the USA scale. A real homemade dough crust even, with a sharp light crunch, followed by that lively gluten pull and chew...the generous size and toppings - an added bonus. This all may seem a bit over the top; but Australia, while being entirely awesome in many, if not most respects, is most certainly a pizza desert, outside of a very few scattered oases of pie-loving goodness (I'm talking to you, Melbourne...). Skinny, lifeless, pre-formed frozen crusts cooked on toaster-like conveyor belts is the norm. The crusts don't actually rise; they simply toast up a bit. Dominos almost counts as gourmet here. Sorry to obsess, but it's been a LONG three years Down Under, counted in pizza-time. So, all love goes out to Papadinos

Pizza, Katoomba, NSW. Just go there, if ever in the region and in need of a genuine pie.

DDU Blog entry: Soon enough it was time to hit the road. We took an alternate high- altitude route back to Sydney on the famous Bells Line of Road, a pioneer route laid down in the 1820's by a 17-year-old surveyor named Bell. Still in use today, it's one of only two major routes crossing the Dividing Range west of Sydney. In fact, the rugged maze of mountains, which rise to over 1100m (3600 ft) turned back successive expeditions, keeping the early settlers crowded on the eastern coastal plains of NSW for twenty-five years before finally being breached. A major destination up here is the Blue Mountains Botanic Garden at Mount Tombah, a cool climate annex of the vast Royal Botanic Garden in the Sydney CBD. It's free and very well done, specializing in cool climate, mountain and sub-polar species. Highly recommended for several hours' relaxed wandering and perhaps lunch.

Very near here, as recently as the 1990s, the botanical world was stunned by the re-discovery of a genus of pine tree thought to be extinct for millions of years, in a remote, isolated slot canyon. The Wollemi Pine, now growing here at Mount Tombah, has since been successfully transplanted to various locations around Australia. I saw one earlier, in Adelaide's Botanic Garden. It's very non-piney looking to me, with flat, sharply tipped primitive leaves, and upright-growing cones. But, for some reason, the botanists consider it a true pine. Imagine that: the botanic equivalent of a living dinosaur being recently re-discovered, and thriving, on the outskirts of the Sydney CBD! In yet another way, Australia is such a remarkable continent!

It would be easy to spend weeks, or months, exploring the Blue Mountains; but our schedule carried us back into Sydney. The STAR conference was being held at MacQuarie University, north of the CBD, so we had an opportunity to explore the nearby Northern Beaches region of greater Sydney. It encompasses a string of small beach towns: Palm, Avalon, Bilgola, Mona Vale and Narrabeen, to name just several legendary Aussie surfing hotspots, each separated by finger-like headlands into distinct, exclusive communities. This fabled stretch of beach-heaven runs up a narrow peninsula for twenty-five kms north from Manly, near the entrance to Sydney Harbor. The entire harbor ecosystem is technically termed Port Jackson; it encompasses the massive, flooded Parramatta River valley - a Ria in geologic terms. This line of beach-side villages terminates north, at the mouth of the Hawkesbury River, at Barrenjoey Head and lighthouse. The more internationally famous stretch of coastline in the popular imagination here in Sydney, containing the iconic Bondi, Bronte, Coogee and Tamarama beaches, is actually referred to as the Eastern Suburbs, and sits dead east of the CBD, south of the Port Jackson harbor entrance. While both areas are certainly among the most expensive and exclusive neighborhoods in greater Sydney, for my money, the Northern Beach communities feel less crowded, greener and have a less urban vibe than those of the Eastern Suburbs. Tough choice, if you have millions to spare!

DDU Blog entry: These Northern Beach breaks can rise impressively and are famous for excellent surfing. The sand here is coarser, and of a curious, deeply orange-salmon hue, the color of fresh arctic char. Because of the rough, dangerous surf, many communities feature a large, open-air saltwater tide pool, built right onto the tidal rocks, and sited just below the high water mark, many years ago. This allows for swim competitions and safety for families, regardless of wind, seas or tide conditions. They are refreshed on each incoming tide and tend to be community social hubs. It's intriguing to watch the breakers crash and spray over the seaward faces of the pool edges while swimmers tread water in the calm, safe spaces within.

Each headland-enclosed crescent of sand here is backed up by a protected green belt, or foreshore park, containing invariably well-maintained playgrounds, restrooms - usually complete with showers - and free gas BBQ pavilions. Across the street from these dreamlike seascapes cluster the small and tidy village CBDs, always containing a lineup of interesting cafes, local pubs and surfwear shops on the main drag, facing seaward. Each village has its distinct personality, and rewards hours of exploration or just settling into the beachy ambiance and relaxing as the day unfolds. One of the true comforts of Aussie coastal living is the predictable order of each village's foreshore park. It's not exactly a competition, but each puts its best face forward for the community and visitor alike. For the traveler, you can be assured of a free and comfortable oasis in virtually every town. If you're not sure how things are laid out, simply drive the leisurely coastal-most road; when you get to the public restrooms and the playground just park - you're there... Everything else you're likely to need is within easy walking distance, including miles of open ocean and widely sweeping, world-class beaches. The one potential wrinkle in this system, depending on your viewpoint, is that overnight camping is uniformly, and strictly, forbidden in these village parks. Sorry, combi-vagabonds; you'll just have to make other sleeping arrangements. Luckily, there's usually a holiday park with camping facilities just nearby.

DDU Blog entry: We had a final day before the RFDS course started, so we headed for new vistas, the Eastern Suburbs beaches of Sydney. Famous for the well-known Bondi Beach, the coastline here feels somehow Mediterranean. Densely packed but livable, with small coastal headlands separating distinct communities, each centered on still more crescent beaches and green public parks. Sweet as...! We somehow stumbled, completely by chance, upon the opening weekend of "Sculpture by the Sea," an annual two-week open air sculpture fest, running along the famous Clifftop Walk between Bondi and Tamarama beaches. It was a bit chockers, i.e., mobbed, but the great weather and festive vibe made for a memorable outing. The sculptures really couldn't compete with the natural beauty of the stunning seascapes below. However, my favorite was a massive frying pan, complete with handle to scale, twenty feet across with an open, sand-filled bottom at Tamarama Beach. You could climb in and get your picture taken lying on the sizzling sand, like a rasher of streaky bacon! A clever, memorable installation. We then headed into town for lunch and explored the Rocks, inner harbor and Opera House. This was Luke's first trip to Sydney, and I'd only been once, several years earlier, so it was a great urban adventure full of new discoveries. It's a teeming and complex harbor metropolis, so we only had time to hit the highest of the high points. Any visit to Australia must include at least several days exploring this fascinating, vibrant, new world city.

The STAR course was being held at the MacQuarie University Graduate School of Management, a green oasis on the north side of Port Jackson Bay, only twenty minutes from the Sydney CBD. The hotel rooms there open directly onto the lawn, allowing guests direct room access into the spacious campus park. The operation's run entirely by the Hospitality Management students as a fully professional, executive conference center. It's a very pleasant setting and comes highly recommended if you're staying north of the Sydney CBD.

DDU Blog entry: The STAR course culminates in an intense multi-casualty, nighttime moulage scenario, using live paramedic actors, resuscitation dummies, buckets of fake blood and prosthetic props, as well as actual rescue supplies and litters. It's as live as a simulation can be. Luke was very excited to be invited to audit most of the classes and was even allowed to role-play as a mass-casualty patient actor.

We apparently caused quite a stir among some of the other hotel guests, as our first after-dark scenario involved a (simulated) drunken and very bloody fall off the hotel roof, complete with a panicked, screaming girlfriend of the injured, who needed to be talked down while the evacuation was commencing by headlamps. I'm not sure the pre-drill warnings were well-circulated, judging by some of the initial non-STAR guest reactions! We also had to stabilize a traumatic mid-thigh amputation caused by a crocodile attack that was sufficiently gory, even for Luke. And finally, a motorcycle accident with a through and through metal rod torso impalement. Seriously... I learned that it's kind of hard to lay a fellow down in a rescue stretcher when a four-foot pole's sticking through his upper chest. Hmmm...what to do...what to do...?

In all, it was a very challenging and realistic exercise for everyone involved. RFDS was really generous to include Luke in almost everything, and even presented him with a Certificate of Attendance, along with the rest of the class. Not bad for a fifteen-year-old boy, skipping out on a week of school. Perhaps a career-changing experience for him? Time will tell, but it sure kept his attention riveted.

Our thanks again to the RFDS crew for being so welcoming of Luke as a junior participant. It was a real eye-opener for him into the world of Emergency Medicine and pre-hospital EMS. Who knows, he might just join the next generation of front-line lifesavers. RFDS is a wonderful and vital service. Please be generous in your support for them. You never know when you, or a loved one, may need their very able assistance somewhere out in the remote Australian bush. But be assured, they will respond efficiently and expertly as required.

CHAPTER 31: A Brief Interlude - Settled Songs, 2014-15

By now, we were fully settled in Australia. Going on three years in-country, we'd made the carefully considered decision to run with the opportunity and see where it led us. The hospital Administration then surprised me by offering to sponsor us for Permanent Residency (PR), which was never part of the original plan. Another example of our being pulled through the system by insiders; they made a potentially nerve-wracking and expensive process feel very organic and like the next logical step. After weighing the offer and considering all options as a family, we agreed to proceed. Stephanie and the kids were now much more integrated into the schools and comfortable in the community. We had a circle of supportive friends from all over the world, many going through the same process of simultaneously welcoming a new life, while letting go of pieces of the old. It has its challenges, believe me.

My songwriting now began to reflect this sense of contentment and settling, of a future open to many new possibilities. When writing lyrics, I often try to universalize what's motivating me as a way to make things feel less self-centric, but mainly to reach out and share. I assume that many other folks must be working through similar challenges and self-doubts in their own lives too. So, here are a few o.g.nolan songs that I look back on fondly, as being a window into a time of relatively settled, still-magical bliss. They say more than I could otherwise.

"Busy" started life as a cool, funky riff, one of the few riff-based songs I've written. Short, upbeat and snappy; it's a bit of a tongue-in-cheek apology to friends, family, myself (?) for having been so preoccupied in life up 'til now. Maybe, it was finally time to get onto Queensland time and enjoy the fruits of all that hard yakka. But probably not...

"Sorry, I've been busy, I've been away too long
This life can make you dizzy; I record it in a song..."

"Living on Luck" Pure autobiography, reflecting on how far I'd come from the old, scrappy and penniless days. I honestly struggled for so many years with almost nothing, I know I must've been living on luck. But when you're young, life's simpler, and we all somehow got by. So, perhaps a wistful longing to return to those less complex days as I get older. This one was straight from the heart, written out on the verandah, overlooking Moreton Bay.

"Kicking back on my hammock, I'm getting pretty tired of chasing a buck
When I think back a long while, I'm pretty sure that I was livin' on luck..."

"Sunday Afternoon" unfolded just like the lyric. Playing out on the shady verandah, watching all the boats coming in from the bay, towards sunset of a sunny Sunday afternoon. I was trying to capture that sun-baked, breeze-blown contentment of ending the perfect weekend with friends and music, with a few more precious hours still to go. It flowed very naturally while writing it, always a good sign.

"Monday morning is still far away
so let's make the most of this fading, amazing day..."

"I Think It's Gonna Rain Tonight" Dreamy and romantic, this is just a simple love song, written in what I consider to be a commercial, Nashville style. Not deep, but still satisfying. Contentment in a song.

"Lover turn out the light, c'mon and hold me tight
I think it's gonna rain tonight..."

"Younger Than I'll Ever Be" A fun, up-tempo, motivational song, written especially for me! And perhaps some others out there? A statement of purpose to remain positive, engaged and moving forward into inevitable aging. There's really no good alternative, and in the end, you'll have a way better time of it.

"I'm getting older now, but I'm younger than I'll ever be

Those crazy times, made me who I turned out to be..."

It also speaks to the importance of real forgiveness, and saying I'm sorry, as a means of letting go of the past and moving forward unburdened by it. I've seen that **not** happen way too often in my own life and family, and it bothers me a lot. Relationships can always improve, until it finally really is too late. I hope the positive sentiment rubs off on others, of whatever age. Also, a full band song; in endless search of said band.

"Forgiveness, forgetting, for God's sake let it go
Saying sorry, and being sorry, can mean more than we will ever know..."

Around this time, we were fortunate to attend a medical conference in Fiji, only three hours' flight dead-east of Brisbane and yet another, entirely different world. By incredible coincidence, it was scheduled to occur over Claire's sweet-sixteenth birthday, so Stephanie and I took her and Cate (then twelve) along for a girls' week in paradise. Of course, they were over the tropical moon, and it was a wonderful, shared experience that we'll always treasure. That got me meditating on the ephemeral nature of good times and shared experience, and how these moments that we treasure are passing even as we enjoy them. **"Mango Smoothie/ Dream Islands"** was the result. I also wanted to contrast the languid, lazy island vibe of being there with the sometimes-frenetic flights, cab transfers etc. required to actually attain paradise, however briefly. So, two songs in one really, flowing back and forth between both realities, while also questioning if we'll ever have such perfect times together again. (Wow o.g., that sure is some heavy shit...!)

Here, it's recorded only in its simplest demo form, but with a nylon string guitar along for the ride. I hope to re-do this one as a proper studio track; somehow, someday, somewhere. But "Vanaka" until then. I hope you all enjoy the island ambiance.

"These islands, passing times in our lives, dream islands, never made to stay.
They drift away, will we return some day..?"

The recorded versions of this set, "Settled Songs" that are available via the o.g.nolan site on Spotify, the DDU website (www.docdownunder.com)

and Amazon music, etc., are pretty sparse, just my vocals and guitar. They're basically demos, done on the run at a friend's home studio, set up in a crumbling oceanside mansion, right there in Raby Bay, QLD sometime in 2015. I've included them in their unfinished versions, as is. Honestly, I'm not sure I'll ever get back around to recording them more properly. It seems my life, and writing, have already moved far beyond them now. But I think they're strong songs, and they mark a settled, if busy, period in our journey, their incomplete form also a part of the story.

"Bright 'n Breezy"

This is perhaps the final number in the contentment series? Time will tell... I listen to a lot of old jazz and country blues, classic American songbook stuff too; now-neglected artists and past legends like Cole Porter, Roy Orbison, Ella Fitzgerald, Hank Williams Sr., the Everly Brothers and such. I love weird jug band music too, like Dan Hicks and his Hot Licks, and the true folky eccentrics, Michael Hurley and John Prine. Old Motown and New Orleans soul. It's great stuff - the absolute shit, IMHO. The chords are cool, the lyrics are witty and real, something that I find lacking in much of today's music. Not to disparage any present-day creators, but those old songs literally brim with real humanity, fresh ideas and cheeky turns-of-phrase. They're also a lot of fun to play. In short, they're also part of the ever- deepening roots of o.g.nolan, should anyone out there even care.

"Bright 'n Breezy" is written in such a ragtime, uptempo style, now some sixty years out of fashion. No worries, I'm lucky, I don't have to do it for a living! I just write what feels right and good. "If it sounds good, it is good." as Duke Ellington so righteously stated. And this one does, at least to me.

It came quickly, in only thirty minutes or so. I already had the lyric; just some sketches about living along the Queensland coast, along with my beautiful gal and kids, where it is indeed very Bright 'n Breezy. Also inspired by memories of day-sailing in Fiji. I sat down, hit the C7 chord, and it was off to the races once again. I hope you can dig the tropical, swingin' vibe on this one. Along with "Busy", it was eventually recorded in a full band session, some years after it was written, and they're included on the "Sea Change" CD on the DDU website.

"Another day without a freeze, onshore breeze, oh swaying palm trees
Love is strong, life is easy; we're going where it's bright n' breezy..."

Looking, and listening back now, it was a happy, calm and productive period for me, and that state of mind remains reflected in these songs.

Meanwhile, work in the ED, always a challenge, was progressing as well. We certainly had our challenges as a department and hospital. And there was now notice of an upcoming void in leadership due to the impending retirement of Dr. Dennis March, my colleague, friend and mentor in Australian Emergency Medicine since we'd arrived. I was approached by him and hospital Administration and asked to consider filling-in as acting ED Director, an honor I cautiously accepted after much soul-searching and some genuine friction between me and Stephanie. She counseled against it, frankly, knowing the stressors I'd experienced as an ED Director back in the USA. At best, it's a very tough role; often simply a no-win, peacekeeping position between the physician staff and Administration, with the added complications of our rapidly growing patient volumes and acuity colliding up against the realities of inevitable budgetary and financial constraints. Doesn't that all just sound like a lark...?

And hadn't I promised "I'll never direct another ED" on my resignation in New York? Yes, indeed, true enough as Stephanie repeatedly reminded me.

But it's my skill set, for better or worse; and the money was good. Much like a sadly aging stripper, you do what you know, however unsavory, to pay the bills. Also, there were no other internal candidates raising their hands and jumping at the opportunity - in retrospect, a clear, early warning sign. But the alternative to my accepting the role was for Administration to bring in an outsider as ED leader - an unknown quality always fraught with hazard. And one that we would all have to live and work with. So, better the devil you know? My FACEM colleagues were all highly supportive of my candidacy, which was gratifying. A new lamb for slaughter, perhaps? She'll be right, mate...

So, in the end, I accepted, and was gradually drawn into the most challenging (i.e., "worst") period of my professional life. Let me just say it right here... Stephanie was **so right**! I sure wish I'd listened to her wisdom now, in hindsight.

And therein lies a bloody tale indeed, perhaps for another day. But for now, "Settled Songs," however fleeting...

CHAPTER 32: Lamington National Park and the NSW Border Ranges

January 2015

DDU Blog entry: A return to O'Reilly's Rainforest Retreat. Aussie schools have summer break from mid-December through the end of January. It's a long spell off in the hot, humid weather. And fortunately, now prime Aussie beach weather. We'd been doing plenty of day trips to various local beaches and decided to get out of the hot, humid coastal zone entirely, and return to Lamington National Park. At over 1000m elevation (3,200 feet), and 50,000 acres, it's the largest intact subtropical rainforest in Australia, and perhaps the entire world. Drive only ninety minutes southwest from Brisbane, and you are in an entirely different world, or epoch.

Our first few days were cool, cloudy and misty. A refreshing change of pace, the suspended moisture coaxing all the dense greenery to glisten and flower, adding to the sense of timelessness and adventure. The free treetop skywalk at O'Reilly's leads to the famous giant Fig tree lookout. You start out on the suspension bridge, rising around sixty feet off the forest floor, and then climb ladders up two more stories to a tiny, swaying lookout, perched high within a crotch of this ancient Fig tree. Certainly not for "fraidy-cats", but a fun challenge for kids of all ages; and one that affords spectacular views of the mountainous ridges sweeping away to the west.

O'Reilly's is also famous for hosting a daily wild bird feeding that's been occurring here since the 1920's. Using specially screened seed to protect the bird's health, it's one of the few places in Australia that allows for the feeding of native rainforest birds. Wild King Parrots, Crimson Rosellas and Rainbow Lorikeets come readily out of the surrounding forest to feast and may even light atop your head and outstretched arms for photos. It's an incredible opportunity to get up close to these normally reclusive species, and very popular. If you are double-lucky, as we were, you might even catch a glimpse of the stunning yellow and black male Regent Bowerbird, the living symbol of O'Reilley's Rainforest Retreat.

World-Heritage listed Lamington NP sits along the northern flank of the massive, long-extinct Tweed Volcano caldera, that last erupted around 23 million years ago. It's only one in a network of dozens of parks that form a continuous preserve running for over a hundred miles along the Border Ranges, so named because the very height of the land forms the state border here between Queensland and New South Wales, to the south. It's one of the premier hiking, or bushwalking, destinations in Australia, containing hundreds of kilometers of trails, traversing through these rare and varied ecosystems.

DDU Blog entry: O'Reilly's farm was also the site of the famous Stimson plane crash in the 1930's. After a massive search was called off as fruitless, one of the O'Reilly brothers, Bernard, struck off on his own through the trackless rainforest and found two living survivors, ten days after the crash. They were carried out to safety and the case made headlines worldwide. There is an interesting museum, statue and even a full-sized airplane similar to the original that crashed, on the grounds today. They schedule occasional guided hikes out to the ruined plane's remote crash site, as well as daily guided bird walks. O'Reilly's started as a remote family dairy farm around 1915 with the release of government lands to settlers. It was soon surrounded by the newly created Lamington National Park. Gradually, the family began housing explorers, tourists and visitors. It's still owned by the original family and is world-renowned for its high standards of hospitality in the middle of this huge wilderness area. It's truly one of the world's first eco-lodges. Plan to stay overnight if ever visiting the area. Once you get up here, you'll want to linger for as long as possible. It's a unique experience in a wonderful part of Australia, and the food and service are to a world-class standard. There are also opportunities for simple camping nearby as well.

Ultimately, any trip to Lamington is all about the magnificent rainforest that surrounds everything here. We did a sixteen km (ten mile) hike on day three up to the very edge of the ancient caldera. As you're starting out already at higher elevation, it's mostly a gradual uphill walk until you get to the very caldera rim, under stunted, moss-festooned trees. The inside face of the caldera is much steeper, with the forested slopes falling away dramatically for hundreds of feet towards its unseen base. A tiny trail leads along this caldera ridgeline, making you feel very much the wild hobbit, as you wend dreamily through this pristine, cloud-swept and little-visited environment.

For the truly fit, this is only the first half of a legendary twenty-four km (fifteen mile) one-way hike across the caldera ridge and down a neighboring spur to the wilderness lodge at Binna-Burra (an Aboriginal term meaning "where the Beech trees grow"). You have to shuttle cars or reserve a space on the resort shuttle buses for the day-long adventure. Most trekkers plan to stay at least one overnight on either end of the hike. As you venture up onto the highest ridges, the forest changes to predominantly moss-covered, ancient Antarctic Beech, which thrive only here, within the cooler, moist cloud cover. Some are dated to being over two thousand years old. They are the last vestige of a lost time, twenty million years ago, when Australia was a cooler, wetter continent. It's a fantastic world to visit, if even for a few hours.

Luckily, the weather held for us, and we were treated to wonderful views of the entire Tweed Volcano caldera, with distant Mount Warning, the cinder cone sentinel, at its very center. The furthest mountain ridges you can see beyond, on the far horizon, are actually the southern rim of this caldera. At almost sixty miles across, it's one of the largest and best-preserved volcanic calderas on earth. The lava flows, some thousands of feet thick, blew out and flowed southeast, forming the rich sugarcane-growing soils of the Tweed River valley around Murwillumbah, NSW, and finally terminating way down the coastline some miles south of Byron Bay. Truly, an epic mountain landscape for anyone so inclined. Do not miss this region if you're nearby on the coast. It's a complementary experience to the sublime beaches down here, and a wonderful natural playground to explore in its own right.

Finally, we took a last, return trip to the big Fig tree, for a final Team Nolan courage trial. Not everybody made the complete climb, names withheld in confidence. Little Owen bravely insisted on climbing all the way up the tree, but I stopped him at the first lookout, some one hundred feet above the ground. He wanted to go all the way up! When the small crowd waiting to climb, in turn below, realized he had made it, at only six, and having the use of only one arm, they were very moved and broke out into a spontaneous round of applause. Aussies really pull for the underdog, and one burly man was nearly moved to tears at Owen's courage, "That's a good little battler, mate", he said with tears welling up on his rough-hewn face. Well earned praise indeed for our brave little battler, Owen, "Goodonyas little buddy..."

As a March 2021 update to the above blog entry from 2015, the Binna Burra region was severely damaged by bushfires during the unprecedented 2019-2020 bushfire season. In September 2019, the heritage-listed, 1930's era, Binna Burra lodge and surrounding heritage cabin complex was entirely destroyed; burned to the ground. The O'Reilly's property was fortunately undamaged. Extensive rebuilding and upgrading efforts are well underway, and the parks are now open. But an irreplaceable chapter of Queensland history was forever altered or destroyed by these devastating bushfires. Please check locally for current conditions if planning a visit to this remarkable Scenic Rim region of Queensland and New South Wales.

DDU Blog entry: Back in Cleveland, work continues steadily in our busy ED. I was recently asked by the hospital Administration, with the support of my FACEM colleagues, to take over as acting ED Director, given the impending retirement of my friend and mentor, Dr. Dennis March. It's a real honor, and a big role to fill. We do have many ongoing challenges as a hospital and a department. The ED here is now rapidly approaching sixty-thousand visits annually and is staffed by some twenty senior FACEM physicians, twenty trainees at various levels, approximately one hundred employees and staff. I had initially embarked on this Oz adventure to take a mid-career break of sorts and attain more balance in our family life. But in life you gotta work at what you know. It is my skill set, for better or worse. So I accepted, though with some reservations. It seems, every time we try to leave this country, they make me a better offer. Lucky us... So here we'll remain for the foreseeable future; still Doc' in Down Under, heading now into our fourth year.

Luke and Claire, ages 15 and 14, recently earned their open ocean scuba diving certificates, finishing up the course with a challenging open ocean, bommie (a large, undersea coral head) dive, where they got up close and personal with Giant Mantas, Lemon Sharks and many other exotic marine species. They are thrilled, and we are so proud of our rapidly maturing teens.

On a musical note, after four years, I've collected a few more guitars here in Australia, mostly crappy ones, some that I've grown fond of. Like kids, they all have their different strengths and annoyances. I found an old Yammie nylon string at the local Salvos for $50, the case worth more than the guitar. But I didn't have a nylon string down here, and I love to fingerpick. You just naturally play different types of guitars in very different ways; finger attack, musical styles, different songs entirely come to mind and emerge. So, variety does inspire learning and new ways forward. "New tools, new tunes" y'might say... It was scratched all to hell, bridge broken, tuners loose. But the cheaper plywood top is much more stable in the humid air than a more resonant, solid grain top. The perfect beach guitar...! Luke and I had a fun few days as we rehabbed it. Surprisingly, I found a blank, genuine bone bridge at the local music store, and taught him how to sand it down, file string notches and reset the string height, lemon oil the desiccated fret board and give her a polish. Turns out to play and sound really good, though definitely not a looker, that one. It's now channeling my inner Jack Johnson and I've been playing it obsessively since - can't put it down. It lies around the house like a cast-off, lonely doggie, and I give it love. And its different voicings have inspired me to write a whole batch of new songs too. I've become quite fond of my ugly little puppy. It's the best $50 I can recall spending in a long, long while.

So, not that anyone has called or written to express concern, but we are doing just fine thanks; as one year evolves into the next, and hopefully, with many more still beyond. We'll likely be here for a while longer yet, manning our duty stations off in the remote South Pacific. Stop in, say hello sometime, even if only by email... Cheers, Doc Down Under

CHAPTER 33: Australian ED Leadership Challenges

February - December 2015

During early 2015, I gradually transitioned into the role of acting ED Director. Dr Dennis March, ever the diligent professional, spent many hours getting me up to speed as he reduced his role in the department. Hospitals are highly complex organisms, and EDs are their front doors to the public. A lot has to be coordinated behind the scenes to make the patients', and their families' journeys through the system feel smooth and satisfactory. My primary role now was to anticipate and ameliorate any complications or patient risks throughout the entire process, from pre-hospital ambulance service interface to final patient disposition, including timely access to specialist care off-site.

It turned out there were many more systemic issues facing the hospital and ED than Dr. March had previously divulged. In short, the hospital was becoming overwhelmed by the rapid growth in our surrounding catchment area; our patient "throughput numbers" were comparatively terrible; the budget was tight; and Queensland Health (QLDH) had other, more pressing priorities. We would simply have to make do and carry on. Fortunately for me, I also had a temporary Director of Medical Services (DMS), who was the consummate professional, and knew the QLDH public system intimately. Not a physician, but a highly skilled administrator, he provided solid, thoughtful counsel, honest feedback and sound recommendations. But ultimately, he was only filling in for a colleague's medical leave of uncertain duration and was not committed to the position for the long haul.

I felt I was in my element, many issues being similar to those back in the States; and that I had valuable perspective and past experience to assist us in getting the ED through this unsettled period. I dug in and got to work. There were daily challenges, both minor and significant. One of the most pressing was trying to raise our profile to the upstream specialty services, based in Brisbane, and help them to understand our need to get critical patients off-site in a safe, expeditious manner. Acute Psychiatry was a particular area of risk, as in many countries. There was simply inefficient patient flow out of the ED and into the wider hospital system; thus, the ED backed up and became bed-blocked. And bed-block is synonymous with poor patient satisfaction and outcomes worldwide. But these specialty services, while sympathetic, also had their own limitations and priorities. We really weren't high on anyone's priority list and had little leverage. Although it sometimes felt as if I were stationed at some remote outpost, the work with this temporary DMS and most of the hospital Department Chairs progressed fairly smoothly. I was assured that, as acting ED Director, I would be interviewed for the permanent role once it was later posted. So, I was all-in, and gave it my best efforts.

Then, after only six months of my being in my new role, we experienced yet another change in leadership at the DMS level. Such administrative "churn" is not uncommon in many healthcare systems, in the USA too. But it can be very disruptive, as new personalities are gradually understood and integrated into the workflow and planning. My able mentor was replaced suddenly, in mid-stream, and unfortunately by a DMS who was more difficult for me to work with effectively. Decisions affecting our department's clinical operations began to be made unilaterally at the administrative level, without my knowledge, or the input or consent of the FACEM group. Control of the physicians' conference and leave schedules was centralized and taken out of the FACEM group's control. Insinuations of our possibly rorting (cheating) the system were made, without basis in fact or evidence. The FACEM group became appropriately alarmed, feeling professionally threatened and restive. Worst of all, I began to understand that much of the rudimentary data the hospital had been collecting on patient waiting and transfer times, clinical outcomes, etc., was being interpreted in ways that didn't correlate with my clinical experiences in the ED. I believed that the data was being misinterpreted to make our clinical performance metrics appear better than they actually were. As a patient-focused clinician, this was unacceptable to me. My philosophy has always been: if you are under-performing, highlight that, attempt to understand why and hopefully, begin to correct it. Honesty and transparency in such matters is paramount to effect genuine improvement.

I've also been surprised over my twenty-five years practicing Emergency Medicine, at how infrequent it is for senior administrators to simply visit clinical areas, spend time with their front-line staff and gain perspective from their own personnel. It's been rare in all my US experience, and here in Australia as well. Yet interpretation of data reigns paramount, and universally informs strategic decision-making, almost unchallenged. Systems can become data-obsessed, relying too heavily on it, and making broad-based assumptions from spreadsheets that don't necessarily translate to a better employee or patient experience at the bedside.

In any centralized, bureaucratic system, (mis)interpretation of data is an area fraught with risk. I recall the Russian grain harvests in the 1970's, under the Soviets. They were breaking all records, yet the people were going hungry. There must be robust dissection and consensus about the accuracy and meaning of such data, coupled with diligent oversight regarding its appropriate application to any proposed clinical changes resulting from its interpretation. I'll just say it here: there wasn't. Or little that I was involved in anyway. And I began to suspect that perhaps there were misplaced incentives, at multiple levels, keeping the reporting of accurate data, and its interpretation, an opaque process. It's been often said that "the first priority of any organization is self-preservation;" and I believe that's true. I attended numerous administrative meetings where I shared my perspectives, to a sometimes unenthusiastic response, or where I simply held my tongue. I began to feel a bit like that pesky Yank, shooting his mouth off again. And for the first time in a long while, I began to feel like an outsider, right here in Australia.

I cautiously relate my experiences here to highlight the sometimes perverse incentives and unfortunate outcomes that can occur in any system under stress. And to caution those who might believe that a government-run, centralized healthcare management system will somehow streamline things and produce outcomes far superior to a privately managed model. Not so, in my personal and professional experience. Good outcomes ultimately emanate from good communication and sound leadership, regardless of the system. And we were experiencing some very bad outcomes, despite our ED staff's best efforts. I raised my increasing concerns at what I believed to be the appropriate forums. After failing to gain traction at the local hospital level, I then brought them to the district level; and was met with some disbelief, frankly. Storm clouds were building on the horizon as we worked through these various conflicts. In retrospect, I should've been more weather-wise. But I guess I'm an idealist, or perhaps naive. There were some improvements made and small victories too; ones that convinced me that positive change was possible within the system. And these kept me motivated to carry on. Bad move, mate...

CHAPTER 34: New Zealand #2: Team Nolan Family Road Trip!

January 2016

I thought I was taking sufficient time off to decompress and bond with my family during this professionally challenging period. But, in retrospect, there was less in terms of travel or blog entries in 2015, as I became consumed with the challenges at work. Stephanie and the kids had been keen to visit New Zealand since arriving in Australia in 2012. Now, four years later, we decided the time was right for a full Team Nolan family adventure "across the ditch." Experiential learning with those you love - a highly effective means of countering burnout. And a heck of a lot of fun too!

After hearing all my tales of the wonders awaiting exploration just across the Tasman, everyone wanted to see New Zealand for a Christmas present. So, we planned an eighteen-night road trip covering both islands for January 2016. Trouble is, that's high summer season down here: camper vans, cabins, almost everything, is booked out six to twelve months in advance. It seemed we were a bit tardy in our planning, and out of luck. A tip for anyone considering a similar trip in high season: even if all the campgrounds are "Sold Out" you can almost always get a spot on short notice if all you're looking for is an unpowered tent space. Going back to basics also gives you heaps of flexibility; you can cancel a reservation or call ahead for a new one even at the last spontaneous minute. Or simply camp off the roadside, if you're really in the middle of nowhere. You never quite know where you'll end up on a trip like this, so some flexibility is highly desirable. Thus, we held a Team Nolan meeting and unanimously decided to do it old school; seven people, three weeks, two mountain tents, one packed Toyota Tarago van. Both islands. New Zealand...Road Trip!!

It was epic, and wonderful, if a bit cramped...

DDU Blog entry: After an easy three-hour flight across the Tasman Sea, Brisbane to Auckland, we started out by driving a Toyota van rental a few hours east, right out of the Auckland airport onto the Coromandel peninsula, a beautiful area with forested mountain ranges above wild beaches and bluffs. Not heavily touristed, it's more of a Kiwi family holiday escape. We were tipped off by some well-traveled Aussie friends. It's well worth checking out. Cathedral Cove is the most famous landmark on this coastline, and pretty impressive; but there are many other fascinating features in this part of the world. And to add a bit of magical wonder to the whole adventure, the Pohutukawa trees, flowering crimson red at Christmastime, were in full, festive bloom - a Kiwi icon and a memorable touch.

We camped a few nights at Tiarua/Pauanui. Two beautiful, small coastal towns on a complex marine estuary. A small volcanic spire affords fantastic views of the surrounding landscapes. Surprisingly "a butt chully" and windy at this season, being so far north. The kids were fully rugged-up and enjoying the outdoors environment, so different to mid-summer Brisbane, only three hours' flight away. As it turned out, the first two nights out were the coldest of the trip by far.

The Kiwi accent is very distinct and hard to mimic. To make it even more confusing to a newcomer, at one time approximately 20% of working-aged Kiwi adults were working "across the ditch" (or "acruss the dutch" in Kiwi...) in Australia, and especially Queensland. The weather and pay are better, and the cost of living, though high, is lower than at home. So, this has created a large population of Kiwi expats of many years standing. Oddly enough, many have acquired a hybrid accent, a sort of "Kiwi-Strine". So, just when you think you're getting the hang of the multiple subtle variations on the English dialect, people with these impossibly mixed accents turn up and send you for a loop. There are some entertaining YouTube videos demonstrating the different accents, for those more deeply interested in such arcana. A few quick examples the kids had fun with while on the road in Nuh Zilla:

The first thing you notice on landing in NZ from QLD is that it's a bit chilly. In Kiwi, this would be pronounced as "a butt chully..." which became a recurring joke while camping around the place; 'cause Nuh Zilla, while certainly beautiful, is indeed "a butt chully." An ice cooler, or "esky" in Strine, is termed a chilly bin, or "chully bun" in Kiwi; fifty cents is approximated "fuffty sunce" That sort of thing. Fun to try to mimic, but difficult to master.

DDU Blog entry: Heading south, still on the North Island, Rotorua is famous for hot springs, geysers, mineral springs and all things geothermal. Hopefully you will camp well upwind, as the dense sulfurous stench is certainly noticeable. This whole town has some really bad gas! Our three Nolan ladies loved spending a leisurely afternoon at the elaborate and posh Polynesian Spa thermal hot spring mineral baths here. The following day, while swimming at a chilly mountain lake, a local woman informed us of the beautiful, free, natural hot springs at Wai-O-Tapu, some thirty km south of Rotorua and right on our way heading south. "It flows right under the small bridge there," she offered. We arrived in a cool, light drizzle, under gray skies to find a lovely, steaming pool of very hot water, which was formed right at the junction with a clear, cold stream. It was a unique experience to find your perfect temperature by moving between the two very distinct water streams. Cold and clear meeting cloudy and simmering... I found that moving up into the purely hot flow was almost excruciating. It certainly made for a memorable hour, soaking in a natural hot springs pool, while surrounded by native Kiwi bushland, and right off an easy side road. It's another highly recommended diversion in these parts. We continued southward around the beautiful, flooded volcano calderas of Lakes Rotorua and Taupo, up onto the high and wild Tongariro plateau and headed into Tongariro National Park. We arrived in a white-out drizzle, right on dark. Luckily, I'd reserved a rustic cabin for this very exposed portion of the trip. Needless to say, it was a very prescient move, as we passed a cold, windy and wet first night happily playing cards and eating popcorn with the kids, while planning the next day's adventures for Team Nolan.

We'd initially planned to hike the stunning moonscape of the Tongariro alpine crossing: it's an eighteen km trail up between two of the three active volcanoes here, and one of nine designated Great Walks in New Zealand. It's considered to be one of the best long day hikes in NZ and is entirely

unique. Brisk winds gusting to 50 km/hr. forced us to choose a lower, less
exposed fourteen km hike to the isolated Tama Lakes, passing by the
picture perfect, and powerful Taranaki Waterfall. The younger kids and
Stephanie breathed a big sigh of relief at this shorter and less exposed
death march. It's hard to capture the vast, windswept austerity of this place
in pictures. In my forty years of serious hiking, I have to say, it's an entirely
unique and intriguing environment. It was also the film location for
Mordor and Mount Doom of the Lord of The Rings fame, and well-chosen
for that role. The active, snow-capped volcanoes dominate the skyline and
add a very exotic feel to the already alien landscape here. It's well worth a
detour and several days of exploring this unique, alpine desert
environment.

Leaving the other-worldly Tongariro plateau and heading still further
south on Route 1 towards Wellington felt like re-entering planet Earth, as
the farmlands gradually reappeared and became increasingly lush with the
drop in elevation. Wellington, aka "Windy Wello" is a small, compact city
sitting along the deep, protected lee of Wellington Harbor, at the
southernmost tip of North Island NZ. It's a cool, arty place where we spent
the night and had a lively pizza party at a colorful, hipster, craft-beer tavern
downtown. One activity not to be missed here is the fabulous collection of
Maori culture, art and architecture at Te Papa Museum, right in the CBD
on the waterfront. It's an exceptional regional museum with a very focused
sense of purpose and place. A real cultural highlight of our NZ adventure.

Although one could spend months exploring this intriguing city and its
surrounds, we were once again on a greater mission: the epic crossing of
Cook Strait, linking the North and South Islands of New Zealand, by ferry.
Approximately fourteen miles across, with an average depth of 420 feet,
but plunging to over 1300 feet, it's considered to be among the most
unpredictable bodies of water on the planet. Miraculously again, we
crossed this infamously treacherous strand of ocean without incident or
even much seasickness, under light sea breezes and placid skies. After
breaching the impressive rolling swells at the inlet to Wellington Harbor
and passing out into Fitzroy Bay, it was smooth sailing indeed, past the
remote sea cliffs marking the terminal end of the North Island and onwards
into the variegated, enforested fiords of the Marlborough Sound region of
South Island New Zealand (SINZ). We landed at the ferry terminus at

pleasant, petite Picton under soft blue skies and calm seas; luckily for us all, as they only cancel the ferries when seas are running over eight meters, or twenty-four feet!

Our route then took us through the bucolic Marlborough wine country near Nelson, world famous especially for their crisp, tangy Sauvignon Blancs. We could not tarry though, as we were headed still deeper - out along the winding northern coastlines of the South Island and further west for several nights of camping and day hiking in the sublime Abel Tasman National Park. Our base in this region was the popular beach resort town of Pohara Beach, where the wide, fine sandy beach and shallow, warm and protected bay proved to be a SINZ rarity. At low tide, Pohara beach reveals an extensive silty mudflat of extremely fine consistency for vast distances offshore. The kids greatly enjoyed slathering themselves up, head to toe, and rolling around in the sun-warmed, slick coating.

The hiking in Abel Tasman NP was also impressively unique; exploring its sandy, calm bays separated by tumbled, forested fingers of rocky headlands was reminiscent of coastal Maine, around Acadia National Park. There are multi-day traverses of the entire coastline here, but we only had time for a few day hikes. Returning from one, we could hear excited screams echoing out on the beach from the forest trail. On arriving at the scene, we witnessed an incredible natural phenomenon. It seems the high tide here regularly fills a large sandy basin, swelling inland. At turn of tide, the water then rushes back out the narrow mouth, being forced back seaward with an almost whitewater velocity. The locals were jumping happily in, being pulled briskly through the river-like narrows and deposited a hundred yards or so out on an offshore sandbar. The sandy bottom here made this a non-life-threatening natural thrill ride; which I did a few times with the older kids. It was a surprising experience unlike anything I'd ever seen or done in the wilds before, or since.

Abel Tasman NP is a very popular (i.e., busy) and highly scenic coastline that one could, again, spend weeks exploring. A bit off the standard tourist track, it's a more subdued, pastoral landscape, in an almost genteel part of the South Island. And it's said to have the most days of SINZ sunshine annually; perfect for growing that lush, citrusy Marlborough Sauvignon Blanc. For these reasons, the region has recently become a popular retirement spot among Kiwis and one that deserves your consideration on a potential visitor's itinerary.

Further along, we headed for the wild west coast, towards Westport and the colorfully named Cape Foulwind, with its seal colony and picturesque lighthouse, (again, under startlingly clear, blue skies). We camped at Cape Foulwind, on a lush, broad green lawn under the finest weather and stars imaginable - especially for a place that looks fortunate to get perhaps a half-dozen or so similar days a year. Lucky for us indeed, as the coastal headlands, open beaches with sea stacks and abundant, varied bird and marine life here were all truly remarkable, and the place almost deserted. Further south along the coastal road, Route 6, Pancake Rocks at Punakaiki, with its unique compressed rock formations, blow holes and sea caves was worthwhile to explore, but under a finally thickening and threatening cloud cover. We explored the quaint, coastal town of Hokitika (famous for its greenstone, aka Pounamu - a highly prized, ornamental jade found locally); and the Franz Josef and Fox Glaciers - fitfully, under truly wretched, and more typical, heavy rainfall and windy conditions. This forced us to seek out a miracle cabin for the night at Fox Glacier instead of our planned tent camping, to keep morale high and to dry everyone out. Considered to be among the very finest coastal drives on Earth, the entire west coast of SINZ did not disappoint; it was remote, stormy, moody and ultimately mystical. No place to live, perhaps; but certainly, a wonderful area to explore. And alas, now locked away now in the confines of my memory alone, after a complete camera failure. For those planning on taking this well-worn, but still wild trip, yes, do - just plan on, and dress for, exceptionally crappy weather and head out...You'll be well rewarded regardless.

DDU Blog entry: Leaving the sublime, but stormy, west coast behind, once again climbing over imposing Haast Pass and heading east and inland towards hip little Wanaka and Queenstown beyond, Team Nolan was working together as a well-oiled road-tripping machine. Great travelers! At this point the trip was going very well. Our five kids all happy, active and engaged. We were hiking and adventuring outdoors, surrounded by wild nature, every day. Stephanie's organizational skills were remarkable: cooking daily for seven on an ancient, two-burner Coleman camp stove is a heroic feat indeed! We camped again at the northern end of Lake Wanaka, near the funky, tiny mountain village of the same name, a quieter, more pristine alternative to fun, but hectic Queenstown, only an hour away.

Next morning, while we were driving along the shores of Lake Wanaka, we passed by the remarkably steep form of Mt. Roy, which I'd hiked prior to the Milford Track in 2014. No wonder it kicked my butt so thoroughly, I reminisced; it rises quite dramatically to an impressive height right above Lake Wanaka. We drove further around the lake than I ever had in the past, completing a fifty km drive to the very end of the gravel road that terminates in Mt Aspiring National Park. The landscape here on the Central Otago plateau is the polar opposite of the wet, wild and windy west coast, only some thirty miles away. Much higher and drier, with a ranchy ambiance. Very reminiscent of western Montana, complete with herds of cattle, sheep and lots of barbed-wired pastures, all backed by the towering, jagged peaks.

Our goal: hiking the Rob Roy Valley Track, a stunning, varied, twelve km trek that's considered one of the very best day hikes in NZ, and that's saying a lot. We headed out under perfect blue skies, and the hike did not disappoint; in fact, was even better than advertised. After crossing the impressive swing bridge (cross your first one and you'll understand... they're well-named), the trail heads steadily up the valley through beech and fern-clad forest. Middle-Earth comes to life! Occasional openings in the forest canopy reveal massive, glaciated peaks, shimmering in the intense sunlight high overhead, and building plenty of anticipation to encourage you to keep moving ever higher. The trail ends above the stunted timberline in a huge glacial cirque. There's plenty of open space to stretch out in the high-altitude sunshine and have lunch with friends while being serenaded by the music of a hundred waterfalls, rivulets and rills. Truly, Rivendell found! It was an enchanting experience that we will fondly remember forever. And a perfect challenge for active kids: tough, but not overwhelming.

The next morning, we all made the short but steep hike up Mt. Iron, right outside of downtown Wanaka. The views of the lake and the central Otago plateau from this flat-topped mesa are panoramic; stunning in 360 degrees. Again, highly recommended for families, and only about a one-hour round trip.

We then made a quick day trip down into Queenstown, as the kids really wanted to see what all the fuss was about. It was a pleasant day exploring the region, and returning again to the birthplace of bungee jumping, since

1988, at Kawarau Bridge. The adrenaline pumping visitor's center is a mandatory free stop, though a single jump will set you back over $100 Kiwi. On this particular day, our older teens deferred from making their leap of faith, even though I volunteered to pay up, if they simply supplied the bravery. Perhaps next time? Visiting Queenstown was an enjoyable outing, but we happily returned again to less frenetic Wanaka to camp by the pristine lake there.

Moving further north, as I had in 2014, the Central Otago plateau gives way to a vast inland grazing area known as the Mackenzie country. This region was settled by pioneering families from Scotland and is still comprised of large, remote sheep stations. Next morning dawned bright and dry. We hiked Mt John for panoramic views of the surrounding Mackenzie countryside, and to check out the telescopes operated by the University of Canterbury due to the purity of the night skies in this region. It was wonderful to repeat this hike, as the payoff in scenery, for effort expended, simply can't be beat. And there's even an excellent summit cafe. Again, highly recommended for almost anyone; as is the Tekapo campground at the foot of Mt John, with adjacent mineral hot springs to soak your weary bones as a post-hike reward. We celebrated the successful trip thus-far with an epic feast at Kohan, which was packed this time with Japanese tour-bus groups. We seemed to be the only non-Japanese patrons there, so they must be doing something right! I initially balked at the $12 desserts, but the kids begged me, so I gave in and shelled out for several. What arrived table-side - fantastically-spun sugar candies, fresh fruits and artfully arranged sorbets - simply blew us all away, and was a high point of the party. If dining at Kohan, you must try one of their desserts, trust me. Worth every blessed penny and calorie... And while shopping next door, at the adjacent Japanese gift shop, be sure to grab a couple of vacuum-packed, smoked Kiwi deer cocks. They are a bit dear, but they might make a fantastic gift, or conversation starter, for the right person. And you can even purchase them with or without, attached deer balls, that is... Dearer still if you want the balls attached too. I assure you the Nolan kids were literally splitting their sides playing along with that fascinating cultural discovery. It was hysterical madness of the most genuine sort and remains a fond family memory. But, in the end, they couldn't convince me to make the deer purchase, either with, or without...

Anyhow, two hours further north brings you back into Christchurch and our final destination. The city is recovering nicely from the devastating earthquakes of 2011. What were depressing vacant lots in the CBD during my visit in January 2014 are now being slowly filled with foundations and rebar forms. Signs of life everywhere, but there's still a very long way to go. Someone mentioned that the rebuilding of the Christchurch CBD was now the largest construction project ongoing in the entire southern hemisphere. From what we saw, I can believe it!

As an update on the city's progress in 2018, the surprisingly iconic Re:START shipping container mall that was first assembled downtown in October 2011, right after the devastating earthquakes, was finally decommissioned, as being no longer necessary, in January 2018, after serving for more than six years as a living symbol of Kiwi resilience in the face of almost overwhelming loss.

DDU Blog entry: The Botanic Garden sustained little damage, and is magnificent now in its full summer bloom, it being January 2016 here in the Southern Hemisphere. Equally impressive, and miraculously undamaged, is the superb Canterbury Museum, on the Botanic Gardens grounds. One of the world's best regional museums, and free, it contains extensive collections of Maori artifacts, Antarctic exploration and New Zealand bird life dioramas. It's unusual, exotic and reminds you yet again of just how unique and isolated a nation New Zealand actually is and is highly recommended by all the Nolan kids.

So, finally, it was time for the ritual end-of-trip celebration. We found a wonderful wood-fired pizza place on Tripadvisor, went right over and gorged out. We'd seen and experienced an amazing amount while traveling rough together over eighteen days across both main islands. It was a real family bonding experience in all the best ways. New Zealand is a very different animal to Australia in almost every regard, and we each carried home with us enough Kiwi and Team Nolan family memories to last a long while yet; so blessed!

To summarize, if you are ever planning on traveling this way Down Under, Australia and New Zealand, though neighbors joined by common heritage and language, are otherwise entirely different places to my mind. My advice is not to miss either, but to plan on spending adequate time, two or three weeks in each country, as a minimum. You could easily spend a lifetime. It seems we are perhaps heading in that direction?!

CHAPTER 35: A Sea Change

By early 2016, it had become increasingly clear that our journey's tides were subtly shifting. Our local ED was under increasing pressure from rapidly growing patient clinical demand and was carrying more of the risk for the remainder of the hospital. Fully half of our critical-care interventions and airway management intubations were being done on inpatients. Bed-block and lengthy access queues were becoming our daily reality. The EM physician group's attempts at effecting operational change, led by yours truly, were met by the hospital's Administration with the almost universal avoidance response, "There's no money in the budget...", or even worse, complete silence. Many of our senior ED staff members were being kept intentionally off-balance on temporary contracts, affecting their buy-in and causing a growing sense of professional unease. Something had to change; many things, in fact. Outside consultants were brought in to help advise on the best ways forward. Recall the old saying, "Once you have to start relying on outside consultants to tell you your own business, you're already going down."

True, that...

Over this six month period, there was a growing philosophical rift between myself and a few members of the local Administration. While I saw myself as a vocal advocate for my beleaguered staff and a champion of badly needed modernization and operational change, some in Administration may have regarded me as being that demanding Yank, who really didn't understand the Aussie way of doing things. Perhaps we were both somewhat correct? It's hard for me to say, as the lack of communication was becoming very apparent. I understood that a change in ED leadership was in the wind and that I was most likely going to be bypassed; so why fight it? Then again, as much of the ruckus boiled down, in my mind, to a personality conflict with the current Director of Medical Service (DMS), why not work to retain my hard-earned position? Think Game of Thrones, but with scalpels. And perhaps, I was the doomed Ned Stark-like figure, idealistically trying to bring order to encroaching chaos, but with a stethoscope instead of a broadsword. Whatever; winter was coming...

Working through a new song **"Sea Change"** helped solidify my feelings of increasing restlessness and resolve. Our period of contentment and settling, so brief in retrospect, was coming to an end.

"I'm feeling like it's time again for a sea change
Tides are moving under me, isn't life strange, you rearrange..."

The song's written in a harder, electric, almost psychedelic style. The keening melody and odd chord changes feel off-kilter, out of sorts... It turned out to be more prescient than I probably realized at the time.

CHAPTER 36: Fiji - Dipping our Toes Further into the South Seas

DDU Blog entry: Well, it was never even supposed to happen. Claire wanted to go somewhere exotic to celebrate her "Sweet 16th". She wanted to go to Thailand, of all places. Even though we'd likely never get closer than we were here in Brisbane, it simply wasn't going to happen, sweetie... Too far, too costly, too complicated. Too, well, everything! Then, suddenly, it occurred that there was a great Emergency Medicine conference being held in Fiji, and right on her big day, and I'd already had a vacation block scheduled. BINGO! Before I knew it, we were on our way to Fiji, an easy, direct, three-hour flight, dead-east from Brisbane. Our first trip into the fabled South Pacific, this was to be another "girls' trip", meaning deluxe, with lots of food and lounging about, and endless selfies. We managed to find the three boys temporary lodgings around Brisbane with friends, another miracle of sorts. It was simply meant to be...

The conference was being held at Denarau Island, a multi-resort area just south of Nadi, on the West Coast of Viti Levu, the largest and most populous of the Fijian Islands. Purists may sniff; it is after all, not the "real" Fiji. But as a quick getaway, it provides a very relaxing and even magical tropical escape. I was in need of some R&R, and starting to think we may not be traveling in these parts for much longer. So, what the heck, let's go! Flying in, direct from Brisbane, landing right at the tropical dusk, you first notice the fragrant air and the warmth and relaxed attitude of the all-Fijian staff. . "Bula" means welcome...

DDU Blog entry: When you wake up to soft warm breezes and gently lapping waves, you've definitely gone full troppo. Over breakfast, Fijian musicians serenade with their distinctly high, lulling harmonies accompanied by acoustic guitars and ukuleles. It's a wonderful way to greet the morning!

Right off, we were booked for a full-day snorkel and catamaran cruise with Coral Cats. They were #1 on Tripadvisor, so we booked ahead, anticipating a great adventure. Stephanie stayed ashore to avoid severe sun exposure and perhaps a touch of sea-sickness. Under picture perfect weather, the girls and I headed out into the Mamanuca Islands a few hours sail west of Nadi. The smaller islands off the west coast are sheltered by Viti and Vanua Levu from the prevailing winds, so we sailed lake-calm waters, under light westerly winds. Claire and Cate were in deep bliss, sunning like lizards on the beanbag lounge chairs resting on the bow netting. Paradise found! The Fijian crew were outstanding, providing animated commentary and platters of fresh tropical fruits on the outbound leg.

DDU Blog entry: On the morning snorkel, the water was warm and calm, with good visibility, fifty-sixty feet. Decent coral with little bleaching, lots of colorful fish, though nothing big - no sharks or rays. It was an easy, comfortable and very beautiful experience. The multiple smaller islands we passed, over shallow, turquoise waters felt somewhat Caribbean, but with a distinct Melanesian/Polynesian flavor....the South Pacific indeed!

Next, we pulled into Musket Cove for a full-on Fijian BBQ lunch ashore. There was an entire grilled fish, pork, tropical fruits and cold drinks; a nice break and after-lunch, a pleasant stretch walking along the crescent sand cove here.

After lunch, the second snorkel was even better: a long, sloping coral bank, covered with soft coral forests, and some large Staghorns, Shelves etc. Clouds of fishes of all sizes and descriptions, including larger Parrot and Triggerfish in the deeper reaches where the corals dropped out of sight. Simply a superb snorkeling experience. The daughties were in heaven, jumping off the boat into the warm, crystalline seas.

The entire day was so well-paced and handled. The crew, company, food, scenery, snorkeling and overall vibe was just one of gentle relaxation, exotic land and seascapes, with a bit of adventure to top it all off. We sailed back towards Denarau Harbor into a freshening breeze, everyone mellowed out by the sun, sea and gently rolling Catamaran. The crew set out a deep-sea trolling rod, which we watched with vague attention, but nothing struck. They said they catch fish about 50% of the time. The athletic Fijian crew members also made quite a show of hanging from the back of the swiftly moving Cat and performing tricks...essentially breakdancing over the skimming waters. Impressive feats of daring and mesmerizing to watch! It really was the perfect day. Coral Cats, is #1 for good reason was and even better than hoped. They are highly recommended if you are ever in Nadi/Port Denarau.

Back ashore, the resorts each have free nightly activities which are wisely focused on traditional Fijian culture. You can witness multiple performances, including full-dress traditional "Meke" ceremonies, fire dances and chants that are only seen today in the more remote villages on special occasions. Staff are all local Fijians, renowned for their genuine warmth and natural sense of hospitality; not a single, disheveled Euro-backpacker server to be seen. Cynics may feel it's all a bit staged, and not "authentic". Whatever... I found this added a lot to creating a specific sense of place and enriched each languid evening. Given the number of tropical resorts springing up worldwide, I think it's vital for any to create a sense of uniqueness of place. Otherwise, why travel to Fiji, versus Bali or Samoa? For me, Denarau Island projected a genuine sense of Fijian identity and hospitality in a classy, understated manner. Very well done.

Another unique feature of Denarau Island is that the six high-end resorts are contiguous and share a mile or so of uninterrupted beachfront facing West and North. You can walk freely among all the beautiful gardens, pools and water features, and use any restaurants and facilities that strike your fancy. All service and approach roads, golf, tennis courts, etc. are on the inside of the complex. Thus, there are no distractions between the open, manicured lawns and the shoreline. On evening, the entire beachfront, facing the glowing embers of a dying South Pacific sunset over the Mamanuca Island chain, is subtly lit by gas tiki torches under swaying coconut palms and tropical flowers. Restaurants and bars are open air, with some setting tables out on the sand. The overall experience is one of soft, green escape. A fantasy perhaps, but a pleasantly persuasive one. I'm in....

DDU Blog entry: Finally, it was time for the grand event; Claire's long-awaited, "Sweet 16" birthday party! It all fell together like it was fated. We managed, with a little intrigue, to source an entire, locally made birthday cake, custom-decorated in chocolate ganache and strawberries, and have it secretly delivered tableside, complete with the Fijian staff singing Happy Birthday to our lovely, blushing Claire. The Fijians are well-known as enthusiastic and excellent singers as a rule, and they did not disappoint. Complete with a tropical "mocktail" toast, the girls were now completely over the Fijian moon, to be held, forever-after, under its magical spell...

A tropical squall had been ominously building all evening. The winds suddenly kicked- up and it broke heavily in a vigorous, but brief downpour; adding excitement to the exotic ambience. Soon after, it dissipated, giving way to a warm, languid evening under southern stars. I'm sure this was a birthday that our beloved Claire will always treasure. I know Stephanie, Cate and I certainly will.

Oh, and the EM conference... That was great too! High-level discussions, good content, engaged, friendly colleagues, nice snacks and afternoons off. The perfect balance.

DDU Blog entry: Suddenly, like all dreams, it was over. The sun rose bright on our last morning in Fiji, the sky the pale, clear blue of the Fijian flag. Up at 0500, for a quick final look around paradise, a few photo snaps and then, reluctantly, into the waiting cab for Nadi airport and a return to reality. But it was a wonderful respite, a luxurious tropical dream; one we hope to revisit someday.

No doubt, given more time and planning, much of the "real" Fiji can still be found in the hinterlands, and especially on multi-day sails into the over three hundred islands that make up this country. Perhaps the subject of a future DDU blog: a fourteen day sail and snorkel/ dive trip through the remote Yasawa Island group? Sigh...one can, and should, always continue to dream...! Vanaka, DDU

So, that's the brief story of our adventures further into the South Seas thus far. Luke has been fortunate enough to attend a school-sponsored immersion trip to rural Samoa, one of the most traditional of the islands, where they brought school supplies to rural kids and slept in communal village Bures, the traditional grass huts. As honored guests, the local villagers slaughtered a pig and held a village-wide celebration for them, an experience he will never forget! He's also been fortunate to travel to the Big Island in Hawaii with friends. So he's pretty widely-traveled at sixteen! One could spend years, exploring the South Pacific islands lying just off the Australian east coast, to say nothing of vast, inscrutable Asia beyond. But those are adventures for another time, or another lifetime...

While paradise might not truly exist in this life, a reasonable approximation for me would be Fiji. As an entrée, Denarau Island was perfect, easy in/easy out, whetting the appetite for future adventures further off the beaten track, in true Doc Down Under fashion. And, for once, no snakes...!

CHAPTER 37: Aussie Citizenship - It's Cool to be Dual

June 2016

DDU Blog entry: In June 2016, we crossed a major milestone by becoming dual citizens of the USA and Australia. No one was more surprised at the outcome than me, except for maybe Stephanie!

As our big day approached, excitement mixed with mild apprehension. It's a major commitment to swear allegiance to another country. Many people have to surrender their native birthright to attain Aussie Citizenship. Luckily for us, both Australia and the USA allow for dual citizenship. I would never surrender my American citizenship for another country. That said, Australia is a wonderfully safe, clean and progressive country with a bright future. Also, a trans-Tasman agreement grants Aussies and Kiwis the mutual right to live, work and retire in either country, thereby opening up future opportunities to live and work in New Zealand with little limitation as well. All in all, it was an offer that was easy to accept.

Attaining Citizenship was a major, if unexpected, corollary benefit of our spending some years Down Under and simply growing to love the people, lifestyle and opportunities available here. Stephanie had more misgivings, and even a touch of melancholy to be honest; but as I reassured her...

"We're not losing our American heritage, just gaining some Australian. All additive, nothing taken away..."

DDU Blog entry: The ceremony itself was really touching and classy. One hundred twenty-eight new residents with families and supportive friends almost filling the Redland Shire performance center auditorium. Dignitary speeches, a few local choirs, patriotic sing-a-longs; it was a full evening - an event even. It was very moving to become accepted as a full-participant in the dynamic historical flow that is the ever-evolving Australian nation. It's remarkable to consider what this young country has been able to achieve: going from impoverished prisoners scraping out a bare living from crude bark huts in the wilderness of Botany Bay in the 1790's, to the modern skyscrapers of Sydney Harbor today, all accomplished in just over two hundred years. A federated Commonwealth only since 1901, and now the world's thirteenth largest economy by GDP. And by some measures, one of the world's wealthiest nations, considering national GDP per capita. The new, New World... A truly remarkable achievement, and a lasting testament to the British genius for engineering and governance. I trust that every member of the Nolan family can and will make some small contribution to the ongoing success of this venture.

In our turn, we all got up to receive the mayor's handshake and an official parchment document from the Redland Shire, and each also received a potted palm to plant as a welcome to our new country. A very nice, green touch. Curiously, there was even a life-sized, cut-out photo of Queen Elizabeth standing on-stage, for those old-school Poms who might want to memorialize their new status with a picture of them standing next to the Queen! "Yah...nah... I'm still American as well, mate. We threw off the royal family a couple a hundred years ago; but, no worries, cheers..." We then went into town for a giant Chinese food banquet at the Nolan kids' request. "The Happy Garden" indeed; and a night that called out for a real multi-cultural celebration of this family milestone.

So, it was a night to remember. A defining moment in our adventures Down Under. Who knows how this trip, these paths taken, will impact and reverberate in our lives and the lives of our kids, and even grandkids, for generations to come? We are now a modern pioneer family. It sure seemed like a good idea at the time, but like many decisions in life, the final repercussions and outcomes are simply unknowable. Good? Bad? It's uncertain, and I'm comfortable with that. Only time will tell. For right now though, we are dual, and that's very cool.

CHAPTER 38: New Zealand #3: Hiking the Routeburn Track

November 2016

I'd planned to attend the 2016 annual Australasian College for Emergency Medicine (ACEM) conference in Queenstown, NZ. It was scheduled for late spring, in a great location - a must attend. We were initially planning for Stephanie to come along, but ultimately, she deferred, due to her burgeoning responsibilities as a mom of five, and now also busy working at the kids' school and supervising multiple teen activities. And even if we could find a sitter, there was no way she would actually leave the country without them all in tow (so unlike me...!). At least I tried. So, Aidan, our fourteen-year-old Huck Finn, happily played hooky to spend ten days road-tripping with his dad, in her place, around South Island New Zealand (SINZ). Experiential learning, the very best kind... It turned out to be a fantastic father-son bonding adventure.

DDU Blog entry: This was the perfect opportunity to schedule the Routeburn Track with Ultimate Hikes for three days prior to the conference. At thirty-five km (twenty-two miles) over three days, including hiking the entire second day above timberline, it's considered one of the very finest of the nine Great Walks of New Zealand, and is said to be "two thirds as long and twice as hard" as the Milford Track. Aidan was over the moon to be going along on the trip of a lifetime with his ever-wandering daddy-o. We flew into Queenstown from Brisbane via Auckland, arriving late on the evening prior to starting out, and so missed the Ultimate Hikes pre-hike orientation. Landing between the tight, sheer mountainsides surrounding Queenstown in a brisk crosswind is an adventure in its own right, believe me! Well, we were off to a vigorous start anyway.

We were up and out by 0500, walking the quiet, chilly streets of Queenstown in the pre-dawn light, to board the Ultimate Hikes bus down to Te Anau, a two-and-a-half-hour ride. It was a bit early, pre-prime hiking season in mid-November, the trails having been open for only a few weeks. So, the hike was only half-booked, and thankfully less crowded, but with the added risk of experiencing less than settled weather. Frankly, the weather was looking a bit iffy, with reports of rain and snow showers, especially in the big mountains to the south; right where we were heading into...

Being early season, there were only twenty-four hikers coming along, making the trip feel pretty relaxed and open. In high season, the forty-hiker limit is filled daily, months in advance. Ultimate Hikes performed as I remembered: friendly, encouraging and very smooth in all respects. I'll admit to being a bit apprehensive, contemplating my hiking over twenty-five rugged miles with a light pack in cold, wet weather. Perhaps a bit too much discomfort to be considered actually "fun"? I'm sure every one of our mostly "over-40" group was silently contemplating the same thoughts as we headed further south on the bus, into the silently brooding, storm-darkening mountains. The hip, young guides were funny, attentive and reassuring, which helped break the mood of cautious anticipation. Aidan was pumped up and enthusiastic, but with no real idea of what lay before us. I began to nod off to the warm, lulling thrum of the bus engine, as we made our journey steadily southwards.

DDU Blog entry: Suddenly, the bus pulls into the trailhead parking lot. In a blur of frenetic activity, you off-load the gear, your drowsy reverie snapped by the startlingly wet and cool breeze outside. It's raining now, as we leave the rustic shelter in small, tight-knit groups; you immediately enter the primeval forest, and the hike begins. The sound of water trickles from everywhere in this green, captivating world. Water music surrounds you and all other concerns soon recede. You focus only on the trail ahead, hiking quickly right out of the gate, to get the blood flowing and your core warmed up. Ahead lie three days of complete separation from the outside world. Hello reality... How rare and marvelous! Parts of the Southwest New Zealand (Fiordland) World Heritage region get over seven meters of rainfall a year, more than in the Amazon basin. It's very, very wet. Plan for that and you're good to go.

Earland Falls, thunderous and bracingly cold in full flood, at 76 meters (250 feet), is a highlight of the first day's gradual ascent above Lake Howden. We carefully pick our way down a slick, boulder-strewn detour out of the main spray coming from off the base of the falls. But it's plenty wet, and even wetter with the misty rain that's falling steadily now. But we are warming up and finding the rhythm of the trail. After a long, steep down section we arrive at Lake MacKenzie Lodge, our stop for the night. The cloud ceiling is lifting a bit, holding out hope for clearing summits tomorrow. It's been a vigorous twelve-km (eight-mile) hike on day one, six hours out in the cold and wet. Call me a wimp if you must, but a hot shower and a dry bunk will be much appreciated tonight!

After a somewhat restless sleep, we awaken to a gray, steady drizzle. This will be the hardest, most exposed day. Through-hikers coming over the ridge in the opposite direction are relaying that they've walked through three days of clouds and rain and saw no peaks at all. A beautiful experience, spiritual indeed, if perhaps not ideal. But, when hiking a long trail, you take what nature throws your way. It's all part of the adventure, and always a unique experience. Aidan and I start out day two, first out of the lodge with the lead guide, Bree, setting a blistering pace, trying to warm up and get the blood flowing. At twenty-one years old, ripped, and raised on a local ranch, she is clearly in her element, as she hops like a mountain sheep from moss-covered boulder to boulder, steadily uphill. She's basically kicking our asses... The trail moderates into a series of long uphill sections, zigzagging steadily up the face of the ridge, now exposed above the timberline. Fellow hikers look like colorful ants struggling, strung out below, as the lake gradually recedes beneath the low-hanging cloud cover. After an hour and a half of hard going, we arrive at a small stone bluff, just under the bare ridgeline, where we have a hot tea and "bikkies" (plain cookies or "biscuits"), adjust clothing to ventilate, and prepare to traverse the very exposed Hollyford Face. This formation stretches along high above the Hollyford Valley and River, now barely visible through the rapidly shifting clouds below. It's a magical, spiritually uplifting environment...truly, my happy place; and it feels wonderful to be back in this rugged, austere backcountry once again. And to be sharing it all with my second son - even better! Aidan is looking tired and a bit uncertain as to what comes next. Steady mate, steady... The raw wind is gusting and swirling dramatically just above our sheltered heads, and I feel reluctant to leave this spot of relative calm. But then again, we can't stay here...

Thus, prepped and energized, we emerge to sprint the remaining hundred meters in full exposure, crossing over the ridge at Ocean Peak Corner, directly into a stinging westerly wind, twenty to thirty km/hr., which is now spitting sleet into my eyes and burning exposed skin. As I'd neglected to put on goggles, my eyeballs and face feel literally on fire, and visibility is ravaged through the tears streaming down my face. Too late to stop now; I move forward as quickly as possible. The force of the wind shakes my entire body like some angry, unseen assailant. It's certainly an invigorating wake-up call! Its ferocity is a bit of a shock but one that soon abates somewhat, once we tuck down onto the slightly more sheltered Hollyford Face. This is a long, exposed trail section, well above timberline, that offers wild, sublime vistas across the Hollyford Valley, over multiple jagged spires and ridges, as the cloud ceiling begins to lift higher. Exciting and enlivening, this intense adrenaline rush is why we venture so, hiking exposed to the raw elements above timberline. It's a world unlike any other. As we traverse, the ceiling, driven by the freshening breeze, now lifts dramatically, exposing the serrated, saw-toothed rooftops of the entire Southern Alps, still brilliant in their late-winter snow cover. Stunning in the broken light, with cloud shadows wind-racing, and the sun-shafts highlighting myriad fissures, remote nooks and gullies in fine detail. It's all simply breathtaking! Heating up now from exertion within my protective shell, driven on by adrenaline and excitement, despite the raw, probing winds, I feel entirely self-contained and preoccupied with the trail before me. Nothing else exists except for this activity, this place, this peak moment and these precious few hours. And this is the very magic of alpine adventuring, why I'm drawn back continually. The distant and complex modern world is of no account, high on these ridges. My mind is totally free, yet completely focused on the moment, and the challenges lying just ahead. If I died in this very instant, well, I would already have been in heaven...

And then suddenly, unbelievably, as if to give physical form to my innermost feelings, a fully complete rainbow appears, arching a thousand feet BELOW us, across the entire Hollyford Valley, building in intensity under the rapidly dissipating cloud cover, and shimmering, literally, at our feet...

The second day on the Routeburn involved a wild, challenging hike, punctuated by sharp winds, rain, sleet and snow flurries. The rapidly changing weather, with sudden sunlit shafts illuminating the ragged peaks overhead, added an unpredictable, exciting edge to the adventure. Much more dynamic and energizing than mere placid, clear blue skies. This was Aidan's first long hike above timberline. He seemed enthralled at the raw environment, chaotic weather and the highly charged energy among the group. The start of a lifelong love affair with the high country I trust. Truly an ultimate hike!

Crossing over the exposed, mountainous Harris Saddle, we entered a relatively calm lee above picturesque Lake Harris. The Routeburn Valley, half-hidden in storm, now stretched out below and beyond, out of view, our way forward. This was the very crux of the hike. We felt strong and capable, with time to spare, so were in no hurry to leave this pristine alpine place. It was all, literally, downhill from here. He and I lingered trailside for over an hour, watching the rapidly changing shadows and light play out below, on a massive scale. A light snow flurry swirled gently around us, as I told him of wild times and wilder friends during my Alaskan years in the late 1970s. Formative experiences now long lost to me. I think Aidan saw a completely different side of his dear old Doctor Dad on that ridge, and the mutual efforts we expended bonded us in a very lasting and genuine way. It was an irreplaceable, peak moment for both of us; hopefully, only one of many more yet to come.

Night two was spent at the stunningly sited, modern Routeburn Falls Lodge. It's situated right below the impressive falls that drain the higher glacial cirques, at gnarled timberline, and overlooking the famed Routeburn Valley below. Large picture windows frame the unique high-altitude forests, highlighting this living Banzai landscape. After a blustery, twelve-km, six-hour hike across the raw, open ridges of the SINZ high country, it was a sublime pleasure to contemplate a hot shower, warm bed and, oh yes, prime New Zealand rack of lamb, served with a glass of central Otago Pinot Noir, of course. Ultimate? Indeed!

Because the trip wasn't chock-full, Ultimate Hikes was also kind enough to give Aidan and me a private room at no additional cost. That really was most appreciated. If you've never been stuck with a snoring, grunting, sleep-apneic stranger for a roommate, it makes for a purely horrendous night, trust me. Another reason to love Ultimate Hikes folks - they are simply the best. After forty years of backcountry adventures, of varying levels of exertion, including actual physical danger, you might think I'd feel guilty about "selling out" on such a posh hike. Well, perhaps aging knees and hard-earned wisdom have banished the purist in me - not in the least! Besides the aforementioned hot shower, bunk and tasty prepared meals and libations, the primary benefit of such an arrangement is the need to carry only ten or fifteen lbs. of kit, allowing one to turn a potentially grueling ordeal into a mere skip down the lane. And after all, you still have to do the hard yakka of trekking the miles, or kilometers, all by yourself. There's simply no way around that. Pure bliss!

Day three involved a wonderfully scenic twelve-km (eight-mile) walk down the broadening, and increasingly lush, Routeburn Valley under clearing skies in bright sunshine. A bit hot actually... The trail follows the crystalline, beautiful Routeburn, and weaves through an ancient Beech forest. Simply lovely, but not exactly the adrenaline- pumping austerity of the high ridges. I actually missed them a bit and would've been happy to spend several more days wandering up in the dramatic high-country. Aidan, his eyes now opened to that unique world, heartily agreed. Perhaps the Keppler Track next, mate? Crossing the final swing bridge to the terminal trailhead, we both felt a strong sense of personal accomplishment and bonding as a team. Lifetime memories with my second son, Aidan; now a budding young man at fourteen. Well-earned mateship. How beautiful!

To make this special day even more memorable, Ultimate Hikes then takes the whole group to the famous Glenorchy tavern at the far end of Lake Wakatipu for a microbrew and snacks, including a lighthearted summing up of trip high (and low) points, certificate ceremony and a final farewell. No one wants the adventure to end, and we linger, exchanging trail notes and travel plans. It's been an amazing three-day journey together. Challenges met and overcome, large and small; lifetime memories made.

DDU Blog entry: So, three days of tech-free, primordial bliss in the deep forests and on the high ridges of Fiordland NP, South Island New Zealand. I'll admit, I had a few doubts about my creaky, aging knees and a gimpy left hip before starting out; medical problems that ended up feeling better after completing the hike than before starting out! That indicates something about these medical ailments - more likely disabilities of inaction, perhaps? I felt a real sense of personal achievement on finishing the Routeburn. My preferred, less-intense version of the Iron Man, I suppose. Aidan, having never been on a multi-day hike, was blown away, in the very best sense, but may have to lower his culinary and service standards for the next several decades of road-trips with grubby, college-aged friends. I've been there many times myself. A bit more low rent, but still, always an amazing journey.

For those readers contemplating a trip to SINZ, just say "YES..." Please do yourself a favor and go, though plan to get a bit damp and "chully". Any excellent weather will just be the icing on a very beautiful cake, indeed. For those with a limber step, a stout heart and a few extra coins in pocket; seriously consider enlisting Ultimate Hikes to assist in logistics, permitting and meal planning. They're truly a most excellent group of people, and the smoothest of operators. Both of my trips with Ultimate Hikes have easily surpassed all expectations and made what could have been a daunting trip to organize and complete, a mere trifle. I have no financial interest in giving them DDU's highest recommendation as an adventure traveler's best friend and resource when on South Island New Zealand.

Flushed with our sense of accomplishment on the Routeburn Track, Aidan and I landed back on our feet back in frenetic, funky Queenstown. It's an outdoor hipster, adrenaline-heaven for the post-college, international outdoors crowd, and sits right on stunning Lake Wakatipu. It was my third trip to Queenstown and there was still so much I had yet to experience! Our first full day in town, we headed up to the Shotover Canyon to take a hair-raising trip on the sleek jet boats that ply these narrow gorges at death-defying speeds. Their prop-less design allows them to skim over gravel banks in only a few inches of water. It was a real adrenaline rush, sitting right up in the very front row; but it did take my aging, less-plastic brain a few hours to sort itself back out, to nearly normal, afterwards. Bungy-jumping was out for me. With my luck, it would result in my having a fatal coronary in mid-drop, leaving the staff with a warm body to dispose of. Being an EM doc, I know very well how that feels...most unpleasant. You can thank me now; a wise man knows his limits. No, thanks. Interestingly, Aidan, who's always had a severe height phobia for some unfathomable reason, was also a non-contender in that department. At least we didn't waste precious hours in a ridiculous game of "dare-ya, double-dare ya..." Dumb and Dumber style. We both agreed to gracefully chicken out. I got yer back mate...

Instead, I'd booked a session online at the Asian-styled Onsen hot tubs high above the same Shotover River. They roll the roofs back in fair weather and it was a sublime, restful hour, soaking in the simmering bath while a cooling, lightly falling drizzle peppered the steaming waters. More our gentlemanly style, Aidan and I could both agree.

Aidan is a rabid fisherman however, so we'd brought our rods along, got local licenses, gear and advice, and headed over Cardrona Pass back up to Wanaka to fish pristine Lake Wanaka. We spent a pleasant, but fruitless morning out, fishing flooded grass banks in the ranch country off the Mt. Aspiring Road, past Glendhu Bay. Being November in the high country, it was now spring; the pristine waters ran high and cold. A ripping wind was coming down off the high peaks, making fly casting impossible. New tactics were called for.

Out on a wide gravel riverbank, at the very head of the lake, we split up. Aidan headed upstream on the braided glacial river flats, out of my sight, looking for promising deep holes; I headed down to the mouth, as close to the lake entrance as I dared wade on the softly collapsing, water-logged gravel bank. I switched to casting with a heavy silver spoon for weight against the wind and distance to get out as far as possible into the deeper channel. If there were big fish cruising, I thought, they're gonna be here...

Lost in thought and memory, the fruitless rhythm of dozens of casts drifted by. Mesmerized by the surrounding glacial mountain scenery, I was transported back to my early twenties, fishing for wild salmon and trout up in Kodiak and Sitka, Alaska. The rhythms of casting and reeling had me in an almost meditative trance, when suddenly, a bracingly hard strike startled me back to reality.

As I looked up, a giant South Island New Zealand Brown trout broke the water, not thirty feet offshore, right in front of me...The fish of my dreams! OMG, I was breathless, not wanting to lose this treasured quarry we'd traveled so far to encounter. The fight was on, brief and savage, similar to many I'd had in Alaska with salmon. You don't let these fish have any line to dive and entangle themselves in underwater snags, or they're gone... like a fleeting phantom, or a broken dream. I horsed him in over the gravel bank - a real monster, over twenty-four inches and brilliantly colored. Perhaps the largest trout I'd ever caught, out of hundreds. I called out to Aidan, the mountains, the heavens; anyone within earshot, "Thank you, thank you, thank you!" and did a little victory dance, right there, out on the gravel bank, to be honest. A fisherman's jig. But only the wind replied... I was entirely alone in my moment of greatest success.

There followed a very comical sequence where I determinedly tried to capture a reasonable selfie photo with my dream fish, out of simple necessity. We were alone together. Imagine trying to control a giant, slimy, muscular fish who doesn't share the attraction, pinched under one arm, while holding your camera in the other, desperately trying to take said selfie while staying somewhat dry and slime-free. It just doesn't work at all... This wasn't going to be the beautifully composed, pristine guide photo - with even the fish smiling - mere seconds after the catch, and moments before the atraumatic release, you see in all the glossy calendars and magazines. No, this was bare-knuckled fish-wrestling, essentially into submission...

"Just PLEASE hold still..."

"No way mate, hands off!"

After all, I planned to release the creature unharmed; but my intentions being unclear, he was in strict survival mode. Aidan wasn't there to assist or translate. In short order, I dropped it onto the gravel bank, but really, it was all his fault... The fish rolled and flapped, rolled and flapped - over and over...becoming wrapped-up in mono fishing line, encrusted with coarse gravel and looking like something out of a grade-B horror movie. By now, it was completely encased in a slimy rubble, with hooked-jaw agape - not a good look for any fish, really...

I tried to rinse it off, which only elicited slime production by the bucket-load. We were a filthy, sticky, fishy pair by the time I managed to get a few reasonable snaps. Anyone watching us pantomime from afar, out on the barren riverbank, would surely think I'd gone starkers - completely mad.

The fish and I were both so exhausted on my releasing him that he nearly went belly up; he actually went head down, initially. Tail up... Not an especially healthy release by any measure. Gills gasping pitifully for some desperately needed oxygen, or mouth to mouth, and perhaps a bit of salmonid CPR, he was sinking slowly away from me...

"Oh shit...!"

Now, feeling very guilty at this ignoble parting with my prized trophy, and not wanting his needless death to be my final, and eternal, memory of our good times together, I then bravely waded out into the ice-cold water, to my waist, in jeans and shirt - no waders - all the while sinking deeper into the collapsing, waterlogged gravel bank. I bent over to grasp his slimy tail, now drifting listlessly in three to four feet of frigid water, thus, essentially dunking my entire chest and face into the ice bath and reacting with an involuntary exhalation of shock.

"Do not drown yourself while trying to save this stupid fish," was my line of thinking at that moment, I clearly recall.

So positioned, I gave my prize the appropriate resuscitative maneuver, basically pulling him backwards a couple of times to force life-giving, oxygen-rich water backwards over his gills. Whereupon, he shuddered in revival, flicked his tail smartly, while silently mouthing a quick, "Thanks a lot, you fucking asshole..." and darted off.

And that's the last I ever saw of him really. He never writes... But I do have this slightly odd photo of us together framed in my study, to remind me of the good times. Off-centered, slightly blurry, both of us scowling into the camera, with mouths agape. If I didn't know any better, I'd swear we were both telling each other to "Just fucking stop it, mate," or something similarly inappropriate.

But it was a peak fishing memory in the end - the very stuff of family legend!

Once back in Queenstown, I checked my phone's email and noticed an item from Human Resources. It was one I'd been anticipating for several weeks: the official announcement of upcoming interview dates for the permanent ED Director's role. I opened it and read the brief notice, followed by the indelible statement that changed our family's entire life trajectory. "Unfortunately, you will not be required to interview for the position. Best wishes in your future career," etc.

It hit like a sudden slap, but I wasn't really surprised. A simple, clean, administrative coup de grace - bloodless, a non-event, arranged by the system. My initial reaction was, "You bastards, use me for a year and a half and then bypass me." There was no justification that I shouldn't be interviewed, at least. I'd launched several successful initiatives and made some real progress. My clinical and personnel records were spotless. Various emotions flooded over me, "It's over. At least Stephanie will be relieved. I don't really want it anymore, anyway..." But also, immediately conflicting thoughts of my contesting the grounds for denial arose. In my heart though, I knew this was a watershed moment; a breach of my trust in the system. My supports were falling away. We really were all alone in a foreign land.

It was all too much to suddenly internalize and process. I was in Queenstown, New Zealand with Aidan. There would be many struggles ahead. I let it lie, cleared my mind and tried to pretend that I'd never read the message.

As if this father-son New Zealand trip could possibly get any better, there was still the matter of the ACEM Annual Scientific Assembly Grand Banquet to attend to. The dress-theme was black and gold. Aidan was introduced to an exceptional group of intelligent, highly-trained and accomplished people. Every one a true success story, and all, I'm proud to say, my colleagues. People who do important, life-saving work, every day. We didn't know exactly what to expect but were suitably impressed when we entered the Queenstown Convention Center ballroom to a full, sit-down, four-course New Zealand sourced, themed dinner for four hundred, with matching Kiwi wine flights and a full-on live band, with acrobats twirling overhead. We were dressed like pirates, complete with gold head scarfs, embroidered black and gold silk vests, even jet-black boa feathers pinched from the table centerpieces. Young Aidan, looking mature for his age, apparently very sneakily drank like a pirate as well, in the wine-fueled chaos that ensued. The band was red hot, and this was the only such function I can recall where the dance floor was packed, and the tables mostly empty, before they'd even served the mains! These folks had their party lights turned way up; to eleven, for sure. Well, in Emergency Medicine we work hard, and we play hard. We know better than anybody: life is precious, weird shit happens, no one knows why; but you can be very dead, very suddenly indeed. Treasure every minute of it. I was all in. Tonight, I needed this. Perfect timing...

Pictures do exist of Aidan, then only fourteen, but tall and mature looking for his age, drinking good Kiwi Reds and dancing ecstatically with several lithe, late twenty-something female EM registrars - but we don't show them outside of the immediate family. If it's possible to have your peak life experiences at the tender age of fourteen, Aidan might just have had his on that night, and on this trip.

As I soberly counseled him the next day, "Hold onto these memories, mate. From here on out, it's all hard work and responsibility ahead for you. Trips like these are as good as it ever gets..." He seemed a bit downcast at the news. Keeping my demeanor composed, I settled into my own thoughts of the options and challenges I now faced, dead-ahead, back home in Brisbane. But the night before, he and I, we were legends; pirate legends in black and gold...

CHAPTER 39: Fractured Notes, 2016-2017

On arrival back in Brisbane, I was now in damage-control mode. I had clearly lost the support of the higher-ups in town and needed time to digest the professional and personal ramifications. "Should I stay, or should I go...?"

But it wasn't quite that simple. Having lost administratively, I now felt very exposed clinically. In such a chaotic work environment as ours had become, what might happen if I were involved in a bad clinical outcome and lacking Administration's support? Thrown to the wolves as payback? Entirely possible; I'd seen it happen before. Recall my observation that any system's primary imperative is self-preservation.

As these highly stressful events played out, a rare state of friction grew between Stephanie and me. What only months before had seemed a stable, certain, five-year pathway towards retirement, now looked to be collapsing as a viable option. Having five school-aged kids in the mix, far overseas, and entirely dependent on my income, raised the stakes considerably. How hard do you negotiate a compromise to stay on, and what are the alternatives? Suddenly, the idea of a return to the States didn't seem so far out of the question.

"Anchor" came to me after our daily one hour walk on the foreshore; a walk that went a bit off track and became pretty heated. It just poured out in one big rush of deep-seated emotion. It's one of the only songs I've ever written as a dialog; in a strong, country-rock ballad style that came straight from the heart. Sometimes we don't realize how much we mean to our partners until the chips are down, and we find ourselves really leaning on, or providing support to, each other. That's when real love shows its strength. Anchor is my way of telling Stephanie just how much I depend on her to keep me on the right path, even if I don't always show her. I love you baby...

"She said, "I'm sorry we're a dead weight on your life"
I said, "Maybe you're an anchor that keeps me safe from strife...""

I decided to take some time off - a mental health break of sorts and contacted my professional physician's union representatives. With their able guidance, we indicated that I was willing to step down as acting ED Director without challenge, based on certain protective employment conditions being met. Events then took a rather Machiavellian turn, and I wasn't certain I could stay on board in any capacity. I'm prevented from revealing more due to a signed non-disclosure agreement between parties; but ultimately, what does it matter? It was time for me to move on. Finally, all that remained was for us to negotiate the separation agreement.

In the end, we negotiated a mutually acceptable resolution to our impasse, and I resigned from my permanent position, eventually regaining my balance somewhat. But only after a prolonged period of mentally stressful re-calibration. I began to consider work as a locums EM doc (traveling moonlighter) in Australia to keep current medically and begin to move on professionally. There were plenty of opportunities, especially as I enjoy the more remote, offbeat and intriguing practice settings. While there remained many complex issues to consider and resolve, it seemed somehow God, or the fates, had laid this most unexpected path before us. And in the end, one must always choose a way forward. "Road, meet Fork..."

I accept that I'm getting older, a worn-out ol' mule still pulling at the emergency medical plow after some twenty-five years; I wanted to begin slowing down in EM anyway. It's definitely not a field for geriatrics. As we contemplated our next moves as a family, one major concern became the high cost of living in Australia. With five kids, you can really burn through piles of cash Down Under, trust me on this. I was no longer making the high income of a full-time ED Director, and it would be very painful to try to replace that level of cash flow by becoming a full-time, locum road-warrior. An occasional exotic foray into the wilder reaches of remote Australia, yes - fun and enlivening. But grinding out a steady forty clinical hours a week while traveling on the road? An immersion into one of the lower circles of EM hell, most certainly.

I suppose this whole Aussie adventure had been my escape and re-animation, into which I'd dragged six other lives. Now it was Stephanie's turn. We were also now facing the inevitable, inter-generational issues around her aging parents depending somewhat on their only daughter being present in their lives. She had her own legitimate needs; I wasn't going to fight it. But it sure gave me whiplash! Here I was, fifty-eight years old, with five kids, ages eight to eighteen, pre-college. Sounds expensive... and I was essentially unemployed. Marketable, but still...

We eventually made the wrenching decision to begin the process of re-locating the family back to our farmhouse in upstate New York. Restarting our lives again at Fairview would be a slower, less costly and far less stressful alternative, and one that I was increasingly ready for. Maybe it was finally time to become a mellow fellow back there in them hills? And perhaps, like Bilbo, to begin writing my book; "There and Back Again" in Hobbit-ish seclusion.

I had some trouble adjusting mentally to all these sudden changes, to be honest. I'm generally a really positive, forward-looking person; full-on, maybe a bit hypomanic. I thrive on that feeling of surging mental energy; it helps in EM, believe me. But this whole turn of events really tossed my head around, once the full implications became clearer.

Although by many measures I was highly successful and accomplished, in reality, I'm just a small fry. We all are. Ultimately expendable. Over time my emotions and understanding evolved. Large organizations and bureaucracies are self-protecting, self-perpetuating organisms. Any significant conflict is judiciously resolved and promptly eliminated. Being right, or even partially right, doesn't matter. Messes are cleaned up, broken things are discarded, and the organization moves on. It's nothing personal, just business. The budgetary impacts of such cleanups are easily rectified; but the emotional costs to any individual so enmeshed remain in flux - to be resolved by them and their loved ones, alone, in private hours. Time and colleagues move on, and you realize that you really are on your own. Ephemeral, fractured notes in life's sometimes bittersweet symphony...

A close EM colleague gently recommended to me a mental health counselor who had helped him over a similarly rough patch; one who was also a fellow physician, i.e., a "shrink". I reveal this tawdry nugget mainly to encourage any fellow physicians navigating similarly wrenching professional changes not to go it alone. We are all ten-feet-tall and bullet-proof, until we're not. Doctor Steve (my shrink) really helped me to gain invaluable perspective, suppress my wounded pride and continue reaching out for support through this transitional process. He even encouraged me to consider a return to the USA, as a stabilizing influence. "You're just another damaged doctor, feeling betrayed by the system. I've seen so many. Sometimes we're just too diligent for our own good," he memorably opined. "It's hard to feel expendable. But that's what we are..."

So, for the first time in my life, I became a patient - and a reluctant daily-doser of Duloxetine, Lorazepam, Lithium (!) and a few other modern pharmaceutical wonders. I'd prescribed heaps of SNRIs, SSRIs and Benzodiazepines to suffering humanity over the years, but had never personally partaken. And it is somewhat weird stuff, I now realize from first-hand experience. I gamely looked at this as being a bit of a medical experiment on myself - sort of a "see one, take one, become one" type of evolution.

The meds did allow me to maintain a Soma-like, steady-state functionality that assisted my re-entry into locum work at far-flung EDs around Australia. It's a career choice that literally defines swimming in an entire ocean of stressful, acidic uncertainty. I found that carefully calibrated doses kept the energy flowing and my mind generally clear, while providing an interesting pharmacological ceiling and tether to my raw emotions. But I hated the deadening "wet blanket" side effects on my creativity and libido. Again, I divulge all this primarily to help fellow healthcare colleagues who may be struggling. You are not alone, and you don't have to solve all of your own challenges. Let go, give in and go with a trusted colleague, please - perhaps even a shrink, God forbid! And while it may sometimes feel, with the entire world seemingly burning down around us, that no one should be overly concerned about the personal life crises of a successful first-world professional, previous status and accomplishments are irrelevant when navigating these turgid waters. Financial security does not guarantee mental resilience. We are all worthy of dignified compassion. You matter. I matter. We all matter. So, I bought in, and began moving ahead through the difficult process of healing and emotional rejuvenation.

Fortunately, within a fairly short period of time, around eight months, I was able to wean myself off of all exogenous pharmaceutical aids, with the possible exception of the occasional stiff G&T. But it was a lot more mentally challenging than I anticipated, with some ebb and flow and outright setbacks, to be honest. But I was committed to regaining my natural homeostasis without pharmacologic support. I wanted Me back... As Doctor Steve reinforced, such major and sustained life stressors literally rewire your physiological response to stressful stimuli. Think PTSD. They tickle the same reflexive neural pathways. Recovery is a slow, methodical process, not a discrete event. In the end, looking back, I do feel my personal experiences in this regard have perhaps made me a more insightful and compassionate physician, at least. Being a patient can be disorienting and demeaning at times. I've lived that now, first-hand. Sometimes, living out our lives ain't so easy.

During this period of professional readjustment and neuro-pharmacologic calibration, I experienced some unusual (for me) psychic lows. There was definitely a sense of personal failure, lurking ever-present in the background, something we physicians have a notoriously difficult time accepting.

I wrote **"(I Don't Mean to) Bring You Down"** during one of my lowest points. Brisk physical exercise always helps sort things out for me. The endorphins kick in, I find a rhythm and my mind turns blissfully to music. I had the entire song by the end of a one-hour seaside walk. It's real and right to the bone. An apology to Stephanie for dragging her along through all this antipodean mud and stuff. And offering this song as some small compensation. It's not maudlin though, building slowly to a positive re-affirmation of love and commitment despite life's gales, or something...

"I'm sorry life can be a stormy sea with me sometimes
in spite of all the rhymes..."

Then, right around this time, someone in my extended family back in the USA committed suicide – shockingly, out of the blue - and at a young age. That put us all on high alert and really affected my own homeostasis. I'm fortunate in being almost always up. I've never had a suicidal thought in my life. I always figure there must be a better alternative to taking your own life. Maybe just to run away and join the circus, or a rock band or such. But, for some, apparently not... Doctor Steve was a bit alarmed at the news, and really kept in close contact with me during my grieving and processing of this tragic event. I thank him for that.

Again, music was my solace and outlet to express sorrow at this sudden death and tragically lost potential. **"Jigsaw Puzzle"** explores how our complex lives and personalities really are a puzzle that we all strive to complete, if that's even possible. But sometimes, the pieces simply don't fit together nice and neatly. The song's actually in a slow, slightly funky blues; as I didn't want it to feel too depressing, and I know the song's muse would appreciate a bit of a groove to their farewell song. So, a bit of a New Orleans funeral then, and a celebration of a life, for CAW... RIP mate. Until we meet again... And a reminder for each of us to hold close to those you love; life really is a fragile, fleeting gift.

"Every life is like a jigsaw puzzle, we work to make the pieces fit
When it all seems too much trouble, work inwards from the edgy bits..."

With all this going on, a feeling of gradual acceptance now began to dawn over the whole affair. Sometimes, true acceptance is the only answer to our prayers for guidance in life. Our one-year Australian adventure had taken on a life of its own, now sprawling out over the past six years. We'd seen and experienced an incredible amount and accomplished far more than we'd initially set out to. And, as we were now dual citizens, any big move back to the USA wouldn't necessarily be final. We could always return at any time, however unlikely that now seemed. There were still other factors dictating that we return to the States now, for a few years at least. Our lonely bachelor farm-sitter and frustrated author had finally found the love of his life and wanted out. The grand, old place simply couldn't be left unoccupied. Our younger kids had spent more of their lives Down Under than in the USA. We were becoming unexpectedly anchored here, but detached from our larger family lives back home, in America.

I pay attention to these confluences of signs in my life. I've found, if you take adequate time, and try to understand all the angles, the decision you make generally turns out for the best. Pretty well, if not perfectly well. Sometimes, there's really no use in trying to push back against the river.

Just let it all go, flow along with the current. Exhale... Let go, let God. Have a little bit of faith...

Still, any such change comes with grieving, and **"Goodbye Southern Cross"** was kind of my exhalation of final acceptance. I've always been a major Stephen Stills fan. At his best, he really was stellar. Even though he's from the generation before mine, his overwhelming excellence still stands out. The first Manassas record, along with the CSNY stuff, and his first two solo albums are among the finest recordings of the late 60's and early 70's in my opinion. They paved the way for much of the California country-rock sound to follow, influencing the Eagles, Joe Walsh, even Fleetwood Mac, while also incorporating deep blues and acoustic folk fingerpicking. It's brilliant American music. One of Stephen's last great creative gasps was the song Southern Cross. It's an iconic song that I treasure; especially when I could simply look up and see it right above me, gleaming nightly in the clear Australian southern sky. One late night, out on the foreshore, I looked up, there it was, standing sentinel as always; and the title just popped into my head, "Goodbye Southern Cross"...

I wanted to expand on, and slightly invert, that image and the idea of it being a beacon leading to a new, exotic life in a different world, far, far away. On the outro I directly quote Southern Cross, to seal the deal. I hope Stephen hears this one day and smiles. It's my o.g. musical tip of the hat then, to a master musician and an unknowing mentor.

"Time moves along, a river of song, and stars to guide my journey on
    Life is just a lucky coin you toss, goodbye Southern Cross..."

Finally, all discussions and planning aside, it was time for our temporary parting. Stephanie was taking the four younger kids back to New York as soon as the school semester ended in Australia, July 2017, to get them ready for the fall start of schools in the USA. I had to stay behind with Luke, who was then a senior in high school, and scheduled to graduate in December 2017 - an event unfortunately missed by the entire family except for me.

I wrote **"Sacred Love"** as a parting love song to Stephanie and the wonderful relationship we've had over the past twenty-five years. It is something rare, to treasure and to celebrate. The melody is very simple and soaring. It perfectly encapsulated what I wanted to say, and thus feels very complete and satisfying.

"The moon is just a gleaming spyglass, looking down from up above
    What she sees she's never telling, a witness to our sacred love..."

So, Luke and I were now unexpectedly batching it for six months, until mid-December, planning on rejoining everyone at Fairview before Christmas. This arrangement allowed me a very rare solo break, to spend supervising Luke, teaching him my many years' accumulation of bachelor hacks and tricks on how to survive, and thrive in life, out on his own. How to shop, cook and eat well for starters; how to do his own laundry, and mix great cocktails too. With a great deal of repetitive and focused experimentation, we were also able to create a new cocktail, the "Nolzie," christened after his Aussie nickname; a beverage which we believe to be a worthy addition to the world's cocktail cannon (see below). I also now had space and time to devote to beginning the book you are currently reading. And fair warning: writing a book's a lot more work than I ever imagined! If I knew then what I know now, I'm not certain I'd have ever started down this winding and treacherous pathway. Any potential authors, be forewarned... Meanwhile, I continued to do regular EM locum stints in various EDs across Australia, far and wide, leaving Luke alone at times - a trial by fire of bachelor living that he passed with flying colors. This helped keep my EM skills up as well as bringing in the ever-vital income.

We also tried to travel as much as possible, while we had this final opportunity, in the southern hemisphere. Believing we were soon to depart this region of the planet, perhaps never to return, we now made time to explore and adventure together further afield in Fiji, Thailand, Hong Kong, Macau and Singapore, in addition to Australia. Another shining example of my life philosophy in action, "You'll know what I value by what I spend my money on." Experiential learning with those you love, forging shared memories - it's simply the biggest bang in happiness for the buck out there. Not just in my opinion but backed up by much psychological research. Those were such great times! Between his school responsibilities, my running a single parent household and our various travels, it was a busy, but irreplaceable bonding time together, helping Luke prepare to fledge into the wide world so very soon. A honeymoon of sorts with my eldest son; our "Sonnymoon," as we jokingly called it.

My best mate PJ then unexpectedly made Luke a very generous offer for Luke to begin working in his family's Queensland based real-estate concern. After careful consideration, Luke made the momentous decision to remain behind, alone in Brisbane, to begin his post-high school career in his adopted homeland. Stephanie's worst fears materialized, and she was already far away, back home in New York!

It took a bit of coaxing, all the way back to America, to get Stephanie to agree that this was the right move for him, but she still had her misgivings. The new plan also required me to extend our boy's solo adventure for an additional three months, allowing time to get Luke graduated in December and then help set him up for a new job and independent living in Brisbane, before I finally jetted back to the USA. Missing another Upstate winter wasn't a major sacrifice, and the bright, hot Aussie summer months soon drifted past, before I finally bought a one-way ticket back to New York, packed up the bay-side house in Brissie, and reluctantly closed the final door on this chapter of our Team Nolan adventures Down Under.

And so here our story pauses; the arc of a journey, the architecture of a life well-lived. We started out somehow, on a wing and a prayer, and returned unexpectedly in the same manner. So many unanticipated twists and turns to the tale, with so many more ahead, in a future as yet undefined. But, in the end, that's what transforms any life into an adventure. I trust that the experiences our five Nolan kids have had along the way will make them into stronger, more resilient, and ultimately more successful young adults. But it's soon up to each of them to define that term, confidently, to their own satisfaction. As we elders diminish, I look forward to celebrating their successes and assisting in their recovery from the inevitable failures life has in store. We are all sometimes fractured, sometimes beautiful, notes in the full, harmonious symphony of life. I embrace this music fully and could never regret living through this major chapter in the journey that ultimately defines us. I trust and fully believe that this is not, in fact, the end, but merely a pause along our way forward.

As the American backwoods philosopher Henry David Thoreau so eloquently stated at the close of "Walden", written in 1854, in my hometown of Concord, Massachusetts:

"Only that day dawns to which we are awake. There is more day to dawn. The sun is but a morning star."

Or, to quote a more contemporary source, our esteemed o.g.nolan, spoken with an irascible Irish twinkle in his eye:

"Life is just a lucky coin you toss..."

Peace, love and blessings to you all, who've made the journey with us thus far. With gratitude.

Cheers! Doc Down Under

The Nolzie

Chill all ingredients beforehand; gin stored in the freezer ideally.

In a large glass, 2/3 filled with ice, add dry London gin, Tanqueray preferred; a good amount to taste.

Double ripe lime wedges, squeezed and dropped in.

Macerate the lime and gin in the ice.

Add 2 tablespoons unsweetened pineapple juice: no more, no less. Stir.

Briskly pour fresh, chilled tonic water, floating the gin and citrus emulsion to the top of the glass. Do not stir. Avoid diet tonic water, please.

Grate finely, fresh ginger to taste; garnish atop.

Sip with gratitude. As the ice melts, it will soften the stronger gin lurking in the depths. Give it proper time.

Give thanks to our gracious Lord for such perfection and solace.

NB: The Nolzie is in no way meant to replace the absolute summer classic G&T. Instead, think of it as a tropical variation on a theme that has been enjoyed countless times over countless summers. Cheers!

EPILOGUE

On concluding this DDU book, now some four years after the final act, in the spring of 2022 and settled back home at Fairview Farm in Upstate New York, various thoughts and feelings come to mind:

Home is where you come from and feel most viscerally centered, in the deepest sense. Recreating a new home in a foreign land and culture is a difficult, if not impossible task. It may be wonderful, but it will never truly be "home." And if you are coming from a relatively comfortable place, I think it's harder still to replace. Being a refugee, or "on the run," changes the calculus entirely. But there will always be compromises to make and losses to endure. In the end you may gain a lot, but you may also give up a lot.

In general, a positive philosophy of seeking new experiences with a flexible outlook will carry you over the inevitable rough bits a lot more surely than going overseas to escape the problems in your current life. What you might be running from may actually reside within you, and thus be carried along for the ride. Engage in some pre-journey introspection. Go for the right reasons.

My intentional documentation of the entire experience as it unfolded, via the DDU blog, o.g.nolan music and this book, has turned out to be a wise investment of time and energy. Otherwise, so much would have been forgotten! The younger kids' understanding of these events has already faded into merely vague memories. While in some ways, it all now feels like some ancient, alien history, in others, our common family experiences have bonded us more tightly than ever as Team Nolan. Ours is a shared story that will be passed down through our generations.

Considering all that we've experienced and know now, both the good and the not so, was it a wise decision to even embark on such an adventure? Would you do it again? This is asked by many family members and friends to this day. To which, I can only reply, most emphatically "Yes!". While it all may have gone suddenly pear-shaped in any number of ways - say if one of the kids had been taken off by the odd Croc or Great White Shark - my overall take-away would be along the lines of the old standby "Nothing ventured, nothing gained." We ventured and risked a lot, but in the end, have gained so much more.

I personally would do it all again, perhaps without taking on the ED leadership bit. That was clearly not a good decision, in retrospect. Keep it simple. And maybe once really is enough, as it could never be repeated in the same way again, in any case. It would become something entirely unique and different. Maybe better, maybe worse.

Finally, we hope you have enjoyed the journey, and thanks for tagging along with us.

Sincerely,

Doc Down Under and the entire Nolan family

An Appreciation:

Everyone needs a mentor, someone to guide them through the maze. I found mine at the American College of Emergency Physicians (ACEP) annual conference in Boston back in 2009, where the idea of living and working in Australia was first planted in my imagination. Dr. BC is an American EM physician and an early adopter, who had made the move to Australia some eight years earlier, with wife and three kids in tow. He was a reassuring presence when negotiations seemed to be going nowhere.

I remember him advising me, "Keep a journal, record it all while it's still fresh and magical. After a while, you forget how special and good life is in Australia, and it just becomes your life." Taking his advice to heart, I've kept that journal, with varying degrees of diligence, over the entire six-plus years of our Australian adventure. Much of the content of DDU is taken from these entries, as well as from my travel blog. Please visit www.docdownunder.com for expanded, fascinating content of American expat life and travels in Oz and NZ, including a copious photo journal of trips made, under the "Blogs" heading. I hope they help deepen the story and provide inspiration for your own trips Down Under to Australia and New Zealand.

So, a special thanks, and note of fondness to my friend and ever patient mentor Dr. BC.

And finally, all thanks and a warm hug to Dr. Trixie, my UVM 1990 Medical School classmate, for her incredibly sharp wit, and even sharper editorial eye. You deserve a bouquet, Doctor Trixie!

SELECTED BIBLIOGRAPHY

Aughton, Peter. *The Fatal Voyage*. Arris Publishing Ltd. Gloucestershire. 2005.

Australia. 11th Edition. Lonely Planet Publications Pty Ltd. Australia. 2002.

Australia's Most Dangerous. Australian Geographic Pty Ltd. 2001.

Alexander, Caroline. *The Bounty*. Harper Perennial. London. 2004.

Bryson, Bill. *In a Sunburned Country*. Broadway Books. New York. 2000.

Chaffey, Will. *Swimming with Crocodiles*. Picador, Pan Macmillan. Australia. 2009.

Hall, Rodney. *Journey Through Australia*. William Heinemann. Australia. 1988.

Herbert, Xavier. *Capricornia*. Harper Collins, Sydney. 1938, 2013.

Hughes, Robert. *The Fatal Shore- The Epic of Australia's Founding*. Alfred Knopf. New York. 1986.

Hunt, David. *Girt- The Unauthorized History of Australia*. Schwartz Media Pty Ltd. Collingwood, VIC, Australia. 2013.

New Zealand. 16th Edition. Lonely Planet Publications Pty Ltd. Australia. 2012.

Queensland and the Great Barrier Reef. 4th Edition. Lonely Planet

Publications Pty Ltd. Australia. 2005.

Shilton, Peter. *Natural Areas of Queensland.* Goldpress Pty Ltd. Mount Gravatt, QLD.2005.

Simpson and Day. *Field Guide to the Birds of Australia.* Viking, The Penguin Group. Australia. 8th Edition. 2010.

South Pacific. 5th Edition. Lonely Planet Publications Pty Ltd. Australia. 2012.

Theroux, Paul. *The Happy Isles of Oceania.* Hamish Hamilton Ltd, The Penguin Group. London. 1992.

Townsend, Derek. *Redlands- The Story of an Australian Shire.* Derek Townsend Productions. 1986.

Wildlife of Greater Brisbane. Queensland Museum. 1995.